Lecture Notes in Artificial Intelligence   5509

Edited by R. Goebel, J. Siekmann, and W. Wahlster

Subseries of Lecture Notes in Computer Science

Michael Kipp   Jean-Claude Martin
Patrizia Paggio   Dirk Heylen (Eds.)

Multimodal Corpora

From Models of Natural Interaction
to Systems and Applications

 Springer

Series Editors

Randy Goebel, University of Alberta, Edmonton, Canada
Jörg Siekmann, University of Saarland, Saarbrücken, Germany
Wolfgang Wahlster, DFKI and University of Saarland, Saarbrücken, Germany

Volume Editors

Michael Kipp
Deutsches Forschungszentrum für künstliche Intelligenz (DFKI)
Campus D3.2, 66123 Saarbrücken, Germany
E-mail: kipp@dfki.de

Jean-Claude Martin
Laboratoire d'Informatique pour la Mécanique
et les Sciences de l'Ingénieur (LIMSI-CNRS)
BP 133, 91403 Orsay Cedex, France
E-mail: martin@limsi.fr

Patrizia Paggio
University of Copenhagen, Faculty of Humanities
Centre for Language Technology
Njalsgade 140-142, 2300 Copenhagen, Denmark
E-mail: paggio@hum.ku.dk

Dirk Heylen
University of Twente, Computer Science, Human Media Interaction
PO Box 217, 7500 AE Enschede, The Netherlands
E-mail: d.k.j.heylen@ewi.utwente.nl

Library of Congress Control Number: 2009935170

CR Subject Classification (1998): I.5, I.4, H.5.2, I.3, I.2, J.5, H.3.1

LNCS Sublibrary: SL 7 – Artificial Intelligence

ISSN 0302-9743

ISBN 978-3-642-04792-3 Springer Berlin Heidelberg New York

springer.com

© Springer-Verlag Berlin Heidelberg 2009

Typesetting: Camera-ready by author, data conversion by Scientific Publishing Services, Chennai, India
Printed on acid-free paper   SPIN: 12747986   06/3180   5 4 3 2 1 0

Preface

The book presents a cross-section of state-of-the-art research on multimodal corpora, a highly interdisciplinary area that is a prerequisite for various specialized disciplines. A number of the papers included are revised and expanded versions of papers accepted to the International Workshop on Multimodal Corpora: From Models of Natural Interaction to Systems and Applications, held in conjunction with the 6th International Conference for Language Resources and Evaluation (LREC) on May 27, 2008, in Marrakech, Morocco. This international workshop series started in 2000 and has since then grown into a regular satellite event of the bi-annual LREC conference, attracting researchers from fields as diverse as psychology, artificial intelligence, robotics, signal processing, computational linguistics and human–computer interaction. To complement the selected papers from the 2008 workshop, we invited well-known researchers from corpus collection initiatives to contribute to this volume. We were able to obtain seven invited research articles, including contributions from major international multimodal corpus projects like AMI and SmartWeb, which complement the six selected workshop contributions. All papers underwent a special review process for this volume, resulting in significant revisions and extensions based on the experts' advice. While we were pleased that the 2006 edition of the workshop resulted in a special issue of the *Journal of Language Resources and Evaluation*, published in 2007, we felt that this was the time for another major publication, given not only the rapid progress and increased interest in this research area but especially in order to acknowledge the difficulty of disseminating results across discipline borders. The Springer LNAI series is the perfect platform for doing so. We also created the website www.multimodal-corpora.org to serve as a permanent information hub for the workshop series, including links to research in multimodality and a mailing list for the announcement of future events.

Empirically based research in multimodality can be viewed as a work pipeline. It starts with collecting video data that are relevant for a specific research question (e.g., how do people express emotions using gestures?), either by filming interactions in a controlled (both technically and scenario-wise) setup or by taking existing material from TV or the movies. These data must then be enriched by human coders, who annotate the corpus with concepts only human competence can recognize and apply (if possible supported by automatic devices such as trackers), and who also explore the potential interconnections between modalities (face, gesture, speech, posture etc.). Since these data will potentially be distributed to a wide spectrum of consumers for research and development, the human-encoded data must be validated for consistency using quantitative measures. Systematic analysis of the observed multimodal behaviors is the central characteristic of multimodal corpora. This allows for the subsequent use of the corpora in creating analytic or generative models. For analysis and modeling tasks, exploratory qualitative and quantitative analysis tools are needed for browsing, viewing, extraction and modeling. Finally, since multimodal interaction is always embedded in a social setting, the intercultural dimension must be taken into account. This means investigating how multimodal interactions change across cultures with different social protocols and possibly different standards and norms.

In this volume, we have carefully selected representative contributions for each step in this pipeline. Accordingly, we have organized the papers along this pipeline and, for the sake of clarity, not assembled all invited papers in one section, but freely interspersed papers from both categories according to their contents. For the topic of collection and distribution of corpora, we have two invited contributions about the SmartWeb corpus (Schiel) and the IFADV corpus (van Son et al.). In the area of coding and analyzing corpora, we invited Blache et al. for an account of the ToMA project. Additionally, three extended workshop papers deal with the multimodal behavior of children (Colletta et al.), politicians (Poggi and Vincze), and multiparty meetings (Matsusaka et al.). Two further included workshop papers deal with the important topic of validating multimodal corpora: Cavicchio and Poesio discuss how to assess coding scheme reliability and Reidsma et al. discuss agreement scores in conjunction with contextual information as part of the AMI project. As multimodal behavior must often be differentiated with regard to the intercultural dimension, we invited Rehm et al. to report on standardized video recordings for this purpose. This is complemented by an analysis of intercultural differences in information and communication technology by Allwood and Ahlsén. In an era of growing availability of large resources, tools for browsing, coding and exchanging data are becoming ever more important. We have therefore included three contributions that present existing tools for visualizing conversational-speech interaction (Campbell), for accessing a large mutimodal corpus (Popescu-Belis et al.), and for exchanging data between different special purpose tools (Schmidt et al.).

Overall, we hope that this "overview by example" volume will provide a unique opportunity for researchers of all related disciplines to gain insight into this active research area where empiricism meets application, and the humanities meet technology. We would like to especially thank all reviewers who contributed their precious time to the excellent quality of the papers.

July 2009

Michael Kipp
Jean-Claude Martin
Patrizia Paggio
Dirk Heylen

Organization

Referees

Jan Alexandersson
Jens Allwood
Elisabeth Ahlsén
Elisabeth André
Gerard Bailly
Stéphanie Buisine
Susanne Burger
Loredana Cerrato
Piero Cosi
Morena Danieli

Nicolas Ech Chafai
John Glauert
Kostas Karpouzis
Alfred Kranstedt
Peter Kuehnlein
Daniel Loehr
Maurizio Mancini
Costanza Navarretta
Catherine Pelachaud
Fabio Pianesi

Isabella Poggi
Matthias Rehm
Laurent Romary
Thomas Schmidt
Rob van Son
Ielka van der Sluis
Rainer Stiefelhagen
Peter Wittenburg
Massimo Zancanaro

Table of Contents

Tools for Browsing, Coding and Exchanging Data in Multimodal Corpora

The SmartWeb Corpora: Multimodal Access to the Web in Natural Environments

Florian Schiel

Bavarian Archive for Speech Signals (BAS),
Ludwig-Maximilians-Universität München,
Schellingstr. 3, 80799 München, Germany
schiel@bas.uni-muenchen.de

Abstract. As a result from the German SmartWeb project three speech corpora, one of them multimodal, have been published by the Bavarian Archive for Speech Signals (BAS). They contain speech and video signals from human–machine interactions in real indoor and outdoor environments. The scenarios for these corpora are a typicial handheld PDA interaction (SHC), an interaction on a running motorcycle (SMC) and another handheld PDA interaction in a human-human-machine setting with face video capture (SVC). The speech was transcribed using the Verbmobil annotation scheme extended by off-talk taggings while the video was labelled for on/off-focus and face boundaries. For all three scenarios the newly developed situational prompting technique SitPro was applied by which spontaneous interactions in different domains can be elicited effectively. This chapter describes the prompting scheme SitPro, the recording technique used to obtain real situation data as well as the properties of the resulting corpora.

1   Introduction

The aim of the SmartWeb project[1] is to enable human users to access semantic Web services via mobile handheld devices by means of a multi-modal user interface [14]. In at least one SmartWeb use case the mobile device not only captures voice and pen input but also the video of the face to derive para-linguistic information about the state of the dialogue, for instance whether the user is addressing the system or other parties, whether the user is watching display output etc. To push the paradigm of mobility to an extreme, another use case involves the access to Internet content while driving a motorcycle by means of within-helmet microphone technology and/or throat contact microphone.

To provide empirical data for training and testing these advanced technologies the SmartWeb multimodal speech data collection was carried out by the Bavarian Archive for Speech Signals (BAS) located at the Institute of Phonetics and Speech Processing (IPS), Ludwig-Maximilians-Universität München, Germany.

In the course of this data collection three new speech resources have been created: The SmartWeb Handheld Corpus (SHC), the SmartWeb Motorbike Corpus (SMC) and the SmartWeb Video Corpus (SVC). As their respective names imply the SHC corpus

---

[1] Funded by the German Ministry of Science and Education (BMB+F) 2005-2007.

M. Kipp et al. (Eds.): Multimodal Corpora, LNAI 5509, pp. 1–17, 2009.

contains a large number of interactions via a PDA or smart phone, the SMC corpus provides a small set of test material recorded on the running motorcycle in real traffic situations while the SVC corpus extends the rather simple scenario of the SHC corpus into a triad communication consisting of two human users and the SmartWeb system and adds an additional modality of user face capture.

These corpora form the empirical basis for the development of the man–machine interface of the SmartWeb system. All three corpora are characterized by

- the natural environment with respect to acoustical and optical background
- the contemporary user interface hardware and data transmission techniques,
- the fact that only naive users have been recorded and
- a common elicitation technique (situational prompting) which allows us to record in a simple and cost-efficient way.

In this contribution we give a detailed description of the recording technique and prompting system SitPro as well as specifics about the resulting multimodal speech resources which can be obtained via the BAS.

Nowadays corpus creation as a resource for applied research in the field of speech technology is subject to two conditions: The process of data collection should be as economical as possible and the resulting data should be as realistic as possible. The latter refers to the properties of the physical signals as well as to the speaking style of the speakers. To summarize, the major cost-intensive parts of such a collection are:

- the annotation
- the realistic recording setup (including transmission lines)
- the realistic task elicitation

For the first point we refer to established annotation schemas derived from the Verbmobil and SmartKom projects (e.g. [8]) as well as distributed web transcription systems like WebTranscribe [3]. A realistic recording setup can be designed based on the given contemporary hardware and infrastructure. Later in this chapter we give a detailed description about the client-server system used for the SmartWeb recordings.

Hence, one of the few remaining challenges in corpus construction is the last point: how to elicit representative utterances from the participants that are as natural as possible in a real situation and to do so in a cost-efficient way. There exist various techniques of speech data collection depending on the purpose of the corpus and of the intended application or target system. Of course, these techniques differ in effort and costs. Furthermore, each technique elicits speech in various speaking styles such as read speech, answering speech, command and control speech, dictation speech, descriptive speech, non-prompted speech, spontaneous speech and emotional speech ([10]). Data collection methods which are designed to obtain natural spoken language data are, for instance, Wizard-of-Oz experiment (WOZ) [13], Video Task (Daily Soap Scenario) [7] and script experiments [9].

WOZ uses a realistic simulation of all functionalities of a fully deployed target system. Script experiments combine features of WOZ and prompting experiments and were applied as one strategy within an iterative data collection approach by [9]. All of these methods are able to elicit spontaneously uttered speech at different levels, but require human support and are therefore expensive and time-consuming. The goal of the SmartWeb data collection is to economically record a variety of naturally spoken requests without human interference and hence at low costs.

The remains of this chapter is organized as follows: In Section 2 we will describe and discuss a new elicitation technique called sit uational prompting' (SitPro) which addresses the above described challenge of creating realistic recordings without resorting to cost-intensive techniques such as WOZ. Section 3 and 4 are dedicated to the client–server system and speaker recruitment as being used in all SmartWeb corpus collections. Section 5 describes the post-processing of the recorded data including alignment of different signal channels and annotation. The final section contains details about the individual corpora SHC, SMC and SVC.

2 Situational Prompting

Situational prompting (SitPro) is a new prompting technique for speech corpus collections that allows task solving data to be obtained in a efficient and cost-effective way. The basic idea of SitPro is to guide the subject through imaginative task situations and elicit user requests within the context of these situations *without providing any prompts for reading or repetition*[2]. Since this can be done automatically by a server software no human intervention is needed during the recording, and more than one recording can be run in parallel.

2.1 Elicitation Method

The development of SitPro is based on the experience we gained in the WOZ simulation of the SmartKom system [13] and in a pilot study [12] of human-human telephone dialogues for the SmartWeb data collection. SitPro combines script methods with interview techniques and speaker prompting (see e.g. [4], chapter 4). Speaker prompting is only used for instruction, information or feedback prompts. Repetition and question prompting are not applied to avoid unnatural speech styles.

SitPro comprises three different prompt categories, called *standard prompts, individualized prompts* and *script prompts.*

In a *standard prompt* the subject is told a topic (see examples in Table 1) to which she/he is supposed to pose a query (see an example in Table 2).

An *individualized prompt* is a prompt for which the subject provides his/her own topic (see example in Table 4).

A *scripted prompt* simulates a three-turn conversation as frequently found in dialogues between human and machine (see example in Table 3).

The fully automatic prompting system simulates two interlocutors: The *instructor* (female voice) gives directions about the situation and the topics, while the *operator* (male voice) answers the subjects' questions or gives feedback like the target system would do.

---

[2] Repeating acoustical prompts leads to unnatural prosody and usually hyper-articulated pronunciation and are therefore to be avoided.

Table 1. Examples for SmartWeb topics

topic	example
soccer	team, group
navigation	public transport, pedestrians
community	restaurant
information	tourist information, points of interest

Table 2. Example of SmartWeb recording dialogue using a *standard prompt* scheme. *pro* denotes the (female) instructor's voice; *rec* indicates a recording of the user's elicited query.

flow	text prompt	pause
pro-010	Please think of the soccer WM. You want to get information about results and games of several teams. First you want to know how the last game of Germany against Costa Rica ended.	4000
rec-010	*What was the result of the match Germany against Costa Rica?*	
pro-010	Now you want to get information about who else plays in the group of England and the Netherlands.	4000
rec-020	*What other teams are in the group of Britain and Holland?*	
pro-031	Next you are interested in the time of the next game of Mexico against Ukraine.	4000
rec-030	*When is the match Mexico against Ukraine*	
...		

Table 3. Example of SmartWeb recording dialogue using a *scripted prompt* scheme. *pro* denotes the (female) instructor's voice; *opr* denotes the (male) operator's voice; *rec* indicates a recording of the user's elicited query.

flow	text prompt	pause
pro-010	In the following block the topic is general knowledge. Please try to find out who painted the ceiling fresco of the Sistine Chapel.	3000
rec-010	*Who did the ceiling painting in the Sistine Chapel?*	
opr-010	The fresco was done by Michelangelo.	1500
pro-020	You were not able to properly understand the name. Please ask for a repetition	2000
rec-020	*Could you say that again?*	
...		

2.2   Prompts Preparation

In this section the detailed generation of the SitPro session is explained.

Structure. The time line of a *prompt unit* consists of a system prompt (pro), a variable silence interval, followed by a recording (rec) and a possible system answer (opr). Five to six prompt units are bundled into a thematic *action unit*. The silence interval at the end of a system prompt allows adjustment of the time between end of prompt playing and start of the recording. The length of this pause depends, on the one hand, on

Table 4. Example of SmartWeb recording dialogue using a *individualized prompt* scheme. *pro* denotes the (female) instructor's voice; *rec* indicates a recording of the user's elicited query.

flow	text prompt	pause
pro-010	Please refer now to the notes with your prepared topics. These topics should be the focus of the following six prompts. Please start by asking a general question about your topic number six.	6000
rec-010	*Where is the new Pinakothek in Munich?*	
pro-020	Now please ask a second, more specific question about this sixth topic.	5000
rec-020	*Uhm ... who was the architect?*	
pro-030	Very good! Now please ask a question about topic number one.	5000
rec-030	*Which country has the largest fresh water consumption?*	
...		

task complexity, script composition and individual prompt structure and, on the other hand, on recording situation and subjects' mental workload. A precise adjustment of these factors is necessary to minimize artefacts in the recordings resulting from subjects' mental overload. Content and timing information of each action unit are coded by hand into an XML file called *text prompt*. For the SmartWeb collection 57 action units (approx. 342 prompt units) covering topics as given in Table 1 were designed and put into an action unit pool.

Audio prompts Generation. Audio prompts are generated from the text prompts using a text-to-speech system of AT&T[3], which allows the choice of two different voices for the interlocutor and the operator. We decided against pre-recorded prompts for two reasons: firstly the situation is more realistic using synthesized voices, and secondly the creation of pre-recorded speech would require much more time and effort than synthesizing the prompts automatically. We selected the German AT&T male voice *Reiner* for the operator and the German female voice *Klara* to impersonate the instructor.[4]

2.3   Recording Procedure

A few days ahead of the recording the recruited subject received preliminary information with a first short explanation about the recording procedure and the request to prepare some topics she/he would like to ask the SmartWeb information system. These notes were necessary for the recording session to manage the *individualized prompts* that are filled by the subject with topics and names of their individual background. During the pilot study [12] we found that subjects easily accommodate to these individualized prompts.

The recordings took place in real environments and with real equipment. This means that the *external context* of the subject is realistic. The subjects are induced to visualize a situation in which they might use an information system like SmartWeb. By the use

---

[3] http://www.naturalvoices.att.com

[4] Unfortunately, it turned out that the spelling of the text prompts had to be adjusted manually so that the synthesized speech can be understood well enough over the UMTS phone line; this applies mainly for proper names and foreign words.

of subjects' imagination of such possible real situations the *internal context* is close to reality. We found that the external and internal context of the participants establish a sufficient communicational context to motivate natural statements.

For each recording session (subject) the server is triggered by a telephone call including a tone coded speaker ID. The server software randomly selects a specified number of action units from the available pool and creates a VoiceXML-like recording script on-the-fly[5]. Then this script is automatically executed by the SmartWeb server and the recorded signals are stored with reference to the given subject ID.[6]

To summarize the SitPro elicitation method:

- external context: real environments
- internal context: imagination of possible real situations
- standard, scripted and individualized prompts bundled in thematic action units
- acoustic prompting only[7]
- synthesized prompt speech
- two interlocutors on system side: instructor and operator
- random selection of action units during recording
- fully automatic server

3   Client Server Architecture

To obtain different levels of quality the recording setup is designed to capture the speech signal several times in parallel; this concerns the signal quality itself as well as to the timing of the recordings (segmentation). Facial video is always captured for the total length of a session in only one quality.

3.1   Signal Sources

The speaker uses a standard UMTS cellular phone[8] in combination with either a wireless[9] or cable connected close talk microphone (headset or helmet). An optional second microphone is attached to the collar or strapped to the throat of the speaker. Both microphone signals, the close talk microphone (after the Bluetooth transmission) and the optional signal, are recorded by a portable hard disc recorder throughout the recording session, which lasts approximately 30 minutes. The close talk microphone signal is then transmitted via WCDMA (UMTS) and the telephone network of the German Telecom to an ISDN speech server at the BAS. Figure 1 depict an overview of the audio signal flow for the SMC recordings.

---

[5] For the remainder of this chapter we will use the abbreviation QXML to denote these VoiceXML-like scripts; 'Q' stands for 'Query'.

[6] For technical reasons not all modalities are transfered to the recording server in realtime but rather stored locally on the client device. See the corresponding sections about the specific SmartWeb corpora for details.

[7] Therefore the user does not have to watch the display, a requirement for the motorcycle recordings.

[8] Siemens U15 or Nokia 6680.

[9] Bluetooth 1.1.

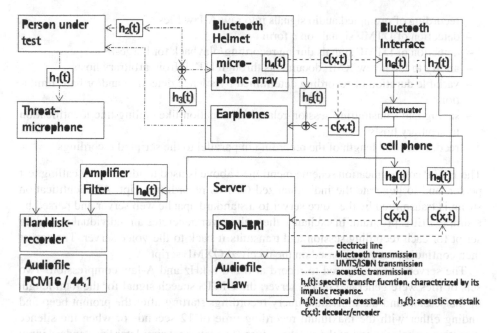

Fig. 1. Example signal flow diagram for motorcycle recording (see Section 6.2 for details)

3.2 High Quality Channels

For high quality recordings the iRiver iHP120 harddisk recorder was used. This device features one analog stereo input and output, one stereo headphone output and one S/PDIF input and output. Input sensitivity can be adjusted over a wide range and the analog input features a 2 V supply voltage for electret microphones. The hard disk recorder was configured to record at 16 bit, 44.1 kHz on the analog input; no compression applied. This results in theoretical capacity of roughly 50h.

3.3 Server Channels

The main server is a PC with *AMD K7 500MHz* and 250 MB RAM running *SuSE Linux 9.0* with kernel 2.4.21. The connectivity to the fixed telephone line network is provided via an *AVM Fritz!PCI v.2.0 (rev 2)* ISDN controller, using the standard kernel driver for CAPI[10]. To record audio signals from the phone line, a special interpreter was developed at our site in Java using JNI. The interpreter is capable of sending and receiving A-law encoded signals to and from a telephone line following simple scripts. The scripts are formatted in QXML to allow simple sequences of prompts and recordings. The properties of the server are:

- parses and interprets QXML
- playback of arbitrary audio files

---

[10] The Common ISDN Application Programming Interface.

- recording of prompted audio signals into raw A-law files
- detection of DTMF signals on a form
- detection of DTMF signals during recording/playback for barge-in
- ability to fetch new XML documents through HTTP from arbitrary hosts
- variable duration of recording determined by silence detection and/or hard limitations.
- saving and transmitting session-related information like calling line identification to arbitrary hosts.
- record the total length of the recording in parallel to the scripted recordings

The HTTP communication scheme mentioned above is used to identify the calling test person and to generate the individualized QXML recording script. An identification string is transmitted by the voice server to a standard apache web server and parsed by a simple PERL program. In exchange the web server generates an individual recording script for each recording session and transmits it back to the voice server. The server then continues processing based on the received QXML script.

The server was configured to record at 8 bit, 8 kHz and A-law compression. Two sets of files were generated by the server: the UMTS speech signal for the total length of the session and the individual query recordings starting after the prompt beep and ending either with the maximum recording time of 12 seconds or when the silence detection signals the end of the speaker's turn. The latter set simulates the standard input behavior of a dialogue system and provides more realistic data with possible incomplete recordings.

This results in four types of recorded speech signals:

- high quality (16bit; 44,1kHz; PCM) recording of close talk microphone
- high quality recording of optional microphone
- UMTS quality (8bit; 8kHz; ALAW) recording of total session
- UMTS quality recording of individual queries

3.4 Facial Video

The facial video signal is captured by the build-in camera of the Nokia 6680 (intended for video conferencing) in 3GPP using the codec H.263 with a picture size of 176x144, 24bpp and 15fps, no audio. The user was not instructed to keep the mobile phone in a certain position; therefore drop outs and partial face coverage are possible. However, a small control display on the client shows the recorded video and therefore provides the user with some intuitive guidance to keep the face somewhere within the video capture area of the camera. We found that this sufficiently influences the user to keep the smart phone in a position where her face was visible most of the time when the user is looking at the display. In case that the user looks elsewhere the face sometimes vanishes totally or partly from the video capture area. Since the user communicates with the system via a headset, the microphone is visible in the video recording; the second optional microphone does not interfere with the facial video.

4 Post-processing and Annotation

The original video file (3GPP) was transformed into an MPEG1 standard video stream and manually synchronized to the audio track recorded by the server. The same video stream is converted into JPG frame sequences. All three video streams are then included into the final corpus. The video stream was manually labeled frame-wise into the categories *OnView, OffView, between OnView/OffView* and *face not visible*.

The individual prompt recordings of the server are automatically synchronized to the harddisk recording using a cross correlation technique thus yielding a segmentation of the harddisk recording into synchronized prompt recordings. Both recordings, segmented and total, are part of the final corpus.

All recorded user output has been annotated using a subset of the annotation scheme used in the SmartKom project [8] covering the following phenomena: foreign words, compounds, spelling, acronyms, numbers, proper names, pauses, pronunciation variants, sound lengthening, hard or non-understandable words, word breaks, neologism, common word reductions, hesitations, interrupted words, technical interrupts. Prosodic markers and markers for superimposed speech have been omitted. The annotation was augmented by phonemic transcripts of all dialectal variants. Also, the annotations of SVC contain an additional set of word tags for 4 different types of OffTalk as well as time markers for the second segmentation of the recording (see Section 6.3 for details). The speech of the prompts server as well as the audible speech of the companion were not transcribed.

Annotations were produced in a three-level scheme where the annotator of the first level produced a basis transcript, the second level added all tags and the third level verified the work of the the the first two levels. Transcripts are stored in text files with extension 'trl' that conform to the Verbmobil and SmartKom transcription format. No inter-labeler agreement measures were derived.

Transcripts are also provided in the BAS Partitur Format (BPF) [11] as well as an ATLAS compatible Annotation Graph [2].

The original *recording script* of each recording is provided in two forms: a simple text file and the original QXML script that was used during the experiment.

Table 5 summarizes all data types provided for each recording session.

5 Subjects and Meta Data

There were only a few restrictions on participating in the SmartWeb data collection: speakers should speak German fluently and be familiar with the use of a cellular phone. Dialect speakers and foreign language speakers with accent were recorded, but not specifically recruited (dialect distribution not controlled). Non-students and persons over 35 years were systematically recruited, to form a counter-balance to the students that typically volunteer for such recordings close to a university. Participants are roughly equally distributed in gender except for SMC. See Table 9 for speaker numbers and age ranges of the SmartWeb corpora.

Extensive speaker information is stored in XML formatted *speaker protocols* for each recorded user: sex, age, handedness, profession, mother tongue, mother tongue

Table 5. Data provided for each recording session

Type	Format
Original face video, 176x144, 24bpp, 15fps (SVC)	3GPP
Video with synchronized audio track (SVC)	MPG1
Video as JPG sequence (SVC)	JPG
OnView/OffView labeling (SVC)	text table
Server recording, total dialogue, close talk microphone via WCDMA	8bit, alaw, 8kHz
ditto for individual prompts	*ditto*
ditto for manual segmentation (SVC, see Section 6.3)	*ditto*
Harddisk recording, total dialogue, optional microphone	16bit, pcm, 44kHz
Server segmentation	text table
Manual segmentation SVC (see Section 6.3)	text table
Transcript SmartKom standard	TRL
BAS Partitur Format (transcript,orthography,canonical pronunciation)	BPF
Annotation graph ATLAS	XML
Speaker protocol	XML
Recording protocol	XML
Recording script	QXML

of both parents, experience with dialogue systems and search engines, glasses, beard, baldness, smoker/non-smoker, piercing, other props.

For each recording session an XML formatted *recording protocol* is provided. It contains the technical setup, experimenter, user and companion[11] IDs, recording date and time, location, recorded audio and video tracks, available annotation as well as environmental conditions during the recording.

Meta data of all three SmartWeb corpora are summarized in the IMDI[12] meta data structure.[13]

6   SmartWeb Corpora

This section provides additional information regarding the three SmartWeb corpora SHC, SMC and SVC which is not covered by the previous sections. Furthermore some problems encountered during the collection and certain characteristics of the resulting data are discussed. At the end of this section you will find a table summarizing the most significant corpus features at a glance.

6.1   SmartWeb Handheld Corpus (SHC)

The main purpose of SHC is to provide data for training and testing the base line interface of SmartWeb. The SHC contains no facial video and comprises simple human-machine interactions in a variety of acoustic environments and domains.

---

[11] SVC only.
[12] See http://www.mpi.nl/IMDI/ for details about IMDI.
[13] http://www2.phonetik.uni-muenchen.de/IMDI/BAS.imdi

Table 6. Number of action units across domains

topic	SUM
community	82
soccer	563
navigation	318
open topic	430
tourist information	295
public transport	129

Table 7. Examples for queries elicited by *standard prompts* in the thematic context of *public transportation*: After being prompted with the text in the top line, the speakers uttered various responses. (translated to English for better readability)

Instructor: **Please check again with SmartWeb whether the information was correct.**
Are you sure that public transportation continues that late?
What time did you say?
... catch you right? Did I catch you right?
Excuse me, until when will there be public transportation tonight?
Until which time will there be public transportation in Leipzig?
You're sure that the underground runs until two o'clock at night?

Table 8. Examples for queries elicited by *scripted prompts* in the thematic context of *navigation*: After being prompted with the text in the top line, the speakers uttered various responses. (translated to English for better readability)

Operator: **There is a bus stop near Hegelstrasse. Would you like to learn more about the schedule?**
Yes.
Yes, I'd love to.
When does the next bus leave towards the train station at this bus stop?
Yes, I'd like to know when the next bus leaves.
Yes. Yes . I wanna catch the last bus that leaves from this bus stop.
Yes, please . What time the buses are leaving there? What number would that be and where does it go?
Nah, just where is that next bus stop? I'll be waiting there for the next bus.
No, thanks.

SHC contains 156 recording sessions with 5871 recorded queries and 57112 token words. 4815 different word forms were encountered; a large number of these are proper names.

Table 6 shows the distribution of action units (6 prompts each) over the SmartWeb domain topics.

The SitPro scheme described above yields satisfying results: The same prompt structure elicits a various range of subject queries. Examples are given in the Tables 7 and 8 which depict a number of recorded queries after the same single prompt (on top).

The recorded data are spoken with natural prosody and contain various features of spontaneously uttered speech like *disfluencies, pauses, hesitations, false starts, ungrammatical sentences, interruptions* etc.

Since we use different combinations of recording equipment — the Siemens U15 cellular phone is combined with five cable and Bluetooth headsets — in different noisy environments (indoors and outdoors), the signal quality varies tremendously. The acoustical environment ranges from quiet office to very noisy train station (with S/N ratio of less than 6dB). Permanent and transient background noise occurs quite frequently as well as strong crosstalk from single or groups of speakers.

6.2   SmartWeb Motorbike Corpus (SMC)

A considerable challenge is to enable motorcyclists to make use of a human machine interface while driving. The SMC was collected in 2005 with the purpose of meeting the requirements the SmartWeb project partners had to dialogue design and testing. To cover the circumstances of real on-the-bike situations, recordings were done during a ride performed by professional test drivers of BMW company in real traffic environment in the City of Munich.

A motorcyclist will access SmartWeb or any other dialogue system in a different way than a pedestrian on a side walk, a person in a car or a building. Motorcyclists use SmartWeb to gather information that is closely related to their current activity, i.e. related to traffic situations, weather, technical state of the vehicle, destination of the journey and similar matters. Complex themes like retrieval of encyclopedic knowledge or general news are less likely to occur although sites of interest might be a major topic. A motorcyclist has to concentrate on steering and has to watch the traffic with high attentiveness. As a consequence dialogues are often interrupted due to traffic situations and speech may be more error prone than in a situation in which the user can hold the mobile device.

Driving on a motorcycle increases the noise level from surrounding traffic, and driving fast adds a significant amount of wind noise. The increased noise causes the speaker to raise his/her voice (Lombard effect) and additional strain may change some characteristics of the voice as well. Since the voice signal is transferred over Bluetooth from the helmet of the driver to the host system of the motorcycle and possibly transferred over UMTS to a server, frequent transmission errors in form of glitches and disruptions will happen, caused by interferences with other Bluetooth channels, UMTS cell hand over and loss of data frames.

The helmet used[14] in the data collection contains two microphones which are located on top of the forehead, embedded into the EPS padding with a distance of approx. 7cm. The two signals are processed by a DSP to achieve a high directivity towards the mouth of the driver; the resulting signal is sent by Bluetooth.

For most of the recordings a throat microphone (Type KEP 33-S) was used as optional second microphone. It consists of a plastic bracket which can be fitted closely around the neck. On both ends it carries a microphone capsule that is 3cm in diameter. These capsules are placed left and right of the larynx.

---

[14] "BMW Systemhelm" with WCS-2 communication controller.

Both the throat microphone and the helmet microphones use standard electret capsules (thus avoiding magnetic field noise).

The signal of the helmet is subject to several influences roughly described in Figure 1. $h_1(t)$ and $h_2(t)$ describe the transfer functions of the acoustic path, while $h_3(t)$ models the acoustic crosstalk between the headphones and the microphones. All other $h_x(t)$ refer to electrical transfer functions, e.g. low pass filters and partially to electrical crosstalk. All functions of the form $c_y(x,t)$ stand for compression and expansion algorithms applied to the signal on digital transmissions. These occur between the helmet and the Bluetooth interface and between the mobile phone and the voice server. Noise sources are not included in Figure 1 but can be considered to influence nearly every part of the transmission except between the UMTS-Network and the server.

After some test drives BMW supplied us with a *R 1200 RT* motorcycle with a 110bhp air cooled engine. The control device was mounted in a water-proof box on top of the tank, the mobile phone was placed in a pocket of the driver and the remaining electronics stored in a small knapsack. There was no galvanic connection to the vehicle's electric system.

Recruitment of speakers was performed by BMW research facilities among a selected list of BMW employees. Public recruitment was not viable due to limitations in insurance policies. To reduce the risk of accidents only experienced drivers were selected who had already performed several test drives in the past. It should be mentioned here that although the percentage of female motorcyclists is rather high in Germany, it turned out to be very difficult to recruit female drivers for the SMC.

46 sessions have been recorded as described above and carefully examined. 10 sessions had to be discarded because of technical problems. Each session consisted of a maximum of 12 action units of 6 prompt units each. A relatively large number of prompts turned out to be useless because the driver did not respond to the prompt, probably being distracted by traffic. In total the recordings resulted in 2315 usable queries with approximately 17175 running words. These numbers seem to be moderate compared to other speech corpora productions. However, considering the limited budget and the effort needed to recruit test drivers a larger number of speakers would have exceeded the scope of this project.

6.3 SmartWeb Video Corpus (SVC)

Portable devices and so called smart phones as well as their respective network infrastructure have matured up to a point where it is possible to capture the video image of the talker's face during a dialogue and send the combined video and voice streams in real time to a server based dialogue system. In large parts of Europe this can be achieved using an effective video coding standard (3GPP) used for mobile phone video as well as the Wide-band Code Division Multiple Access (WCDMA) transmission protocol (commonly known as 'UMTS') and an infrastructure which is by now in operation from a number of telephone providers. This technique not only makes video conferencing from handheld devices possible but also allows — in principle — a speech dialogue system not only to capture the human user's voice input but also her facial gestures such as eye direction, lip movement, head movement, movement of eyebrows etc. One

Fig. 2. Left: captured frame with OffFocus; right: captured frame with OnFocus behavior (recording *i055*)

interesting application of face video capture is the automatic detection of so called On-Focus/OffFocus [5,1], meaning basically the answer to two questions:

> *Is the user's focus on the display?*
> *Is she addressing the system or rather a third party or is speaking to herself?*

Figure 2 shows two captured video frames taken during a user–machine interaction; in the right picture the user is OnFocus, in the left picture she talks to her companion and is therefore OffFocus.

Assuming a dialogue system with no push-to-talk activation — that is, the microphone is always 'open' for voice input of the user — it is of vital importance to detect utterances that are not addressed to the system to avoid misinterpreted voice input to the dialogue engine. On the other hand, a dialogue system using combined acoustic and visual output modalities might alter its output modality depending on information about whether the user is looking at the display or not: visual display output may for instance be replaced by speech synthesis output if the user's focus is definitely not on the device.

To provoke head movements and facial expressions combined with speech directed to the system and to third parties we chose a triad communication scenario: the system and two human subjects (the user and a companion). The user interacts directly with the system while her companion tries to interfere with the communication through remarks and additional requests for information. Thus the recorded user is often distracted from her task (to gather information about a certain topic), looks to and from the display and addresses her companion to answer questions. The companion is not allowed to watch the display's output. Therefore the user often paraphrases or reads given system output to her companion.

The SmartWeb annotation (see Section 4) was augmented by a set of word tags for different types of OffTalk:

> <SOT> spontaneous Off-Talk
> <POT> paraphrased Off-Talk
> <ROT> read Off-Talk
> <OOT> other Off-Talk

where *spontaneous Off-Talk* denotes speech directed to the companion, *paraphrased Off-Talk* is a special case of spontaneous Off-Talk where the user is relaying information

Fig. 3. From left to right: two different OffFocus situations, OnFocus behavior (recording *i077*)

provided by the system to her companion. *Read Off-Talk* denotes reading (literally) from the display while *other Off-Talk* builds the garbage class (e.g. muttering to himself).

About half of the uttered words were classified as OffTalk which indicates that the triad communication scheme of SVC works fine (see table 9). As can be expected, spontaneous OffTalk is the most frequently occurring form of OffTalk. The high percentage of paraphrasing and read OffTalk is caused by the explicit instruction to the speakers; in a natural setting we would expect a much lower frequency for these types of OffTalk. Finally, at 3.1% of the total OffTalk the percentage of other OffTalk (muttering to himself etc.) is very low, probably caused by the (possibly embarrassing) presence of the companion. In other studies [6] where no third party was present this percentage was significantly higher.

OffTalk always implies OffFocus, while OnTalk (everything that is not tagged as OffTalk) always implies OnFocus. Unfortunately, this does not mean that Talk and Focus are equivalent, since the user might be OffFocus while being silent (e.g. listening to her companion).

The equivalent to OnTalk is OnView labeled in the facial video stream. As mentioned earlier the video stream was manually labeled frame-wise into the 4 categories *OnView, OffView, between OnView/OffView* and *face not visible*.

Figure 3 illustrates two different instances of OffFocus behavior. The left picture shows OffFocus with almost no head movement; only the eye focus changes. The middle picture shows a clearly visible case of OffFocus: the user moves her head towards her companion. For reference, a typical OnFocus situation is shown in the right picture.

Since the user is often being distracted, many user inputs do not fit within the recording windows of the QXML script. Furthermore, all OffFocus related speech is naturally outside the server recording windows as well. Therefore the total server recording was manually segmented into speech chunks independently of the QXML script. This second segmentation of the session is also incorporated into the annotation of the user's speech so that the transcripts are closely aligned to this segmentation.

7   Conclusion

Three speech corpora SHC, SMC and SVC produced within the SmartWeb project have been described in detail. Table 9 summarizes the most prominent figures of the SmartWeb corpora. In the scope of this book the SmartWeb Video Corpus (SVC) bears the potential

Table 9. The SmartWeb corpora in numbers

	SHC	SMC	SVC
number of sessions/speakers	156	36	99
female / male	56/70	2/34	63/36
age	13–70	24–57	15–64
indoor/outdoor sessions	62/94	0/36	72/27
number of queries	5871	2315	2218
number of words	57112	17175	25151
number words spontaneous OffTalk	-	-	5177
number words paraphrasing OffTalk	-	-	4385
number words read OffTalk	-	-	2917
number words other OffTalk	-	-	404
percentage OffTalk	-	-	51.2%
total size	55.1GB	9.8GB	19.2GB
media	15 DVD-R	3 DVD-R	6 DVD-R

to investigate turn handling and user focus based on speech (OnTalk/OffTalk) and face video capture data (OnView/OffView) in real environments. Also the rarely investigated triad communication scenario where two humans interact and also interact with the machine can be analysed here. Data from the SHC corpus may act as training or benchmark data for the 'normal' case where one single human interacts with the machine in the same setting as in the SVC corpus. The SMC corpus may be used as test data for an extreme case of human computer interaction which main characteristics are extreme background noise, high mental distraction and channel disturbances.

The SmartWeb corpora are distributed for scientific or commercial usage on DVD-R via the BAS[15] and the ELDA[16]. Since the corpus was 100% funded by the German government, only the BAS distributions fees apply[17].

Acknowledgements

The work presented in this chapter as well as the resulting speech corpora were funded by the German Ministry for Education and Science (BMBF) under grant number 01 IM D01 I as well as by the Bavarian Archive for Speech Signals (BAS). The author thanks all colleagues within the SmartWeb project and the BAS for their help and support.

References

1. Batliner, A., Hacker, C., Kaiser, M., Mögele, H., Nöth, E.: Taking into Account the User's Focus of Attention with the Help of Audio-Visual Information: Towards less Artificial Human-Machine-Communication. In: Krahmer, E., Swerts, M., Vroomen, J. (eds.) International Conference on Auditory-Visual Speech Processing 2007, pp. 51–56 (2007)

---

[15] http://www.bas.uni-muenchen.de/Bas
[16] http://www.elda.org
[17] At the time of writing EUR 256 per distributed medium.

2. Bird, S., Day, D., Garofolo, J., Henderson, J., Laprun, C., Libermann M.: ATLAS: A flexible and extensible architecture for linguistic annotation. In: Proceedings of LREC 2000, Rhodes, Greece (2000)
3. Draxler, C.: WebTranscribe - An Extensible Web-Based Speech Annotation Framework. In: Matoušek, V., Mautner, P., Pavelka, T. (eds.) TSD 2005. LNCS (LNAI), vol. 3658, pp. 61–68. Springer, Heidelberg (2005)
4. Gibbon, D., Moore, R., Winski, R.: Handbook of Standards and Resources for Spoken Language Systems. Walter de Gruyter, Berlin (1997)
5. Hacker, C., Batliner, A., Nöth, E.: Are You Looking at Me, are You Talking with Me – Multimodal Classification of the Focus of Attention. In: Sojka, P., Kopeček, I., Pala, K. (eds.) TSD 2006. LNCS (LNAI), vol. 4188, pp. 581–588. Springer, Heidelberg (2006)
6. Oppermann, D., Schiel, F., Steininger, S., Beringer, N.: Off-Talk - A Problem for Human-Machine-Interaction. In: Proceedings of the EUROSPEECH 2001, Scandinavia, Aalborg, Danmark (2001)
7. Peters, B.: Video Task oder Daily Soap Scenario. Ein neues Verfahren zur kontrollierten Elizitation von Spontansprache (2001), www.ipds.uni-kiel.de/pub_exx/bp2001_1/Linda21.html (Cited February 13, 2009)
8. Rabold, S., Biersack, S.: SmartKom Transliteration Manual (2002), www.phonetik.uni-muenchen.de/forschung/SmartKom/Konengl/engltrans/engltrans.html (Cited February 13, 2009)
9. Rapp, S., Strube, M.: An Iterative Data Collection Approach for Multimodal Dialogue Systems. In: Proceedings of the 3rd International Conference on Language Resources and Evaluation, Las Palmas, Canary Islands, Spain, pp. 661–665 (2002)
10. Schiel, F., Draxler, C.: Production and Validation of Speech Corpora. Bastard Verlag, Munich (2003)
11. Schiel, F., Burger, S., Geumann, A., Weilhammer, K.: The Partitur Format at BAS. In: Proceedings of the 1st Int. Conf. on Language Resources and Evaluation 1998, Granada, Spain, pp. 1295–1301 (1998)
12. Steininger, S.: Data collection pilot study - human-human telephone dialgoues. SmartKom Technical Document No. 01 Version 1.0, University of Munich, Institute of Phonetics (2005)
13. Türk, U.: The Technical Processing in SmartKom Data Collection: a Case Study. In: Proceedings of Eurospeech 2001 Scandianavia, Aalborg, Denmark, pp. 1541–1544 (2001)
14. Wahlster, W.: Smartweb: Mobile applications of the semantic web (2004), http://www.springerlink.com/content/l15mexmr5gd6cy8u/ (Cited February 13, 2009)

Promoting *free* Dialog Video Corpora: The IFADV Corpus Example

R.J.J.H. van Son[1], Wieneke Wesseling[1], Eric Sanders[2],
and Henk van den Heuvel[2]

[1] ACLC/IFA, University of Amsterdam, The Netherlands
R.J.J.H.vanSon@uva.nl
[2] SPEX/CLST, Radboud University Nijmegen, The Netherlands

Abstract. Research into spoken language has become more visual over the years. Both fundamental and applied research have progressively included gestures, gaze, and facial expression. Corpora of multi-modal conversational speech are rare and frequently difficult to use due to privacy and copyright restrictions. In contrast, *Free-and-Libre* corpora would allow anyone to add incremental annotations and improvement, distributing the cost of construction and maintenance. A freely available annotated corpus is presented with high quality video recordings of face-to-face conversational speech. An effort has been made to remove copyright and use restrictions. Annotations have been processed to RDBMS tables that allow SQL queries and direct connections to statistical software. A few simple examples are presented to illustrate the use of a databases of annotated speech. From our experiences we would like to advocate the formulation of "best practises" for both legal handling and database storage of recordings and annotations.

1 Introduction

Fundamental and applied research have progressively included visual aspects of speech. Gestures, gaze, and facial expression have become important for understanding human communication. Such research requires corpora of multi-modal conversational speech. But such corpora are rare and frequently difficult to use due to privacy and copyright restrictions. Creating such a corpus is an expensive and time-consuming effort. Free, as in *freedom*, corpora would allow anyone to add incremental annotations and improvement. This way the burden of construction and maintenance of the corpus can be distributed over a wider user community. Such a distribution of efforts is also seen in other communities that freely share expensive information resources, e.g., Genbank [1], web based community resources like Wikipedia [2], and Free and Open Source software like the Linux kernel [3,4,5].

In the context of a research project into spoken language understanding in conversations, a corpus of visible speech was needed. Reaction time experiments were planned where experimental subjects watch and listen to manipulated recordings and react with minimal responses. For these experiments video recordings

M. Kipp et al. (Eds.): Multimodal Corpora, LNAI 5509, pp. 18–37, 2009.

of informal conversations were needed. Neither ELRA [6] nor the LDC [7] had any conversational video material available. The corresponding entity in the Netherlands, the Dutch TST centrale [8], also had no conversational video corpus available. Nor were we at the time able to obtain another video corpus.

In the world, several corpora exist that contain annotated video recordings of conversational speech. For instance, the HCRC Map Task Corpus [9] does contain video recordings, but, according to their web-site, these have not been made generally available due to privacy concerns. Also, the French Corpus of Interactional Data, CID [10,11], is an annotated audio-video recording of conversational speech which is currently available to other researchers at no cost. It is distributed under a license that intends to *"guarantee the undividedness of data distributed by CRDO and the follow-up of its utilisation for the benefit of its producers"*. As such, the license does not allow redistribution and sharing of the corpus and requires that the distribution of upgrades and changes should go through the CRDO [12].

Within our project, we have created a visual version of the friendly Face-to-Face dialogs of the Spoken Dutch Corpus, also known as CGN [13]. Within the bounds of our budget, the procedures and design of the corpus were adapted to make this corpus useful for other researchers of Dutch speech. For this corpus we recorded and annotated 20 dialog conversations of 15 minutes, in total 5 hours of speech. To stay close to the very useful Face-to-Face dialogs in the CGN, we selected pairs of well acquainted participants, either good friends, relatives, or long-time colleagues. The participants were allowed to talk about any topic they wanted.

In total, 20 out of 24 initial recordings were annotated to the same, or updated, standards as the original CGN. However, only the initial orthographic transcription was done by hand. Other CGN-format annotations were only done automatically (see below). As an extension, we added two other manual annotations, a functional annotation of dialog utterances and annotated gaze direction.

The remainder of this paper is organized as follows. Sections 2 to 5 will describe the construction and structure of the corpus. Sections 6 and 7 contain a discussion on the legal aspects of creating and distributing (spoken) language corpora. Section 8 presents some illustrative examples of corpus use. The last sections, 9 and 10, contain a general discussion and conclusions drawn from our experiences with creating this corpus.

2   Recordings

For the recordings, the speakers sat face-to-face opposite of each other in an audio studio with a table in between (see Figure 1) The recording studio had a sound-treated box-in-a-box design and noise levels were low. The distance between the speakers was about 1m. Recordings were made with two gen-locked JVC TK-C1480B analog color video cameras (see table 1). Each camera was positioned to the left of one speaker and focused on the face of the other (see Figure 2). Participants first spoke some scripted sentences. Then they were instructed to

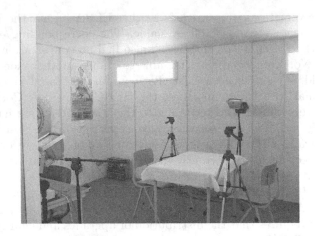

Fig. 1. Recording studio set-up. The distance between the speakers was around 1 m. Photograph courtesy of Jeannette M. van der Stelt.

Table 1. Recording equipment, two gen-locked JVC TK-C1480B analog color video cameras with following specifications and peripherals

Image pickup :	1/2 type IT CCD 752 (H) x 582 (V)
Synchronization :	Internal Line Lock, Full Genlock
Scanning freq. :	(H) 15.625kHz x (V) 50Hz
Resolution :	480 TV lines (H)
Screen size :	720x576 BGR 24-bit, 25 frames/s
Camera A :	Ernitec GA4V10NA-1/2 lens (4-10mm)
Camera B :	Panasonic WV-LZ80/2 lens (6-12mm)
AD conversion :	2 Canopus ADVC110 digital video conv.
Microphones :	Samson QV head-set microphones

speak freely while preferably avoiding sensitive material or identifying people by name.

Gen-lock ensures synchronization of all frames of the two cameras to within a half (interleaved) frame, i.e., 20 ms. Recordings were digitized, and then stored unprocessed on disk, i.e., in DV format with 48 kHz 16 bit PCM sound.

Recording the videos of the dialogs introduced some limitations to our participants. For technical reasons, all recordings had to be done in our studio, instead of in the participant's home, as was done for the CGN Face-to-Face recordings. The position of the cameras, as much as possible directly in front of the participants, did induce a static set-up with both participants sitting face-to-face at a table.

Figure 2 gives an example frame of each of the two cameras. Notice the position of the camera focussed on the other subject. The position of the head-mounted microphone was such that it would not obstruct the view of the lips. The posters on the back-ground were intended to suggest conversation topics

Fig. 2. Example frame of recordings (output camera A, left; B, right). In the frames shown, the speakers are looking at each other, i.e., a Gaze annotation label *g* (see text).

when needed. In practice, subjects hardly ever needed any help in finding topics for conversation. They generally started before we were ready to record, and even tended to continue after we informed them that the session was over. After the interruption by the instructions and scripted sentences that started each recording, the subjects in all dialogs initiated a new conversation on a new topic. Recordings were cut-off 900 seconds after the start of the conversations following the scripted sentences. Consequently, no conversation open and closing parts were recorded.

The result of these procedures was that the conversations are probably as free-form as can be obtained in a studio setting. The quality of the sound and video is high and even the gaze direction can easily be identified. This makes this corpus useful for many types of research, from classical conversation analysis to automatically detecting gaze direction and emotion in facial expressions.

Annotated recordings are limited to 900 seconds (15 min). Each recorded DV file is around 4 GB in size. The diaphragm of the B camera overcompensated the lighting and most of the B recordings are, therefore, rather dark. However, there is enough range in the brightness left to compensate for this. Dropped frames during recording offset the synchrony of the two recordings, and all occurrences of frame drops have therefore been identified. For each recording, a SMIL [14] file is available that specifies how the original frame timing can be restored by repeating frames to replace dropped frames.

3 Participants

The corpus consists of 20 annotated dialogs (selected from 24 recordings). All participants signed an informed consent and transferred all copyrights to the Dutch Language Union (Nederlandse Taalunie). For two minors, the parents too signed the forms. In total 34 speakers participated in the annotated recordings: 10 male and 24 female. Age ranged from 21 to 72 for males and 12 to 62 for females. All were native speakers of Dutch. Participants originated in different parts of the Netherlands. Each speaker completed a form with personal characteristics. Notably, age, place of birth, and the places of primary and secondary education were all recorded. In addition, the education of the parents and data on height and weight were recorded, as well as some data on training or experiences in relevant speech related fields, like speech therapy, acting, and call-center work.

The recordings were made in-face with a small offset (see Figure 2). Although participants never looked directly into the camera, it is immediately obvious when watching the videos whether a person looks at the other participant or not. Video recordings were synchronized to make uniform timing measurements possible. All conversations were "informal" since participants were friends or colleagues. There were no constraints on subject matter, style, or other aspects. However, participants were reminded before the recordings started that their speech would be published.

4   File Formats

Like archives, corpora are constructed with an aim of long term access. Obviously, the first and foremost concern is the preservation of the original recordings, metadata, and other materials. This principle extends to the annotations, which should be added cumulative. The combined requirements of source preservation and cumulative annotations leads to the principle of *stand off annotation*, the separation of annotations and source materials [15].

For long term access, all data must be available in well understood, preferably open, formats [16,17]. It is essential that access and processing of the files is not restricted to specific applications or computer platforms as this will compromise the long term access and integrity of the corpus. Data stored using proprietary codecs and file formats faces a considerable risk of losing support from the technology's "owner" at some moment. Data stored in such legacy formats might become inaccessible in only a few years [16]. Being proprietary, it is often impossible to find or build supporting software from other sources.

Exclusionary proprietary restrictions are obviously a problem with codecs or file formats that are only available from a single vendor for selected platforms, e.g., Microsoft's VC-1 codecs and ASF file format. In the distribution of on-line broadcast media content, such exclusionary choices of formats and codecs are quite common. For instance, the codec chosen for the on-line broadcast of the 2008 Olympics in Beijing was at the time only available for Microsoft Windows and Apple OSX and excluded users of other platforms. Therefore, the designers of multi-modal corpora should be wary to take an example from media distribution on the internet.

Where possible, international standards should be supported in corpus construction and distribution, e.g., SMIL, MPEG, PDF, or ODF. However, the use of some standards, like MPEG, is restricted by patents which might be an issue for some users. It is therefore advisable to include an option for accessing

Table 2. Annotations in the IFA DV corpus. Annotations have been made by *Hand* and *Automatic*. Where possible, the annotations were made in a *CGN* format. Annotations *not* in the CGN used new formats.

Orthographic transliteration:	Hand *CGN* chunk aligned
POS tagging:	Automatic, *CGN*
Word alignment:	Automatic, *CGN*
Word-to-Phoneme:	Automatic, *CGN*
Phoneme alignment:	Automatic, *CGN*
Conversational function:	Hand, *non-CGN*
Gaze direction:	Hand, *ELAN, non-CGN*
End intonation:	Automatic, *non-CGN*

copies that are unencumbered by Intellectual Property (IP, e.g., copyrights and patents) claims. For the current IFADV corpus this was an issue only for the processed, i.e., compressed, versions of the recordings. Therefore, these are offered in several different formats, one of which was always "open" [18,19], e.g., Ogg formats and codecs .

For the IFADV corpus, we chose to preserve the original DV format recordings with audio and video as they were obtained from the AD converters. For each recording, a SMIL markup file [14] was created that described the frames that were dropped. These SMIL files will recreate the original timing by redoubling frames to stand in for the lost ones. The original recording files are large (> 3GB) and rather cumbersome to distribute and manage. Therefore, frame corrected files are made available in DV format. These are also available as compressed files in avi (DivX3) and Ogg (Theora) format, with normalized brightness and contrast levels. The audio is available seperately as 48 kHz WAV (RIFF) files and a selection of compressed versions (FLAC, Ogg, Speex, MP3). All these file formats, and codecs, are widely used and available for all platforms.

There is currently no accepted standard file format for speech and video annotations. Work on such an international (exchange) standard has only just been presented [20]. For practial reasons, all annotations were stored in the Praat TextGrid format and the ELAN EAF file format (original gaze annotations). Both applications are widely used and sources are available. These annotation file formats are well documented and easy to parse automatically.

Where possible, the annotation labels and procedures of the CGN were used (see table 2).

5 Annotations

20 conversations have been annotated according to the formalism of the Spoken Dutch Corpus, CGN [13], by SPEX in Nijmegen. A full list of the annotations can be found in table 2. The computer applications used for the automatic annotations were different from those used by the CGN, but the file format and labels were kept compatible with those in the CGN. The manual orthographic

transliteration and rough time alignment of 5 hours of dialogs took approximately 150 hours (30 times real time).

The basic unit of the transliteration was the utterance-like *chunk*. This is an *inter-pausal unit* (IPU) when short, up to 3 seconds. Longer IPUs were split on strong prosodic breaks based on the intuition of the annotators. For practical purposes, these chunks can be interpreted as *utterances*, c.f., figure 3. To improve readability, we will refer to *utterances* in this text when we, strictly speaking, are referring to *chunks*, as defined in the Spoken Dutch Corpus [13]. The annotations are either in the same formats used by the CGN [13] or in newly defined formats (*non-CGN*) for annotations not present in the CGN (table 2).

The functional annotation was restricted to keep the costs within budget. A HRC style hierarchical speech or conversational acts annotation [21,22] was not intended. The idea behind the annotation was to stay close to the information content of the conversation. How does the content fit into the current topic and how does it function? The label set is described in table 3. The hand annotation of the chunk functions in context took around 140 hours ($\sim$30 times real time).

Each utterance was labeled with respect to the previous utterance, irrespective of the speaker. Some labels can be combined with other labels, e.g., almost every type of utterance can end in a question or hesitation, i.e., u or a. Note that a speaker can answer (r) her own question (u). Labeling was done by naive subjects who were instructed about the labeling procedure. We are well aware that this annotation is impressionistic.

Gaze direction was annotated with ELAN [23]. The categories were basically g for gazing at the partner and x for looking away. For some subjects, special labels were used in addition to specify consistent idiosyncratic behavior, i.e., d for closing the eyes and k for stereotypical blinking. The start and end of all occurrences where one subject gazed towards their partner were indicated. This hand labelling took around 85 hours for 5 hours of recordings (17 times real time).

```
F59H: heel melancholieke sfeer.
M65I: hoe was 't uh met de muziek op Kreta?
F59H: nou uh we zaten dit keer in 'n uh we
      hebben een huis gehuurd 'n
      traditioneel uh boerenhuis een stenen huis.
      en dat was een uh
M65I: wat je kende of niet zomaar uh?
F59H: nou we hebben 't van het internet
      geplukt en toen 'n beetje
      gecorrespondeerd met de eigenaar en
      dat leek ons wel wat.
      ja 't blijft natuurlijk altijd een gok.
      maar dat bleek dus heel erg leuk te zijn.
      in 'n heel klein boerendorpje*n
      helemaal noordwest uh Kreta.
```

Fig. 3. Example transcription of recordings, formatted for readability (originals are in Praat textgrid format). The transcription of a chunk ends with a punctuation mark. M65I: Male subject, F59H: Female subject.

Table 3. Conversational function annotation labels and their distribution in the corpus. Both u and a can follow other labels. 52 Chunks did not receive a label when they should have. Labels u and a can be added to other labels and are counted separately ($n = 13{,}669$).

Label	Description	
b:	Start of a new topic	735
c:	Continuing topic (e.g., follows b, or c)	8739
h:	Repetition of content	240
r:	Reaction (to u)	853
f:	Grounding acts or formulaic expressions	213
k:	Minimal response	2425
i:	Interjections	27
m:	Meta remarks	61
o:	Interruptions	138
x:	Cannot be labeled	27
a:	Hesitations at the end of the utterance	1374
u:	Questions and other attempts to get a reaction	1028

Summary *DVA6H+I*

Relation Speakers: *Colleagues*

List of Topics: *Leiden, Russian, Storage of documentation, Edison Klassiek, Crete, Greek, Restoration, Noord/Zuidlijn, Sailing*

Summary: *2 Speakers (F59H and M65I)*

...

Then they discuss the chaos on Amsterdam Central. A tunnel for a new metro line, the 'Noord/Zuidlijn', is built there. F59H says to M65I that he doesn't have to take a train anymore. He says that he will take the train to Amsterdam every now and then. M65I is going sailing soon. He describes the route that they are going to take.

Fig. 4. Example extract from a summary of a recording session. Female and Male subject.

The intonation at the end of an utterance is an important signal for potential turn switches, or Transition Relevance Places (TRP) [24]. Therefore, an automatic annotation on utterance end pitch was added (*low*, *mid*, and *high*, coded as 1, 2, 3), determined on the final pitch (in *semitones*) relative to the utterance mean and global variance, i.e., $Z = \left(F_0^{end} - \overline{F_0}\right)/stdev(F_0)$ with boundaries for *mid* $-0.5 \leq Z \leq 0.2$ [25].

An identification code (ID) has been added to all linguistic entities in the corpus according to [26,27,28,29]. All entities referring to the same stretch of speech receive an identical and unique ID. See table 4 for an example[1]. Although

---

[1] Syllables are counted S, T, U, ... and divided into <u>O</u>nset, <u>K</u>ernel, and <u>C</u>oda using a maximum onset rule. So the ID of the first (and only) phoneme of the kernel of the first syllable in a word ends in *SK1*.

Table 4. Example encoding scheme for item IDs. The /e/ from the first word /ne:/ (*no*) of the utterance "nee dat was in Leiden." (*no, that was in Leiden*) uttered by the left subject (*A*) in the sixth session as her third chunk is encoded as:

Item	ID code	Description
phoneme	*DVA6F59H2C1SK1*	First vowel
syllable part	*DVA6F59H2C1SK*	Kernel
syllable	*DVA6F59H2C1S*	First syllable[1]
word	*DVA6F59H2C1*	First word
chunk	*DVA6F59H2C*	Third chunk
Tier name	*DVA6F59H2*	-
Recording	*DVA6F59H2*	(this subject's)
Speaker	*DVA6F59H*	Female H
Session	*DVA6*	Recording session 6
Camera	*DVA*	Left subject
Annotation	*DV*	Dialog Video Audio

the ID codes only have to be unique, they have been built by extending the ID of the parent item. That is, an individual phoneme ID can be traced back to the exact position in the recording session it has been uttered in. The gaze direction annotations run "parallel" to the speech and have been given ID's that start with *GD* (Gaze Direction) instead of *DV* (Dialog Video). In all other respects they are treated identical to speech annotations.

These codes are necessary to build RDBMS (Relational Database Management System) tables for database access [26,27,28,29]. Such tables are available for all annotations as tab-delimited lists. The RDBMS tables are optimized for PostgreSQL, but should be easy to use in other databases. Through the unique ID, it is possible to join different tables and perform statistics directly on the database (see Figure 5). For example, statistical scripts from *R* can connect directly to the database [30]. All numerical data in this paper have been calculated with simple SQL database queries and demonstrate their usefulness.

Transcripts are available in standard text form for easier reading (see Figure 3). Summaries were compiled from these transcripts (see Figure 4). Meta data for all recordings are available. These have been entered into IMDI format [31].

6 Copyright and Privacy Concerns

One of the aims of our corpus effort was to create a resource that could be *used*, *adapted*, and *distributed* freely by all. This aim looks deceptively simple. It is, however, fraught with legal obstacles. The law gives those who perform, create, or alter what is now often called *intellectual content* broad control over precisely *use*, *adaptation*, and *distribution* of the products of their works. In legal terms, "intellectual content" is described by the Berne Convention as [32]:

> ...every production in the literary, scientific and artistic domain, whatever may be the mode or form of its expression, ...

```
SELECT
      avg(delay) AS Mean,
      stddev(delay) AS SD,
      sqrt(variance(delay)
           /count(properturnswitch.id)) AS SE,
      count(properturnswitch.id) AS Count
FROM
      properturnswitch
      JOIN
      fct
      USING (ID)
WHERE
      fct.value ~ 'u' AND fct.value ~ 'a';
```

Fig. 5. Example SQL query. This query generates the results displayed in the right hand (PSTS) side of the *ua* row of table 5. *properturnswitch*: table with the chunk ID's and the turn switch delays; *fct*: table with the functional labeling.

With the added requirement that it is "fixed in some material form" [32]. In practise, this can often be interpreted as anything that can be reproduced and is not automatically generated. It does not help that the relevant laws differ between countries. In addition, there are also *performance* and *editorial* rights for those who act out or process the production [33] as well as *database* rights [34,35,36]. When creating corpora, these additional rights can be treated like copyrights. Most countries also allow individuals additional control over materials related to their privacy.

On the surface, the above problems could be solved easily. It only requires that all the subjects and everyone else involved in the creation and handling of the corpus, agree to the fact that the corpus should be free to be used and distributed by anyone. The copyright and privacy laws allow such an arrangement, provided that these agreements are put in writing and signed by everyone involved. And it must be clear that everybody, especially naive subjects, actually understood what they agreed to. Therefore, the problem shifts to what the written and signed agreements must contain to legally allow free *use*, *adaptation*, and *distribution* by all, and who must sign them.

In recent years, the interpretations of copyright and privacy laws have become very restrictive. The result is that the required written agreements, i.e., copyright transfers and informed consents, have become longer and more complex and have involved more people. There are countless examples of (unexpected) restrictions attached onto corpora and recordings due to inappropriate, restrictive, or even missing copyright transfer agreements or informed consent signatures. Experience has shown that trying to amend missing signatures is fraught with problems.

The solution to these problems has been to make clear, up-front, to subjects how the recordings and the personal data might be used. In practise, this has meant that the different options, e.g., publishing recordings and meta data on the internet, have to be written explicitly into the copyright transfer forms. A good guide seems to be that corpus creators are specific about the intended uses whenever possible. At the same time, an effort should be made to be inclusive and prepare for potential, future, uses by yourself and others. All the "legal" information has to be made available also in layman's terms in an informed consent declaration. Obviously, subjects should have ample opportunity to ask questions about the procedures and use of the recordings.

For logistic reasons, signatures are generally needed before the recordings start. However, the courts might very well find that subjects cannot judge the consequences of their consent before they know what will actually be distributed afterwards. For that reason, subjects should have an opportunity to retract their consent after they know what is actually recorded and published.

As to who must all sign a copyright transfer agreement, it is instructive to look at movie credits listings. Although not authoritative, the categories of contributors in these credits listings can be used as a first draft of who to include in any copyright transfer agreement. It might often be a good idea to *in*clude more people, but it is better to consult a legal expert before *ex*cluding possible contributors.

The requirements of privacy laws are different from those of copyrights. It is both polite and good practise to try to protect the anonymity of the subjects. However, this is obviously not possible for video recordings, as the subjects can easily be recognized. In general, this fact will be made clear to the subjects before the recordings start. In our practise we pointed out to the subjects that it might be possible that someone uses the recording in a television or radio broadcast. A more modern example would be posting of the recordings on YouTube. If the subjects can agree with that, it can be assumed that they have no strongly felt privacy concerns.

All our participants were asked to sign copyright transfer forms that allow the use of the recordings in a very broad range of activities, including unlimited distribution over the Internet. This also included the use of relevant personal information (however, excluding any use of participant's name or contact information). Participants read and accorded informed consent forms that explained these possible uses to them. To ensure that participants were able to judge the recordings on their appropriateness, they were given a DVD with the recordings afterwards and allowed ample time to retract their consent.

7   License and Distribution

To be able to use or distribute copyrighted materials in any way or form, users must have a license from the copyright holder. Our aim of giving *free* (as in *libre*) access to the corpus is best served by using a Free or Open Source license [19]. We chose the GNU General Public License, GPLv 2 [37], as it has shown to protect the continuity and integrity of the licensed works. It has also shown to be an efficient means to promote use by a wide audience with the least administrative overhead. This license ensures the least restrictions and simplifies the continued build up of annotations and corrections.

In almost all respects, the GPLv2 is equivalent to, and compatible with, the European Union Public Licence, EUPL v.1.0 [38]. However, the GPLv2 is only available in English, while the EUPLv1 is available in all official EU languages where versions have the (exact) same legal meaning. So, future corpus building efforts in Europe might consider the EUPL for their license.

According to an agreement with the funding agency, the Netherlands Organization for Scientific Research (NWO), all copyrights were directly transferred to the Dutch Language Union (NTU). The Dutch Language Union distributes the corpus and all related materials under the GNU General Public License [37].

The GPLv2 allows unlimited use and distribution of the licensed materials. There is however a condition to (re-) distributing partial, adapted, or changed versions of the "works". Whenever changes fall under copyright laws, i.e., when they create a *derivative work* in the sense of the law, they *must* be distributed under the same license, i.e., the GPLv2. And that license requires the release of the "source" behind the works.

This condition raises the question of what the source of a corpus recording or annotation is. The short answer is, everything needed to reproduce the changes in whatever format is customary for making changes. Examples would be Praat TextGrid or ELAN EAF files. A long answer would include audio, video, and document formats and associated codecs. Basically, if the receiver has more problems making changes than the originator, there is reason to add additional sources.

The corpus is currently freely available from the TST-centrale [8]. This includes raw and processed video recordings, audio, and all annotations. In addition, there are derived annotation files available that combine different annotations. Summaries and IMDI metadata records have been made for all annotated dialogs. Relational database tables have been constructed from the annotations and stored in tab-delimited lists. These and all the scripts needed to process the annotations and tables are also available at the TST-centrale. All materials are copyrighted by the Dutch Language Union (Nederlandse Taalunie) and licensed under the GNU GPLv2 [37]. All materials are available free of charge. Pre-release development versions of all materials are available from the University of Amsterdam at URL http://www.fon.hum.uva.nl/IFA-SpokenLanguageCorpora/

8   Examples

An important aim that guided the construction of the IFADV corpus was to make the corpus easy accessible for research purposes. The approach chosen was to store all meta-data and annotations in database tables (RDBMS). As a result, many research questions can be directly answered using standard SQL queries using common tools. Such an approach to spoken language corpora is not yet standard practice. To illustrate the usefulness of annotation databases, we will present three practical examples of simple research questions that can be tackled using database searches.

Table 5. Distribution of durations in seconds over the most important conversational functions. Chunks (Chk, left) and PSTS delays (right). Labels u and a can be added to other labels and are counted separately. Mean: mean duration; SD: Standard Deviation; SE: Standard Error; #: Number of occurrences; All: all functional labels.

Label	Chk Mean	SD	SE	#	PSTS Mean	SD	SE	#
b	1.535	0.648	0.024	735	0.425	0.633	0.039	262
c	1.367	0.667	0.007	8739	0.233	0.670	0.011	3682
h	0.773	0.531	0.034	240	0.122	0.564	0.051	121
k	0.312	0.288	0.006	2425	0.307	0.507	0.016	1009
r	0.937	0.687	0.024	853	0.251	0.644	0.032	409
f	0.539	0.318	0.022	213	0.271	0.713	0.075	90
a	1.194	0.667	0.018	1374	0.167	0.754	0.038	388
u	1.189	0.668	0.021	1002	0.278	0.613	0.023	733
ua	1.747	0.679	0.133	26	0.053	0.574	0.117	24
All	1.119	0.739	0.006	13669	0.256	0.643	0.008	5752

To start with the contents of the database. In total, 13,373 (IPU based) verbal *chunks* with 69,187 words were recorded (excluding non-verbal noises). 589 Words were transcribed as incomplete ('*a' in CGN). The original orthographic transliteration chunks were combined with the automatic word alignments to create word aligned chunks.

8.1   Example: Simplified *Proper Speaker Turn Switches*

Many important aspects of conversations are localized around, potential, speaker turn switches. Determining such places is non-trivial, but it is possible to automatically mark all overt speaker switches. Simplified *Proper Speaker Turn Switches* (PSTS) were defined as succeeding pairs of utterances from different speakers where the next speaker started an utterance *after* the start of the last utterance of the previous speaker that continued beyond the end of that last utterance. Non-verbal noises were ignored. These PSTS events were automatically determined by sorting verbal chunks on their end times and selecting those turns that start after the start of the preceding turn.

Such PSTS events are cardinal places in dialogs and the delay between the end of the last turn and the start of the new turn contains important information about the dynamics of the conversation. We will use the distribution of PSTS (turn) delays to illustrate the use of the IFADV corpus. The basic distribution of the PSTS delays as found in the IFADV corpus is given in figure 6 (circles). The modal turn switch delay time is visible around 300 ms. The distribution is broad and falls to half its height at delays of 0 and 500 ms.

To be able to evaluate the distribution of PSTS delays, the statistics of observed turn switch delays must be compared to some null hypothesis of random, or unrelated, turn switches. Features of interest, e.g., the variance, can be extracted from the PSTS delays and related to some other aspect of the

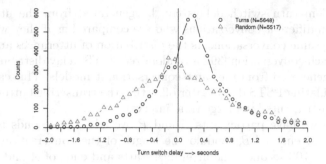

Fig. 6. Distribution of turn switch delays (PSTS), circles, and randomized turn switches, triangles. Bin sizes: 100ms.

Table 6. Distribution over the most important dialog functions of the time between the speaker looking towards the addressed dialog partner and the end of her turn (PSTS). Delay statistics calculated over the interval $[-2, 2]$ only. Labels u and a can be added to other labels and are counted separately. Mean: mean delay; SD: Standard Deviation; SE: Standard Error; #: Number of occurrences; all: all function labels.

Label	Mean	SD	SE	#
b	-0.534	0.854	0.079	117
c	-0.328	0.916	0.024	1506
h	0.199	0.930	0.164	32
k	0.646	0.627	0.040	242
r	-0.116	0.850	0.071	142
f	0.254	0.730	0.141	27
a	-0.296	0.908	0.0718	160
u	-0.318	0.957	0.065	220
ua	-0.316	1.137	0.343	11
all	-0.181	0.935	0.020	2139

conversation, e.g., the expected mental processing effort based on the transcription. This relation would than have to be compared to the null hypothesis, that there is no relation between the two features investigated.

To do this comparison, the statistics of the delays under random delay timings should be known. That is, the statistics of a real conversation will be compared to the same statistics for a sample of random, or unrelated, turn switches. The statistical difference between the feature measurements in the real, observed and the randomized turn delays can then be used to indicate whether the presence or size of the feature is convincingly shown. For instance, the question whether the PSTS delay distribution in figure 6 indicates that speakers wait for each other to end a turn can only be answered if we have a distribution of PSTS delays of people who do *not* wait for each other but start speaking randomly. That would be our null hypothesis.

Such random turn switch delays can be generated from the utterances of speakers from different conversations who are compared as if they were participating in the same conversation. As the distribution of utterances and pauses is specific for each conversation [39], a randomized PSTS delay distribution should actually be generated from the same conversation it models. This can easily be done by calculating PSTS delays after offsetting the transcribed utterances from one of the participants by a large time interval.

That is, if we have participants A and B, we add 100 seconds to all utterance starts and ends of B, modulo the length of the conversation (i.e., wrap around). After 100 seconds, the utterance starts and ends of A and B have become uncorrelated and the new "PSTS" delays are a model of the distribution of unrelated, random, turn switches. The resulting distribution shows a clear maximum close to a delay of 0s (triangles in figure 6). The differences between real and random PSTS delays seem obvious, and can be quantified with measures like the Kullback-Leibler divergence, but the statistics are not always straightforward.

8.2   Example: Gaze Direction

The gaze direction annotation is combined with the speech annotation by linking every gaze event, starting to look towards or away from the dialog partner, to word annotations. For each start and end of a gaze label, the corresponding automatically aligned words or pauses are located that were annotated for the *same* (looking) and the *other* subject. The distribution of gaze delays between the speaker looking towards the partner and the end of the nearest turn of the speaker is presented in figure 7. There were 5,168 discrete time spans in total where one subject looked directly at the other (and equally many where they looked away). Dialog participants gazed at each other for almost 75% of the time and at the end of 70% of all of their utterances. However, speakers gaze at the listener preceeding 79% of the turn switches (PSTS), which is more than expected ($p \leq 0.001$, χ^2 test).

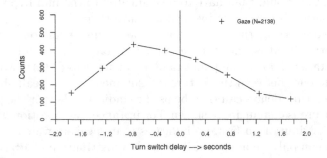

Fig. 7. Distribution of gaze delays from the last speaker (see text). Bin sizes: 500ms.

8.3   Example: Functional Annotation

Most of the annotations used in this corpus were taken from the Spoken Dutch Corpus (CGN) [13], and are well understood. Gaze direction is straightforward and we do not expect problems with its interpretation. However, the functional annotation of the dialog chunks was newly developed for this corpus. Therefore, the categories used have not yet been validated. The aim of this annotation was to add a simple judgement on the discourse function of individual utterances. We will try to find internal support in other annotations for the relevance of this functional labeling for the behavior of conversational participants.

The distribution of verbal chunks over conversational function is given in table 3. Around 18% of all utterances are classified as minimal responses. A lot of non-verbal sounds (transcription: *ggg*) were labeled as minimal responses. As expected, utterance duration depends on the functional label, as is visible in table 5. The most marked effect is expected between utterances adding content to the discourse, i.e., *b*, *c*, and *h* (*begin*, *continuation*, and *repetition*). These type labels are intended to describe those utterances that contribute directly to the subject matter of the discourse. Their difference lies in their relative positions with respect to content matter. *b* Indicates the introduction of a new topic at any level of the discourse. *c* Signifies utterances that contribute to an existing topic. *h* Labels utterances that mainly, word-by-word, repeat a message that has already been uttered before.

Obviously, it is expected that the predictability, or information content, of the utterances decreases from *b* to *c* to *h*. This should affect the duration, turn switches, and other behavior. The differences between the average utterance durations for these conversational function categories, *b*, *c*, and *h* are indeed statistically significant (table 5, $p \leq 0.001$, Student's t-test: $t > 6.5$, $\nu > 8000$). Indeed, the average duration of a type *b*, topic start, utterance is twice that of a simple repetition utterance, type *h*.

A distribution of the PSTS time delays over functional categories is given in table 5. Those for gaze timing in table 6. The PSTS delays in table 5 too show the marked effects of functional categories on dialog behavior. Less predictable utterances, like *b*, induce delays in the next speaker that are almost twice as long as more predictable utterances, like *c*. The difference in delay duration is much larger than the corresponding difference in utterance duration, as can be seen in table 5. However, interpreting the delays is complicated by the generally negative correlation between stimulus length and response times.

The gaze delays in table 6 show the opposite behavior to the turn delays. Where the next speaker tends to wait longer before starting to speak after a *b* utterance, the speaker that actually utters it starts to look towards her partner earlier. Again, the relation between gaze delay and utterance lengths might not be simple.

More work is obviously needed to disentangle the effects of utterance duration and conversational function, e.g., *b*, *c*, and *h*, on the gaze and next speaker timing.

9   Discussion

With the advent of large corpora, e.g., the Spoken Dutch Corpus [13], speech communication science is becoming a *big data* science [40]. With big science come new challenges and responsibilities, as distribution and access policies are required to unlock the collected data, e.g., [1]. For language corpora, see also the discussion and references in [28,29].

At the moment, comprehensive mechanisms for statistical analysis are urgently needed. For the IFADV corpus, we have chosen to prepare the annotations for relational database access, RDBMS [26,27,28,29]. For many questions related to statistical tests and distributions such access is both required and sufficient. However, there are cases where the hierarchical nature of linguistic annotations, e.g., syntax, would demand searching tree-like structures. We suggest that the use of XML databases would be studied for such use cases. The above examples show, again, the usefulness of integrating standard linguistic annotations and low cost dialog annotations into a searchable database. This opens an easy access to a host of statistical and analysis tools, from Standard Query Language (SQL) to spreadsheets and R [30].

The method used to create a RDMS for the IFADV corpus is arguably ad-hoc, c.f., [26,27,28,29]. We would prefer that *best practises* were formulated for preparing annotations for relational database access. With increasing corpus size, database storage will only increase in importance.

A simple, low cost, functional annotation of dialogs into very simple content types was introduced for this corpus. A first look shows that these chosen categories seem to be relevant for interpersonal dialog behavior (see section 8.3). But real validation will only come from successful use in explaining the behavior of the participants or experimental observers. The current results show the interaction between the functional annotation categories and the behavior of the speakers. These first results support the relevance of the functional label categories. These categories are at least predictive for some aspects of dialog behavior.

The bare fact that this paper spends more space on legal and license matters than on the annotations shows that, here too, there is a need for *best practises* for the handling of copyrights, informed consent, and privacy sensitive information in the context of corpus construction. Anecdotal reports emphasize the restrictions of the current laws where proper preparations might very well have prevented problems.

In the end it is the courts that decide on the boundaries of copyright and privacy laws. For a researcher of speech or language, little more can be done than listen to legal experts. During the construction of this corpus, we have tried to incorporate previous experiences with legal questions. This included attempts to inform our subjects about the full possible extent of the distribution and use cases of the recordings, as well as about the legal consequences of their signatures. Moreover, we allowed our subjects ample time to review the recordings and retract their consent. None of the subjects did retract their consent. We used (adapted) copyright transfer forms that were prepared by legal staff of the Dutch Language Union for the CGN.

Copyright protects many aspects of recordings and annotations. It must be emphasized that almost everyone who has in any way contributed to, adapted, or changed the collected recordings or annotations has to sign copyright transfer forms.

10 Conclusions

The speech and language community can gain a lot from widely available corpora of language behavior. Experience in other fields have shown that gains in efficiency can be obtained by sharing information resources in a *free/libre* fashion. An example of a *free/libre* annotated corpus of conversational dialog video recordings is presented and described. For this corpus, it has been tried to overcome several known legal hurdles to freely sharing and distributing video recordings and annotations. With close to 70k words, there was a need for database storage and access for efficient analysis. This was tackled by using identification markers for every single item in the annotations that link the annotations together and to specific time points in the recordings. A few simple examples are presented to illustrate potential uses of such a database of annotated speech. Corpus construction has only recently been finished, so there are currently no data about any effect of it's liberal license on use and maintenance.

Acknowledgements

The IFADV corpus is supported by grant 276-75-002 of the Netherlands Organization for Scientific Research. We want to thank Anita van Boxtel for transliterating the dialogs and labeling gaze direction, Stephanie Wagenaar for compiling the summaries of the dialog transcripts, and Maaike van Naerssen for the IMDI records.

References

1. Benson, D.A., Karsch-Mizrachi, I., Lipman, D.J., Ostell, J., Wheeler, D.L.: Genbank. Nucleic Acids Research 35(Database-Issue), 21–25 (2007)
2. Kolbitsch, J., Maurer, H.: The transformation of the web: How emerging communities shape the information we consume. Journal of Universal Computer Science 12(2), 187–213 (2006)
3. Lerner, J., Tirole, J.: Some simple economics of open source. Journal of Industrial Economics 50, 197–234 (2002)
4. Ciffolilli, A.: The economics of open source hijacking and declining quality of digital information resources: A case for copyleft. Development and Comp. Systems 0404008, EconWPA (April 2004)
5. Rullani, F.: Dragging developers towards the core. how the free/libre/open source software community enhances developers' contribution. LEM Papers Series 2006/22, Laboratory of Economics and Management (LEM), Sant'Anna School of Advanced Studies, Pisa, Italy (September 2006)

6. ELRA: European Language Resources Association: Catalogue of Language Resources (2004–2007), http://catalog.elra.info/
7. LDC: The Language Data Consortium Corpus Catalog (1992–2007), http://www.ldc.upenn.edu/Catalog/
8. HLT-Agency: Centrale voor Taal- en Spraaktechnologie, TST-centrale (2007), http://www.tst.inl.nl/producten/
9. MAPtask: HCRC Map Task Corpus (1992–2007), http://www.hcrc.ed.ac.uk/maptask/
10. Blache, P., Rauzy, S., Ferré, G.: An XML Coding Scheme for Multimodal Corpus Annotation. In: Proceedings of Corpus Linguistics (2007)
11. Bertrand, R.: Corpus d'interactions dilogales, CID (2007), http://crdo.fr/voir_depot.php?langue=en&id=27
12. CRDO: Licences (2008), http://crdo.up.univ-aix.fr/phpwiki/index.php?pagename=Licences
13. CGN: The Spoken Dutch Corpus project (2006), http://www.tst.inl.nl/cgndocs/doc_English/topics/index.htm
14. SMIL: W3C Synchronized Multimedia Integration Language (2008), http://www.w3.org/AudioVideo/
15. Ide, N., Romary, L.: Outline of the international standard linguistic annotation framework. In: Proceedings of the ACL 2003 workshop on Linguistic annotation, Morristown, NJ, USA, Association for Computational Linguistics, pp. 1–5 (2003)
16. Schmidt, T., Chiarcos, C., Lehmberg, T., Rehm, G., Witt, A., Hinrichs, E.: Avoiding data graveyards: From heterogeneous data collected in multiple research projects to sustainable linguistic resources. In: Proceedings of the E-MELD 2006 Workshop on Digital Language Documentation: Tools and Standards: The State of the Art, Lansing, Michigan (2006)
17. Rehm, G., Witt, A., Hinrichs, E., Reis, M.: Sustainability of annotated resources in linguistics. In: Proceedings of Digital Humanities 2008, Oulu, Finland, pp. 27–29 (2008)
18. IDABC: European Interoperability Framework for Pan-European eGovernmentservices (2004), http://europa.eu.int/idabc/en/document/3761
19. Ken Coar: The Open Source Definition, Annotated (2006), http://www.opensource.org/docs/definition.php
20. Schmidt, T., Duncan, S., Ehmer, O., Hoyt, J., Kipp, M., Loehr, D., Magnusson, M., Rose, T., Sloetjes, H.: An exchange format for multimodal annotations. In: (ELRA), E.L.R.A. (ed.) Proceedings of the Sixth International Language Resources and Evaluation (LREC 2008), Marrakech, Morocco (May 2008)
21. Carletta, J., Isard, A., Isard, S., Kowtko, J., Doherty-Sneddon, G., Anderson, A.: The reliability of a dialogue structure coding scheme. Computational Linguistics 23, 13–31 (1997)
22. Core, M., Allen, J.: Coding dialogs with the damsl annotation scheme. In: AAAI Fall Symposium on Communicative Action in Humans and Machines, pp. 28–35 (1997)
23. ELAN: ELAN is a professional tool for the creation of complex annotations on video and audio resources (2002–2007), http://www.lat-mpi.eu/tools/elan/
24. Caspers, J.: Local speech melody as a limiting factor in the turn-taking system in dutch. Journal of Phonetics 31(2), 251–276 (2003)
25. Wesseling, W., van Son, R.J.J.H.: Early Preparation of Experimentally Elicited Minimal Responses. In: Proceedings of the 6th SIGdial Workshop on Discourse and Dialogue, pp. 11–18 (2005)

26. Mengel, A., Heid, U.: Enhancing reusability of speech corpora by hyperlinked query output. In: Proceedings of EUROSPEECH 1999, Budapest, pp. 2703–2706 (1999)
27. Cassidy, S.: Compiling multi-tiered speech databases into the relational model: Experiments with the EMU system. In: Proceedings of EUROSPEECH 1999, Budapest, pp. 2239–2242 (1999)
28. Van Son, R., Binnenpoorte, D., van den Heuvel, H., Pols, L.: The IFA corpus: a phonemically segmented Dutch Open Source speech database. In: Proceedings of EUROSPEECH 2001, Aalborg, pp. 2051–2054 (2001)
29. Van Son, R., Pols, L.: Structure and access of the open source IFA Corpus. In: Proceedings of the IRCS workshop on Linguistic Databases, Philadelphia, pp. 245–253 (2001)
30. R Core Team: The R Project for Statistical Computing (1998–2008), http://www.r-project.org/
31. IMDI: ISLE Meta Data Initiative (1999–2007), http://www.mpi.nl/IMDI/
32. WIPO: Berne Convention for the Protection of Literary and Artistic Works (1979), http://www.wipo.int/treaties/en/ip/berne/index.html
33. WIPO: 5: International Treaties and Conventions on Intellectual Property. In: WIPO Handbook on Intellectual Property: Policy, Law and Use, 2nd edn., pp. 237–364. WIPO (2004), http://www.wipo.int/about-ip/en/iprm/ (Date of access: March 2008)
34. Maurer, S.M., Hugenholtz, P.B., Onsrud, H.J.: Europe's database experiment. Science 294, 789–790 (2001)
35. Kienle, H.M., German, D., Tilley, S., Müller, H.A.: Intellectual property aspects of web publishing. In: SIGDOC 2004: Proceedings of the 22nd annual international conference on Design of communication, pp. 136–144. ACM, New York (2004)
36. EC: First evaluation of Directive 96/9/EC on the legal protection of databases, DG Internal Market and Services Working Paper (2005), http://europa.eu.int/comm/internal_market/copyright/docs/databases/evaluation_report_en.pdf
37. FSF: GNU General Public License, version 2 (1991), http://www.gnu.org/licenses/old-licenses/gpl-2.0.html
38. IDABC: European Union Public Licence, EUPL v.1.0 (2008), http://ec.europa.eu/idabc/eupl
39. ten Bosch, L., Oostdijk, N., Boves, L.: On temporal aspects of turn taking in conversational dialogues. Speech Communication 47(1-2), 80–86 (2005)
40. : Community cleverness required. Nature 455(7209), 1 (2008)

Creating and Exploiting Multimodal Annotated Corpora: The ToMA Project

Philippe Blache[1], Roxane Bertrand[1], and Gaëlle Ferré[2]

[1] Laboratoire Parole & Langage, CNRS & Aix-Marseille Universités
29, av. Robert Schuman, 13100 Aix en Provence
[2] LLING Université de Nantes
Chemin de la Censive du Tertre, BP 81227, 44312 Nantes cedex 3
{blache,roxane.bertrand}@lpl-aix.fr, gaelle.ferre@univ-nantes.fr

Abstract. The paper presents a project aiming at collecting, annotating and exploiting a dialogue corpus from a multimodal perspective. The goal of the project is the description of the different parameters involved in a natural interaction process. Describing such complex mechanism requires corpora annotated in different domains. This paper first presents the corpus and the scheme used in order to annotate the different domains that have to be taken into consideration, namely phonetics, morphology, syntax, prosody, discourse and gestures. Several examples illustrating the interest of such a resource are then proposed.

1 Introduction

In recent years, linguists have become aware that a theory of communication describing real interactions should involve the different domains fo verbal and non-verbal description. This is the reason why linguistics and natural language processing have turned to multimodal data where human communication is represented in its entire complexity. By multimodal data, we mean a complex annotation in the auditory-visual domains, not only visual information, Each domain is itself composed of a set of parameters and must be related to the other dimensions of speech. However, annotating such inputs remains problematic both for theoretical and technical reasons. First, we still need a linguistic theory taking into account all the different aspects of multimodality, explaining in particular how the different linguistic domains interact. At the same time, we need to specify a standardized way of representing multimodal information in order to give access to large multimodal corpora, as richly annotated as possible. What is meant by large corpora is however quite a relative notion since in some linguistic fields such as syntax for instance, corpora of several million words are used whereas in prosody where most of the annotations are made manually, a few hours of speech are considered as a large corpus.

This paper describes the first results of the ToMA project[1] which aims at answering these different issues. In this project we propose to specify the different requisites and

---

[1] ToMA stands for "Tools for Multimodal Annotation" (the French acronym is "OTIM"). Project supported by the ANR French agency, involving different partners (LPL, LSIS, LIMSI, LIA, RFC and LLING).

M. Kipp et al. (Eds.): Multimodal Corpora, LNAI 5509, pp. 38–53, 2009.

needs in the perspective of multimodal annotation. Different from many other projects, ToMA does not focus on a specific problem such as information structure, gesture studies or prosody-syntax interaction. Our goal is the development of generic and reusable annotated resources, providing precise annotations in all possible domains, from prosody to gesture. We propose transcription conventions and information encoding as well as tools helping in the annotation process and access to information.

In the first section, we specify a coding scheme adapted for multimodal transcription and annotations. In the second part, we describe the automation of the production of multimodal resources by means of a platform integrating different annotation tools. This platform consists of a sequence of tools leading from raw data to enriched annotations in each linguistic domain. We illustrate the application of this environment by the description of a large multimodal annotated corpus for French. Finally, we present some first results obtained thanks to this resource.

2 Multimodal Resources and Coding Schemes

Several projects address the question of multimodal resources and their annotation. For example, the LUNA project (cf. [Rodriguez07]) focuses on spoken language understanding. The corpus is made of human-machine and human-human dialogues. It proposes, on top of the transcription, different levels of annotation, from morphosyntax to semantics and discourse analysis. Annotations have been done by means of different tools producing different formats that become interoperable thanks to the use of an interchange format called PAULA (cf. [Dipper05]). SAMMIE (cf. [Kruijff-Korbayova06]) is another project aiming at building multimodal resources in the context of human-machine interaction. Annotations are done using the Nite XML Toolkit (cf. [Carletta03]); they concern syntactic and discourse-level information, plus indication about the specific computer modality used in the experiment. A comparable resource, also acquired following a Wizard-of-Oz technique, has been built by the DIME project (cf. [Pineda02]) for Spanish. In comparison with previous ones, this resource mainly focuses on first-level prosodic information as well as dialog acts.

These three examples are quite typical of multimodal resources development. The main differences with ToMA are first the nature of the source (in our case human-human natural interaction) and second the richness of the annotation (much more exhaustive and precise for ToMA).

Annotating corpora first requires to specify what kind of information it is necessary to represent and how it is organized. This problem consists in defining a coding scheme. Several of them have been developed in different projects such as MATE, NIMM, EMMA, XCES, TUSNELDA, etc. What comes out is that they are very precise in one or two modalities. However, they usually do not cover the entire multimodal domain nor the very fine-grained level of annotation required in every modality. We propose to combine several existing schemes and to extend them so as to obtain a coding scheme that would be as complete as possible.

- *Corpus metadata*: we use a TUSNELDA-like coding scheme ([Tusnelda05]) in which all the information such as speaker name, sex, region, etc. is noted.
- *Morphology and Syntax*: we propose to adapt the Maptask coding scheme for French in the morphological dimension, completed with syntactic relations and properties.
- *Phonetics*: some annotations are a completed version of MATE ([Carletta99]). The phonetic representation is coded in SAMPA.
- *Phonology and Prosody*: we adopt the coding scheme proposed in [DiCristo04] in which prosodic information is annotated both in an automatic (MOmel-Instsint algorithm, [Hirst00]) and manually.
- *Gesture analysis*: we adapt the MUMIN coding scheme ([Allwood05]), which provides an extensive description of gesture forms, but we propose to code gestures and discourse tags separately. The gesture typology is encoded following the scheme proposed in [McNeill05]. A gesture lexicon is compiled from the existing descriptions found in the literature ([Kendon04], [Kipp04], [Krenn04]).
- *Discourse and conversation analysis*: we use the Maptask ([Isard01]) and DAMSL coding schemes, extended to other discourse types such as narration, description, etc. Using the framework of conversation analysis, we also annotate conversational units (turn-constructional units, [Selting00]). We follow the MUMIN coding scheme again to annotate backchannels phenomena.

On top of these schemes, we also take into account different proposals in our encoding like the one elaborated in Potsdam (cf. [Dipper07]) which covers many of the annotation domains used in ToMA. The following descriptions illustrate, in the manner of the TEI formalization, some annotation conventions at different levels:

Morphosyntax

```
Token::        attributes: orthography
               content: Lex*
```

```
Lex:: attributes: id category lemma rank prob. freq. phon. reference
      content: msd

      category: {Adj Det Noun Pron Adv Prep Aux Verb Conjunction
Interjection Ignored Punctuation Particle Filled pause}
```

Gestures

```
Head::
      attributes:Movement_Type        Frequency        Horizontal_Plane
Vertical_Plane Side_Type
      Movement_Type: {Nod, Jerk , Tilt , Turn , Shake , Waggle ,
Other}
      Frequency: {Single , Repeated }
      Horizontal_Plane: {Forwards , Backwards , Sideways}
      Vertical_Plane: {Up, Down}
      Sid_Type: {Left , Right}
```

Our coding scheme, still under development, proposes then a general synthesis taking into account all the different levels of annotation for multimodal corpora such as phonetics, prosody, syntax, or gestures, as well as annotations at the discourse level (humor, backchannels, narrative units, conversational turns, etc.).

A general coding scheme is of deep importance not only in terms of standardization and knowledge representation, but also for practical matters: it constitutes the basis for a *pivot language*, making it possible for the different tools (Praat, Anvil, etc.) to exchange formats. This is one of the goals of the PAULA format (cf. [Dipper05]). From the same perspective, starting from an adaptation of this format, we are developing tools implementing such interoperability, relying on a translation between the source format of the tool and this language.

3   The ToMA Annotation Process

Until now, corpus annotation has been essentially based on written corpora, the annotation of oral corpora being very limited. Some transcribed oral corpora exist, but they rarely contain precise phonetic and prosodic information on top of transcription. The Switchboard corpus has been recently annotated in such perspective (see [Carletta04]) and constitutes an exception. As for multimodality, only few initiative try to build large broad coverage annotated corpora, including such level of precision in each domain. The AMI project is one of them (see [Carletta06]), even though the annotations does not seem to be at the same precision level in the different domains. Our project aims at building such large resource, trying to answer to the needs of researches in each domain (in other words being as precise as possible in the annotations) and at the same time making possible the analysis of domain interaction (annotating as many domains as possible). The problem first comes from the lack of annotation tools and second, the difficulty in integrating annotations into a common format.

The ToMA project's aim is to develop a platform providing help at each step of the process, from raw data to high-level annotations. ToMA specifies conventions for manual annotation steps and is based on freely available tools from different sources for the automatic ones. Most of the tools have been developed by the project partners and are adapted for the specific needs of spoken language processing. They will be distributed under the auspices of ToMA, as well as the annotated corpora. The experiment described in this paper has been used for the annotation of a corpus (*Corpus of Interactional Data – CID*) which is already freely available from the CRDO[2]. Figure 1 describes the state of the general process in which the status of each step, automatic (auto) or manual (manual) is specified. We briefly sketch in what follows the main steps of the process:

- *Segmentation in Interpausal-Units*: Transcriptions are made starting from an automatic pre-segmentation of the speech signal into interpausal-units (IPU) that are blocks of speech bounded by silent pauses of at least 200 ms. IPU segmentation makes transcription, phonetization and alignment with the signal easier. Moreover, speech overlap phases are extracted from IPUs.
- *Transcription*: conventions are derived from [Blanche-Benveniste87] on top of which other information is added (such as elisions, particular phonetic realizations, etc.). From this initial *enriched orthographic transcription* (EOT), two

---

[2] http://www.crdo.fr/

transcriptions are derived: one is phonological, the other is phonetic. The following example illustrates this step:

- EOT: et c(e) qu(i) était encore plus le choc c'est que en
  [fait, faiteu]
            (what was even a greater shock was that...)
- Phonologic version: et ce qui était encore plus le choc c'est que en fait
- Pseudo-phonetic version: et c' qu était encore plus le choc c'est que en faiteu

- *Phonetization*: This step produces a list of phonemes. After a tokenization, the symbolic phonetizer (see [DiCristo01]) provides a list of tokens and their phonetization labeled in SAMPA. The EOT may sometimes be difficult to use, and a direct phonetic transcription can be, in some cases, simpler for the transcriber; the phonetizer therefore accepts mixed orthographic and SAMPA symbols as an input.
- *Alignment*: The aligner (cf. [Brun04]) takes as input the list of phonemes and the audio signal. It then localizes each phoneme in the signal.
- *Prosody*: Prosodic annotations essentially encode the prosodic categories (intonational and accentual phrases [Jun02]) and the intonation contours associated to them. Such annotations are exclusively done by experts. The intonative level is also encoded with the Momel-Intsint algorithm ([Hirst00]) in an automatic way: from a phonetic representation of the fundamental frequency curve, INTSINT provides a level of surface phonological representation where the melody is represented by a sequence of discrete symbols ([Hirst05]). Because of the lack of consensus on the phonological system in French, we use the MOMEL-INTSINT system which precisely does not suppose any a priori knowledge of the phonological system of the language. The interest to have both manual annotations and automatic INTSINT annotations is to improve INTSINT itself, but also the knowledge, which is still very fragmentary, of the prosodic domains in French.
- *Morphosyntax*: Morphosyntactic annotation is done automatically, using a POS–tagger (LPLsuite, cf. [VanRullen05]) which has been adapted to spoken language. The system has been trained with appropriate data, and custom correcting code heuristics has been developed. It is then checked and corrected manually.
- *Syntax*: We have developed an original statistical parser, adapted to the treatment of spoken data. This is done in two different phases. The first consists in parsing a spoken language corpus by means of a symbolic parser (cf. [Blache05]). In a second stage, the output is corrected manually, the result being a treebank for spoken language. Finally, the statistical parser is trained on these data. The tool we obtain is used in order to generate the trees of the corpora to be annotated automatically. This output also has to be checked manually.
- *Gesture*: The annotation of the gestures made by the participants is being done manually using ANVIL as shown in Figure 3 below. Facial movements (eyebrow, head), gaze direction and facial expressions (smiles, etc) are encoded as well as hand gestures. For the latter, McNeill's typology [McNeill05] was used (metaphorics, iconics, deictics, beats) and completed with emblems and adaptors. It has also been decided to annotate gesture phases (preparation, stroke, hold, retraction), as well as gesture apex as proposed by [Loehr04], although this annotation will come in a second step.

- *Discourse*: Discourse events (narrative units, speech particles, etc.) are annotated manually in distinct tiers either in Praat or in Anvil depending on the need for video information (for instance, verbal and vocal backchannels were annotated in Praat whereas gestural ones were annotated in Anvil. After all the annotations are made, they were grouped into a single file for the queries to be made). Annotations are created from the aligned orthographic transcription.

4 The CID: A First Multimodal Annotated Corpus in French

The Corpus of Interactional Data is an audio-video recording of spontaneous spoken French (8 hours, 8 pairs of speakers). It features data recorded in an anechoic room and containing 110.000 words. Each speaker of the dialogue is equipped with a head-set microphone enabling the recording of the two speakers' voices on two different sound tracks. This enables the study of speech at a phonemic and prosodic level. It also enables the study of overlapping speech which is frequent in spontaneous interactions but seldom analyzed because of the difficulty to separate the intertwined voices of the two speakers a posteriori. Yet, overlapping speech plays a major role in conversation and requires experimental investigations.

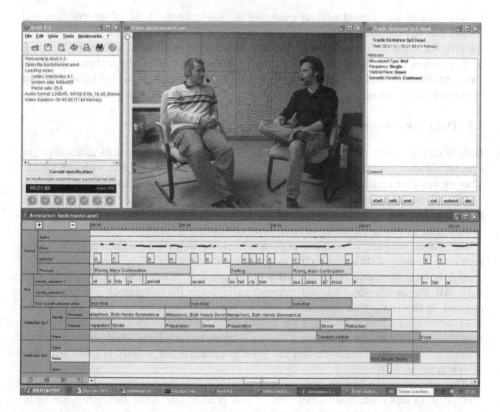

Fig. 2. CID annotation board

In this corpus, we aimed at collecting useful data for the investigation of all the levels under study: the audio quality is optimum and they have been videotaped with a high quality digital camera. The corpus, described in [Bertrand08], has been annotated following the different steps described above.

We then aligned the orthographic and phonetic transcription with the signal and added information from different linguistic fields (prosodic units, intonative contours, morphosyntactic categories, syntactic phrases, etc.). These annotations have been done separately on the audio files and constitute the basis for our present project which consists in the annotation and processing of the corpus from a multimodal / multi-dimensional perspective.

The annotation of the gestures made by the participants is being done manually using ANVIL as shown in Figure 2. The tiers bear different information, from the f0 curve and pitch targets coded with INTSINT (tier 3) to the conversational units (tier 5). Tier 4 encodes the function of the rising contour (RMC: major continuation rise). The following tiers encode the gestural information and the last tier refers to the interlocutor which produces a gestural backchannel signal (nod).

5   Exploiting Multimodal Annotations

In this section we present several examples to illustrate the kind of information and results that can be obtained thanks to such multimodal resources. In the first subsection we propose some observations which can be done from these data concerning the relations between different levels, in particular prosody and syntax. After this subsection, three studies will be presented: the first study on backchannelling has led to the analysis of some general extenders in French and to the question of reinforcing gestures.

5.1   Data Synchronisation

Before entering into data description, it is necessary to tell how data alignment (or synchronization) is done. In our approach, all information is aligned with the signal. This means that identifying interaction between objects requires a temporal comparison. In most cases, an intersection of the temporal segments of the objects to be considered is the sign of an interaction. For example, an intersection between a deictic gesture and a pronoun specifies a referential relation.

Of course, we have to take into consideration that objects have been aligned on the signal by means of different techniques. In some cases, the alignment is done automatically (e.g. syntactic units aligned with words and phonemes, then with the signal). All the annotations aligned automatically from the phonemes can be strictly aligned in the sense that they share exactly the same boundaries. For example, we have developed a tool segmenting the input on the basis of morpho-syntacitc information. Segments correspond to what we call "pseudo-sentences" that show a certain syntactic coherence. Pseudo-sentences' right boundaries are strictly aligned with that of syntactic groups.

The situation is different when at least one of the annotations has been created manually. In this case, boundaries can be less precise and some flexibility has to be taken into account when identifying the synchronisation between the different annotations. For example, contours and syntactic units usually do not have the same boundaries in our annotations, so that when looking for synchronisation this parameter has to be taken into account.

5.2 Prosody/Syntax Interaction

Different kinds of prosodic information are available in the CID. At a first level, relations between prosodic units and contours can be underlined. Here are the different categories that have been used:

- *Units* : accentual phrase (AP), intonational phrase (IP),
- *Contours*: mr (minor rising), m0 (other minor contours), RMC (major continuation), RL (list rising), fl (flat), F (falling), R (rising), RF1 (rising-falling), RF2 (falling from the penultimate), RQ (interrogative rising), RT (terminal rising).

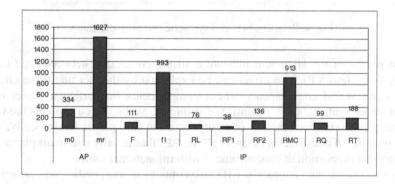

Fig. 3. Relations between contours and prosodic units

Figure 3 illustrates the distribution of the different contours in one of the dialogue of the CID. This distribution shows that flat and major rising contours are the most frequently used ones at the right boundary of an IP. Conversely, minor rising contours are by far the most frequent type in association with APs.

Figure 4 includes syntactic information on top of these prosodic relations. More precisely, it shows the distribution of syntactic units in relation with the different contours. Syntactic annotation of our corpus has been done by means of a stochastic chunker adapted from the techniques developed by the LPL (see [Vanrullen06]). Chunks are non recursive units, defined by the PEAS formalism (see [Paroubek06]) used for the parsing evaluation campaign regularly organized for French parsers. Concretely, we have shown that chunks correspond to a certain kind of supertags (see [Blache08]) or, in other words, identify left boundaries together with the nucleus of the corresponding phrases. The evaluation campaign shows good results for our parser as for spoken language parsing (F-score 80%).

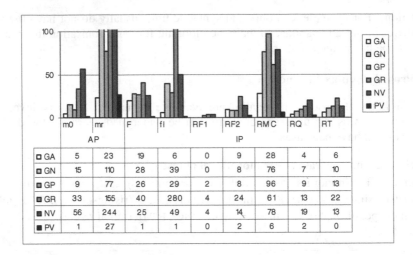

	m0	mr	F	fl	RF1	RF2	RMC	RQ	RT
◻ GA	5	23	19	6	0	9	28	4	6
◻ GN	15	110	28	39	0	8	76	7	10
◻ GP	9	77	26	29	2	8	96	9	13
◻ GR	33	155	40	280	4	24	61	13	22
◼ NV	56	244	25	49	4	14	78	19	13
◼ PV	1	27	1	1	0	2	6	2	0

Fig. 4. Relations between syntactic and prosodic contours

The results of the alignment indicate a strong correlation between /mr/ contours and /NV/ (nucleus VP). This effect can be explained by the fact that these chunks do not contain verbal complements. These complements (in particular direct objects) have a strong syntactic (and semantic) relation with verbs, which explains the fact that no strong prosodic boundary or contour occurs in this place. Reciprocally, chunks corresponding to constituents (such as NP or PP) that usually end main phrases show an important proportion of cooccurrences with intonational phrases.

Beside general annotations, the CID also contains more specific ones, added for the study of precise phenomena. For example, detachment constructions have been identified and located (this is an ongoing study, lead by Lisa Brunetti). Among different detachment types, figure 5 focuses on lexical and pronominal dislocated subjects. It shows a relative low level of cooccurrence with intonational phrases and a high

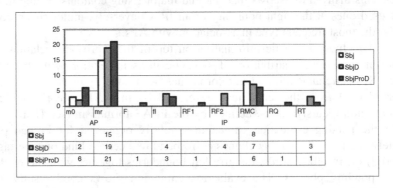

	m0	mr	F	fl	RF1	RF2	RMC	RQ	RT
◻ Sbj	3	15					8		
◼ SbjD	2	19		4		4	7		3
◼ SbjProD	6	21	1	3	1		6	1	1

Fig. 5. Relations between detachments and prosodic contours

proportion of minor rising contours. These data tend to illustrate the syntactic cohesion between the dislocated element and the matrix sentence. This figure also gives indications concerning canonical lexicalized subjects (that are relatively rare in spoken language corpora). What is interesting is that these subjects seem to have the same prosodic characteristics as dislocated ones, including the ones which occur in intonational phrases. This observation should be refined, but it seems that it could illustrate the fact that the detachment construction could become marked in spoken language.

5.3 Backchannels

Backchannel signals (BCs) provide information both on the partner's listening and on the speaker's discourse processes: they are used by recipients to express manifest attention to speakers in preserving the relation between the participants by regulating exchanges. They also function as acknowledgement, support or attitude statement, and interactional signals in marking specific points or steps in the elaboration of discourse. Until recently, they were still considered as fortuitous, but recent works showed that they have a real impact on the speaker's discourse (see [FoxTree99]).

Although they can be verbal like "ouais" (*yeah*), "ok", etc, vocal ("mh") or gestural (nods, smiles, etc), most of the studies on BCs only concern one modality. Our aim is to integrate the different nature of BCs in order to draw up a formal and functional typology. Such information helps in automatically labelling BCs, as well as understanding more accurately the communication strategies (see [Allwood05]). Moreover, we also try to have a better understanding of the BC context which can also inform on its function and contribute to the study of the turn-taking system.

The following example, taken from the CID, illustrates the interest of a multimodal study of BCs. Verbal BCs are represented in italics, gestural ones in frames.

```
A ah ouais nous on est rentré à (...) dix heures dix heures et demi
je crois du soir (...)
B                                                           nod
A et elle a accouché à six heures je crois (...)
B                                    ah quand même ouais
B                                    head tilt / eyebrow raising
A donc c'était ouais c'était quand même assez long quoi (...)
B head tilt

[A] oh yeah we were admitted at 10, 10.30 I think pm
[A] and she had the baby at 6 I think
[B] [oh yeah right?]
[A] so it was yeah it was quite long indeed
```

Several questions can be raised: in what context do backchannels appear, do verbal and gestural BCs behave similarly, etc. Such problems require the study of the different levels of information. Among them, the prosodic and discourse layers seem to play an important role for backchannels. Figure 6 shows the relations between these prosodic-unit levels, prosodic contours and conversational turns. By conversational turns, we mean the different units of turn (the turn-constructional units) defined as points of completeness from a syntactic, prosodic and pragmatic point of view [Selting00].

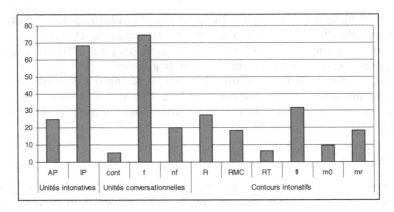

Fig. 6. Relations between backchannels, prosody and discourse

A TCU may be labelled as final (complete from the three criteria), as non final (incomplete from the pragmatic point of view for instance) or as cont(inuation) to refer to cases of adds-on or completion of turn (after a final TCU). As for prosody, the figure shows that BCs are realized preferentially after IPs and /fl/ contours. Concerning discourse, they are realized after final turns, in other words when the speaker reaches a certain level of completion in discourse.

In [Bertrand07], we have shown that vocal and gestural BCs have similar behavior, in particular concerning the morphological and discursive production context. They appear after nouns, verbs and adverbs, but not after connectors or linking words between two conversational units. As for prosody, gestural BCs can occur after accentual phrases (AP) and intonational phrases (IP) whereas verbal BCs only occur after IPs. Both BCs seem to be favoured by rising and flat contours.

However, rising contours (R, which brings together the whole rising contours RMC + RT) exhibit a specific behavior according to the nature of BC. Proportion tests with a z-score to measure the significant deviation between the two proportions confirm that significant relevant typical contours at points where BC occur are: RT (z-score = 3.23 for vocal BC and 2.18 for gestural BC); RMC (z-score = 2.9 for vocal BC and 4 for gestural BC); and fl (z-score = 2.8 for vocal BC and 3.9 for gestural BC).

By producing preferentially a gestural BC after a RMC contour, the recipient shows that not only does he understand that the speaker has not finished yet but he does not want interrupt him. On the other hand, by producing more frequently a vocal BC after a terminal rising contour, the recipient displays a minimal but sufficient contribution. But thanks to it the recipient also shows his willingness to stay as recipient at a potential transition relevance place. These first results show that different cues at different levels of analysis are relevant for BCs occurring. More generally they confirm the relevance of a multimodal approach for conversational data and corpus-based investigations.

5.4 Adjunctive General Extenders

The study on BCs has led to an analysis of specific French locutions on 3 hours of the corpus. These locutions are a set of *adjunctive general extenders* (cf. [Overstreet00])

such as "(et) tout (ça)" ("*and all that*") and "et cetera", which are favorable contexts for the production of BCs by the hearer. Two issues are at stake concerning them: (1) whether they should or not count as a category of discourse markers (DM), and (2) what their function is. Our aim is to refine existing work mainly based on syntax and discourse analysis, adding prosodic and gestural descriptions of the extenders.

There is yet no consensus concerning the classification of general extenders as DMs (also sometimes called *pragmatic markers* or *pragmatic particles*). Whereas some do consider they are, they do not meet all the criteria defined by [Schiffrin87] and [Fraser99] to enter the category of DMs: for instance, they cannot be inserted at the beginning of an utterance, and their meaning in context is not always different from the core meaning of the locution.

Yet, they fully meet other criteria such as the fact that they cannot stand alone as subject or object of a VP, they show a range of prosodic contours, etc. An intermediate standpoint consists in considering some instances of general extenders as DMs, but not all of them. This is the point of view we adopted in this study, one coder determining the status of DM whenever the locution showed prosodic dependence with the intonation unit which preceded or followed it. This first annotation would of course have to be cross-examined by other coders as well but our preliminary results are quite interesting to mention here.

They show that DMs are almost systematically de-accented (they do not carry nuclear stress and a number of items are phonetically reduced although this is not systematic: for instance "tout ça" [*tu sa*] is often pronounced [tsa] in this context) and usually follow a rising contour, which is not the case of locutions. They are also significantly accompanied with reinforcing gestures, either head movements or hand gestures. As will be shown in the next section, reinforcing gestures reveal discourse structure and this is also the role of "tout ça" in the following example. It is written in capital letters, is accompanied by a metaphoric hand gesture and is produced just after another DM "et tout" with which it forms a single prosodic unit. The example however should not be considered as a case of reduplication of the locution for emphasis.

Example: tu sais tout ce qui était Provence et tout TOUT CA
            "*you know all the stuff made in Provence and all that TOUT CA*"

When it comes to the second issue concerning general extenders, i.e. their linguistic function, we adopted the typology proposed by [Overstreet00] who suggested that the items have three main values:

1. List extenders (extending a list without naming all the items): "ceux qui font les courses ceux qui font la vaisselle et cetera" ("*the people who do the shopping, the ones who wash the dishes et cetera*")
2. Illustration (giving an example): "c'est comme les marrons qu'on bouffe tout ça c'est des châtaignes aussi" ("*it's like the horse chestnuts that we eat and stuff they are indeed chestnuts*")
3. Intersubjectivity (relationships between the participants to the dialogue): "il avait perdu ses parents tout ça" ("*he had lost his parents and stuff*")

Each general extender was assigned a function on the basis of semantics only (on the written script) with Praat by one coder. Out of 104 occurrences of general extenders, only 4 instances could not be decided on. Our aim was to see if the intuitive annotation of the functions of general extenders would meet any pattern in prosody and gesture.

In prosody, we expected to find congruence between the LIST function and the enumerative contour for instance, although the results concerning the correspondence between contours and values need to be developed. But as far as gestures are concerned, we do have preliminary results which are very encouraging. The gestures, which accompany 40 % of the adjunctive general extenders in this corpus, are only head movements (head shakes and head tilts) and hand gestures (metaphorics and iconics).

We never met any eyebrow rising for instance or any smile. We will have to think about such a gestural specificity on general extenders since in other contexts in the corpus, movements and gestures are much more varied. What is more, although head movements were equally distributed among the different functions, we found a much higher proportion of hand gestures reinforcing extenders with an intersubjective value, especially metaphorics.

At last, to loop the loop, since DMs are used to express the pragmatic relationships in dialogue, we expected a higher proportion of DMs than locutions to have an inter-subjective value, since this value is the one which is the farthest from the core meaning of general extenders, and this is exactly what our results show.

5.5 Reinforcing Gestures

As we have seen in the previous subsection, some gestures can be interpreted as discourse reinforcement devices (cf. [Ferré07], [Ferré09]). To illustrate our point, let us say that there is a difference, for instance, between a head nod produced by the audience as backchannel, and a nod produced by the speaker without any prompt, when this nod doesn't stand for the emblem of "yes". This is the case of the example provided below, where the nod slightly anticipates "super strict", and can be understood as reinforcement of the degree adverb "super".

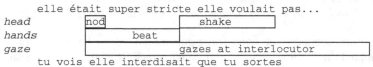

```
          elle était super stricte elle voulait pas...
head      nod              shake
hands              beat
gaze              gazes at interlocutor
          tu vois elle interdisait que tu sortes
  [A]  "she [the teacher] was super strict she didn't want... you see
she forbade us to leave the room [during lessons]"
```

We started with annotating what we intuitively felt were reinforcing gestures, in order to adopt a more gestural perspective rather than a discursive or a prosodic one. Here, we wanted to know what exactly would be reinforced, e.g. instead of focusing on semantic and morphological criteria for intensification, we wanted to find out if there were other possible production contexts for reinforcing gestures. We also wanted to know if gestural and prosodic reinforcement would be simultaneous.

The study showed that intensive gestures are more liable to accompany degree adverbs and negation particles, as well as connectors (DMs which show the discursive or pragmatic links between speech turns). Considering this, we concluded that the gestures we looked at — which were head and eyebrow movements as well as gaze direction — rather played a discursive role of intensification, especially since none of these gestures were associated with any specific stress type. The study also showed that intensive gestures are not redundant in their expression of emphasis: the segments they highlight do not fall under intonational focalization, for instance, with which they are in complementary distribution. This does not mean that reinforcing gestures are never used at the same time as prosodic focalization: in the example above, for instance, there actually is a focal accent on the first syllable of "super" which is also reinforced by the nod. What it means however, is that there are many other contexts, especially negation particles, which are unstressed but yet reinforced by a gesture. Yet, when looking at the gestures themselves and their distribution, one wouldn't speak of emphasis. Indeed, whereas a large gesture could be considered as emphatic (or giving the accompanying speech some emphasis), these movements are not necessarily large at all. Most of the time, they are even very slight. What counts here rather seems to be a question of gesture density, pretty much in the same way as S. Norris [Norris04] speaks of modal density, e.g. the accumulation of body movements on certain parts of speech, listener-oriented.

This study was actually a pilot experiment which must be extended and this will be done in two ways: (a) the rest of the corpus should be annotated in the same way and (b) at the time of the study, the syntactic annotations were not ready to allow their being taken into account, and as they have been done since, they would certainly refine enormously the analysis of the co-occurrences of reinforcement gestures with adverbs and connectors.

6 Conclusion

Annotated multimodal corpora now constitute an essential resource in linguistics. The understanding of language mechanisms (both in production and perception) needs to take into account very precisely the interaction between all the different domains or modalities (phonetics, prosody, lexicon, syntax, pragmatics, gestures, discourse, etc.). Producing such resources represents however a huge amount of work. It is then necessary to specify a precise framework, identifying the different tasks, the kind of information they have to produce and to what extend they can be automatized.

We have presented in this paper the main characteristics of the ToMA project, providing a general framework for building richly annotated multimodal corpora. The main characteristic of ToMA is that it aims at the description of natural human-human interaction. In order to do this it is necessary to exploit a set of precise and high-level annotations in each linguistic domain. This annotation process has been made possible thanks to a precise definition of different steps, each coming with a set of recommendations and tools.

We have shown in this paper that new results can be obtained from such resources: several examples have been presented here illustrating the importance of a description which brings together information from different levels. It now becomes possible to specify linguistic information in a new perspective, in which phenomena are described in terms of interaction between objects from different domains. This we hope to become an open door for *multimodal grammars*.

References

Allwood, J., Cerrato, L., Dybkjaer, L., et al.: The MUMIN Multimodal Coding Scheme, NorFA yearbook 2005 (2005),
   http://www.ling.gu.se/~jens/publications/B%20files/B70.pdf
Bertrand, R., Blache, P., Espesser, R., et al.: Le CID - Corpus of Interactional Data - Annotation et Exploitation Multimodale de Parole Conversationnelle. In revue Traitement Automatique des Langues 49(3) (2008)
Bertrand, R., Ferré, G., Blache, P., Espesser, R., Rauzy, S.: Backchannels revisited from a multimodal perspective. In: Proceedings of Auditory-visual Speech Processing (2007)
Blache, P., Rauzy, S.: Influence de la qualité de l'étiquetage sur le chunking: une corrélation dépendant de la taille des chunks. In: Proceedings of TALN 2008 (2008)
Blanche-Benveniste, C., Jeanjean, C.: Le français parlé, Transcription et édition, Didier (1987)
Brun, A., Cerisara, C., Fohr, D., Illina, I., Langlois, D., Mella, O., Smaïli, K.: Ants: le système de transcription automatique du Loria, in actes des XXVe JEP (2004)
Carletta, J., Isard, A.: The MATE Annotation Workbench: User Requirements. In: Proceedings of the ACL Workshop: Towards Standards and Tools for Discourse Tagging (1999)
Carletta, J., Evert, S., Heid, U., Kilgour, J., Robertson, J., Voormann, H.: The NITE XML Toolkit: flexible annotation for multi-modal language data. Behavior Research Methods, Instruments, and Computers 35(3) (2003)
Carletta, J.: Announcing the AMI Meeting Corpus. The ELRA Newsletter 11(1) (2006)
Carletta, J., Dingare, S., Nissim, M., Nikitina, T.: Using the NITE XML Toolkit on the Switchboard Corpus to study syntactic choice: a case study. In: Proceedings of LREC 2004 (2004)
Di Cristo, A., Di Cristo, P.: Syntaix, une approche métrique-autosegmentale de la prosodie. TAL 42(1), 69–114 (2001)
Di Cristo, A., Auran, C., Bertrand, R., et al.: Outils prosodiques et analyse du discours. In: Simon, A.C., Auchlin, A., Grobet, A. (eds.) Cahiers de Linguistique de Louvain 28, Peeters, pp. 27–84 (2004)
Dipper, S.: XML-based stand-off representation and exploitation of multi-level linguistic annotation. In: Proceedings of Berliner XML Tage, Berlin (September 2005)
Dipper, S., Götze, M., Skopeteas, S.: Information Structure in Cross-Linguistic Corpora: Annotation Guidelines for Phonology, Morphology, Syntax, Semantics, and Information Structure. Interdisciplinary Studies on In formation Structure, Working Papers of the SFB 632. University of Potsdam, vol. 7 (2007)
Ferré, G., Bertrand, R., Blache, P., Espesser, R., Rauzy, S.: Gestural Reinforcement of Degree Adverbs and Adjectives in French and English. In: Proceedings. of AFLICO (2009)
Ferré, G., Bertrand, R., Blache, P., Espesser, R., Rauzy, S.: Intensive Gestures in French and their Multimodal Correlates. In: Proceedings of Interspeech 2007 (2007)
Fraser, B.: What are discourse markers? Journal of Pragmatics 31 (1999)
Fox Tree, J.E.: Listening in on Monologues and Dialogues. Discourse Processes 27(1) (1999)
Hirst, D., Di Cristo, A., Espesser, R.: Levels of description and levels of representation in the analysis of intonation. In: Prosody: Theory and Experiment. Kluwer, Dordrecht (2000)

Hirst, D., Auran, C.: Analysis by synthesis of speech prosody: the ProZed environment. In: Proceedings of Interspeech/Eurospeech (2005)

Jun, S.-A., Fougeron, C.: Realizations of accentual phrase in French intonation. Probus 14 (2002)

Kendon, A.: Gesture: Visible Action As Utterance. Cambridge University Press, Cambridge (2004)

Kipp, M.: Gesture Generation By Imitation. From Human Behavior To Computer Character Animation, Florida, Boca Raton (2004),
http://www.dfki.de/~Kipp/Dissertation.html

Krenn, B., Pirker, H.: Defining The Gesticon: Language And Gesture Coordination For Interacting Embodied Agents. In: Aisb 2004 Symposium On Language, Speech And Gesture For Expressive Characters (2004)

Kruijff-Korbayova, I., Gerstenberger, C., Rieser, V., Schehl, J.: The SAMMIE multimodal dialogue corpus meets the NITE XML toolkit. In: Proceedings of LREC 2006 (2006)

Loehr, D.P.: Gesture and Intonation. Doctoral Dissertation, Georgetown University (2004)

McNeill, D.: Gesture and Thought. University of Chicago Press, Chicago (2005)

Norris, S.: Analyzing Multimodal Interaction. A Methodological Framework. Routledge, New York (2004)

Overstreet, M.: Whales, candlelight, and stuff like that: General extenders in English discourse. Oxford University Press, Oxford (1999)

Paroubek, P., Robba, I., Vilnat, A., Ayache, C.: Data Annotations and Measures in EASY the Evaluation Campaign for Parsers in French. In: Proceedings of LREC 2006 (2006)

Pineda, L.A., Massé, A., Meza, I., Salas, M., Schwarz, E., Uraga, E., Villaseñor, L.: The DIME Project. In: Coello Coello, C.A., de Albornoz, Á., Sucar, L.E., Battistutti, O.C. (eds.) MICAI 2002. LNCS (LNAI), vol. 2313, p. 166. Springer, Heidelberg (2002)

Rodriguez, K., Dipper, S., Götze, M., Poesio, M., Riccardi, G., Raymond, C., Rabiega-Wisniewska, J.: Standoff Coordination for Multi-Tool Annotation in a Dialogue Corpus. In: Proceedings of Linguistic Annotation Workshop (2007)

Schiffrin, D.: Discourse Markers. Cambridge University Press, Cambridge (1987)

Selting, M.: The construction of 'units' in conversational talk, Language in Society 29 (2000)

Tusnelda, Tübingen collection of reusable, empirical, linguistic data structures (2005),
http://www.sfb441.uni-tuebingen.de/tusnelda-engl.html

Vanrullen, T., Blache, P., Balfourier, J.-M.: Constraint-Based Parsing as an Efficient Solution: Results from the Parsing Evaluation Campaign EASy. In: Proceedings of LREC 2006 (2006)

Multi-track Annotation of Child Language and Gestures

Jean-Marc Colletta, Ramona N. Kunene, Aurélie Venouil, Virginie Kaufmann,
and Jean-Pascal Simon

Lidilem – IUFM and Université Stendhal
BP25 – 38040 Grenoble Cedex 9, France

Abstract. This paper presents the method and tools applied to the annotation of
a corpus of children's oral and multimodal discourse. The multimodal reality of
speech has been long established and is now studied extensively. Linguists and
psycholinguists who focus on language acquisition also begin to study child
language with a multimodal perspective. In both cases, the annotation of
multimodal corpora remains a crucial issue as the preparation of the analysis
tools has to be in line with the objectives and goals of the research. In this paper
we present a coding manual aimed at the annotation of linguistic and gesture
production of narratives performed by children and adults of different
languages, with emphasis to the relationship between speech and gesture and
how it develops. We also present a third coder (3-coder) validation method for
gesture annotation.

Keywords: coding manual; annotation tool; gesture transcription; cross-
linguistic comparison; child development.

1 Introduction

This paper deals with a cross-linguistic and intercultural perspective of child's speech
development in its multimodal and semiotic aspects. It is grounded on the multimodal
reality of speech as established by gesture researchers (Kendon, 1980, 2004; McNeill,
1992), as well as on the evidence of the complementary semiotic nature of speech
signs and gesture signs (McNeill, 1992; Calbris, 2003). Research on gesture as well as
cognitive science has shown data which reveal that the listener, or speaker, integrates
auditory and visual information from linguistic, prosodic and gesture sources into a
single message (McNeill et al. 2001; McNeill, 2005; Beattie & Shovelton, 2006; Kita
& Özyürek, 2007).

In relation to child language development, several researchers have shown
evidence that a gesture-speech system begins to operate from 16–18 months of age
(Capirci, Iverson, Pizzuto & Volterra, 1996; Butcher & Goldin-Meadow, 2000;
Volterra, Caselli, Capirci & Pizzuto, 2005; Ozcaliskan & Goldin-Meadow, 2006).
Furthermore, there is additional evidence that co-speech gesture – hand or head
gestures as well as facial expressions linked to speech – develop as well as vary as the
child grows older (McNeill, 1992; Goldin-Meadow, 2003, 2006; Guidetti, 2005).
More precisely, the relationship between gesture and speech appears to be modified
under the influence of new linguistic acquisitions and new communicative behaviour,

M. Kipp et al. (Eds.): Multimodal Corpora, LNAI 5509, pp. 54–72, 2009.
© Springer-Verlag Berlin Heidelberg 2009

as is suggested in our own work on the development of multimodal explanatory and narrative abilities.

As a preliminary observation, the use of co-speech gesture varies a lot as a function of the type of language production that is performed by the speaker (Colletta, 2004). Studying primary school children in interviews with an adult, we found significantly more concrete representational gestures ('iconic gestures' in McNeill's 1992 classification) in spontaneous verbal depictions and narratives compared to spontaneous verbal explanations, and significantly more abstract representational gestures ('metaphoric gestures' in McNeill's classification) in the latter. The use of abstract representational gestures in verbal explanations was also reported by Goldin-Meadow (2003) studying math problem solving and piagetian tasks in children at primary school.

In order to gain more insight on the multimodal development of explanatory abilities, two types of data were collected in nursery and primary schools: video recorded classroom interactions and activities whom teachers often use to elicit explanations from their young pupils (3 to 6 years), and video recorded interviews of children aged from 6 to 11 years, who had to give explanations about family and social topics. The collected data allowed us to build a video corpus of 500 explanations (Colletta & Pellenq, in press). We measured the time length of each explanation, as well as its verbal (number of syllables, clauses, connectors) and gestural information content. The results showed a strong effect of age on all measures, which was interpreted as a growing ability in children to produce verbal explanations filling discourse properties. As for gesture, by the age of 7 years, one gesture out of two was a gesture of the abstract, symbolizing abstract concepts or filling cohesive properties (Colletta & Pellenq, 2007). The observation of gesture thus renders visible the emergence of both new cognitive abilities and new discourse abilities.

As for narrative development, 32 event reports freely verbalised by 6 to 11-years-old French children during interviews with an adult in school settings were extracted from a video corpus (Colletta, 2004). Every report was analysed on four dimensions: discourse construction, voice and prosodic features that accompany utterances, facial expressions and co-speech gestures, gaze direction. Our analysis led us to distinguish between three levels of narrative performance which were well correlated with age (Colletta, in press). To summarise, narratives performed by children aged 9 years and over were more detailed than those performed by younger children, and they often included backtracking through the event frame and various types of parenthetical statements and comments. Older children commonly used bodily behaviour to enliven the retelling of the story and to mark the transitions between processing the event frame and commenting on the narrative or on the narration itself.

In other words, discourse development is intimately related to gesture development. Although psycholinguists did not pay as much attention to gesture until recently, new investigations of later language development need to integrate a multimodal analysis. In order to study discourse development in French children, our research team in Grenoble (France) collected a substantial corpus of multimodal narratives produced by children and adults (French ANR Multimodality Project NT05-1_42974, 2005-2008). This research also includes a cross-linguistic comparison.

Generally, in the cross-linguistic multimodal study of language, all speakers are required to plan for their 'thinking for speaking' and all languages employ different approaches (Slobin, 1996; Kita, 2002). All languages of the world use lexical aspects such as ground, manner, path of motion as well as figure, to segment features of a motion event and to organise it in a hierarchical fashion in line with the properties of the given language (Özyürek et al., 2005). Talmy's typology of languages (1985) shows that in some languages, a motion event may require one clause (i.e. satellite framed languages) and in other languages, the same motion event may require several clauses (i.e. verb framed languages).

In a cross-linguistic study of American English, Turkish and Japanese narratives, Kita (1993) found that gestures used to describe the same motion event were influenced by two factors, namely:

1)   how each language expresses motion events.
2)   the spatial information in the stimulus (animated cartoon) that was not
       verbally expressed.

As such, the Interface Hypothesis, as proposed by Kita & Özyürek (2003: 18) predicts that "for a given gesture one can observe the simultaneous influence of both the linguistic formulation possibilities and the spatio-motoric properties of the referent that are not verbalized in the accompanying speech."

However, in the case of typically developing children, when and how does culture influence the development of gesture and speech? Four research teams from France, Italy and the United States, joined forces in order to tackle these questions through the comparative study of multimodal narratives performed by children and adults (same ANR Multimodality Project as mentioned above). The aim is to study and compare the verb framed romance languages (French and Italian), the satellite framed Germanic language (American English) and a Bantu language (isiZulu) which we propose to be a verb framed language.

Nevertheless, such investigations need proper annotation tools, which enable linguists and psycholinguists to transcribe and annotate for gestures as well as for words. Within the past ten years, a growing number of researchers have shown considerable awareness in the multimodal complexity processes of oral communication. This issue has brought about increased interest amongst researchers aiming to transcribe and annotate different kinds of multimodal corpora, for instance, researchers in computer sciences take into account the multimodal clues in order to improve the Embodied Conversational Agents (cf. Ech Chafai, Pelachaud & Pelé, 2006; Kipp, Neff & Albrecht, 2006; Kopp et al., 2006; Vilhjalmsson et al., 2007). In the course of the collaboration as stated above, we were faced with the need for an annotation tool, designed to efficiently transcribe and annotate the corpora. The main objective for this paper is to present the methodological procedures and coding manual we devised for this research project on the cultural aspects of language and gesture development.

Our data collection is based on a protocol aimed at collecting spoken narratives from American, French, Italian and Zulu children and adults under controlled experimental conditions. A 2 minute extract of an animated "Tom & Jerry" cartoon was shown to each subject. The participant was then asked to recount the story to the interviewer. Each interaction was filmed with a camcorder. From the French language group, 120 narratives produced by 40 children aged 5-6 years, 40 children aged 9-10 years, and 40 adults were collected. From the isiZulu language group, 60 narratives produced by 20 children aged 5-6 years, 20 children aged 9-10 years, and 20 adults were collected. From the American and Italian language groups, each collected 40 narratives produced by 20 children aged 5-6 years and 20 children aged 9-10 years. A total number of 260 narratives were collected, corresponding to 11 hours of film (mean duration of each file: 2.5min). The data were then analysed using the software ELAN (EUDICO Linguistic Annotator)[1]. Two main levels of transcription were selected for annotation: a verbal level and a gesture level (see Fig.1 below and Table 1 in the Appendix). We briefly present the verbal level and then we shall elaborate on the gesture and the validation method, as the latter were the most challenging aspects of the coding process.

The mean duration for the annotation of the verbal level, which included the transcription of the words of the speakers, syntactic analysis, discourse analysis and validation of all annotations, was 6 hours per file (2.4h/min). The mean duration for the annotation of the gesture level, including the validation and final annotation, was 12 hours per file (4.8h/min). The duration time varied a lot and was certainly dependant on the subject's communication behaviour, as some children and adults gestured far more than others.

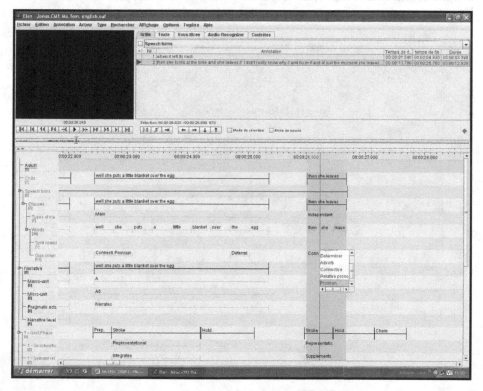

Fig. 1. Extract from ELAN annotation window file

---

[1] Available from http://www.mpi.nl/tools/. Also see Brugman and Russel (2004).

2 Annotation of the Verbal Level

The main aim of our work is to study narrative abilities and the way they develop in children. As children grow older, their linguistic performance in narratives develops because they use longer, more complex sentences (Diessel, 2004; Jisa, 2004). There are also changes in the use of tense, determiners and connectors (Fayol, 2000; Hickmann, 2003). The pragmatic and discourse performance also evolves, as the children include changes on the processing of ground information: background versus foreground, more freedom in the processing of the event frame (Fayol, 1997), and various speech acts such as narrating, explaining, commenting on the narrative or on the narration (Colletta, 2004). The verbal level of our annotation scheme thus includes not only an orthographical transcription, but also a syntactic analysis and a narrative analysis (see Fig. 2).

That being said, the question of selecting relevant linguistic variables remains problematic when working from a cross-linguistic perspective. In Italian, for example, the subject is not always marked, which creates implicit anaphors (zero anaphora). In isiZulu, an agglutinative language, it is extremely difficult to proceed with a division of words as we can for English or French, thus it is necessary to segment in morphemes. In each instance, the linguistic coding must be adapted to the considered language.

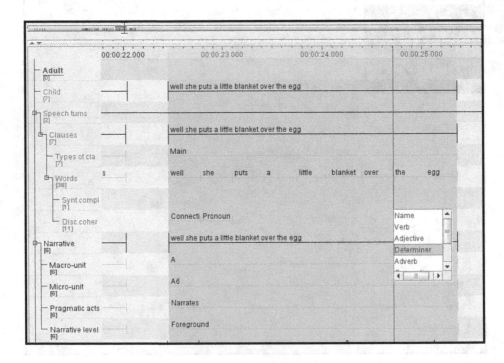

Fig. 2. Annotation of the verbal level

2.1 Speech Transcription and Syntactic Analysis

The transcription of the speakers' words appears on two tracks: one track for the interviewer and one for the child or the adult. The transcription is orthographical and presents the entirety of the remarks of the speakers.

In order to study age related changes in the subject's narrative performance, we first segmented the speech into speech turns. To annotate and segment speech turns is important to study from what age the child is able to achieve an autonomous monologic narrative task, without assistance from the adult (on the development of monologic discourse, see Jisa & Kern, 1998; Hickmann, 2003; Colletta, 2004; Jisa, 2004). We then segmented the speech into clauses and words. The number of clauses or the number of words contained in an account provides a good indication of its informational quantity, which is likely to grow with age. We also classified the clauses of the corpus in order to check whether there is or not a change towards complex syntax in the course of age development. We annotated the words to identify clues of subordination such as conjunctions, relative pronouns or prepositions. Our coding scheme relies on Berman & Slobin's work (1994), as well as Diessel's analysis of the children's syntactic units, in Diessel (2004). The annotation of words also serves to identify connectors and anaphoric expressions (pronouns, nouns, determiners, etc.) which play an important role in discourse cohesion (de Weck, 1991; Hickmann, 2003).

2.2 Narrative Analysis

Before the annotation grid was completed, the extract of the Tom & Jerry cartoon was segmented into macro and micro-episodes. During the annotation process, each clause with narrative content was categorised as processing one of these macro and micro-episodes in order to have an estimate of the degree of accuracy of the retelling of the story by each subject as well as to study his/ her processing of the event frame (Fayol, 1997). Each clause was also categorised as expressing the part or whole of a speech act (narrating, explaining, interpreting or commenting) and as expressing foreground versus background of the story (Colletta, 2004; Weinrich, 1989). It is a question of studying how age and culture affect pragmatic and discourse dimensions of the narrative activity, as also seen in Berman & Slobin (1994) and Hickmann (2003).

3 Annotation of the Gesture Level

In most cases, the annotation schemes developed by researchers in computer sciences focuses mainly on the description of corporal movements and the form of gestures. It is a question of capturing, as finely as possible, the corporal movements, to allow for an automatic synthesis. (Kipp, Neff & Albrecht, 2006; Le Chenadec, Maffiolo, Château & Colletta, 2006; Kipp, Neff, Kipp & Albrecht, 2007; Le Chenadec., Maffiolo & Chateau, 2007). Our objective for this developmental and cross-linguistic study is very different as the annotation has to allow us to study the relationship between gesture and speech. As a consequence, only the bodily movements maintaining a relation to speech – co-speech gesture – as well as the function of the gesture are of interest to us.

The gesture annotation was carried out in parallel by two independent well trained coders 1 and 2, who annotated on five stages (see Fig.2). Why five stages? In our developmental perspective, the five following parameters proved to be interesting. To begin with; the number of co-speech gestures, which as one would expect, increases with age as we see longer, more detailed and more complex narratives (Colletta, 2004, submitted). Another key parameter is the function of gesture. If the hypothesis of a gesture-word system is valid, then we ought to observe age related changes in gesture, with more gestures of the abstract and gestures marking discourse cohesion in the older children's and the adults' performance. The third important parameter is the gesture-speech relationship, which should evolve in parallel with linguistic acquisition and provide evidence of the evolution of language performance towards a more elaborated pragmatic and discursive use (McNeill, 1992; Colletta & Pellenq, 2007). The fourth parameter which is likely to vary with the age of the subjects is the manner which gestures and speech occur on the temporal level (synchrony and anticipation). The fifth parameter is gesture form, which in addition to representational accuracy (for representational gestures) in the older children and the adults, should gain more precision in use (see our three criteria in 3.1).

In addition to the developmental perspective, every one of these five parameters is likely to vary with the language and culture of the subjects. The study of the interactions between age on one hand, and language and culture on the other hand, should lead us to a better understanding of the role played by linguistic, cognitive and social factors in multimodal language acquisition.

3.1 Identification of the Gestures

In Kendon's work (1972, 1980, 2004), a pointing gesture, a representational gesture or any other hand gesture (an excursion of the body during speech) is called a *gesture phrase* and it possesses several phases including the preparation, the stroke, i.e., the meaningful part of the gesture phrase, the retraction or return and the repositioning for a new gesture phrase. Yet, some gestures are nothing else but strokes: a head gesture or a facial expression, for instance, are meaningful right from the start till the end of the movement and have no preparatory nor any retraction phases. As a consequence, our premise is that a gesture is any co-speech gesture phrase or isolated gesture stroke that needs to be annotated.

To identify the gesture, each coder took into account the following three criteria (based on Adam Kendon's proposals in Kendon, 2006):

> (i)   If the movement was easy to perceive, of good amplitude or marked well by its speed (on a scale of 0 to 2, 2 being the strongest value),
> (ii)   If location was in frontal space of speaker, for the interlocutor (on a scale of 0 to 2, 2 being the strongest value).
> (iii) If there was a precise hand shape or a well marked trajectory (on a scale of 0 to 2, 2 being the strongest value).

Once a gesture had been identified (total score > 3), the coder annotated its phases using the following values (based on Kendon, 2004):

Stroke » the meaningful height of the excursion of the gesture phrase of a hand gesture, or a movement of the head, shoulders or chest, or a facial display.

Prep » the movement which precedes a hand gesture stroke, which takes the hand(s) from its (their) initial position (at place of rest) to where the gesture begins. Contrary to hands, the position of head, the bust or shoulders is fixed. These movements can therefore not be "prepared" as hand movements and consequently can only be annotated as "strokes".

Hold » the maintaining of the hand(s) in its (their) position at the end of a hand gesture stroke, before the returning phase or a chained gesture.

Chain » the movement which brings the hand(s) from its (their) initial position at the end of a hand gesture stroke to the place where a new stroke begins, without returning to a rest position between the two strokes.

Return » the movement which brings back the hand(s) from its (their) position at the end of a hand gesture stroke to a rest position, identical or not to the preceding one (called "recovery" in Kendon, 2004).

3.2 Attributing Function to Gesture

The coder then attributed a function to each gesture stroke. In literature about gesture function, there generally appears to be agreement amongst gesture researchers, although they do not always agree on terminology. According to several researchers, Scherer (1984), McNeill (1992), Cosnier (1993), Calbris (1997), Kendon (2004), 4 main functions are always mentioned:

> (i)   gestures that help identify (pointing gestures) or represent concrete and abstract referents;
> (ii)   gestures that express social attitudes, mental states and emotions and that help perform speech acts and comment on own speech as well as other's;
> (iii)   gestures that mark speech and discourse, including cohesion gesture;
> (iv)   gestures that help to synchronise own-behaviour with interlocutor's in social interaction.

Our gesture annotation scheme mostly relies on Kendon's classification and covers the whole range of these functions. The coders had to choose between:

Deictic » hand or head gesture pointing to an object present in the communication setting, or to the interlocutor, or to oneself or a part of the body, or indicating the direction in which the referent is found from the actual coordinates of the physical setting. Not all pointing gestures have a deictic function as deictic pointing gesture strictly implies the presence of the referent or its location from the actual physical setting. Thus, gestures which locate a virtual character, object or action (like in sign languages of deaf communities) are to be annotated under <representational>.

Representational » hand or facial gesture, associated or not to other parts of the body, which represents an object or a property of this object, a place, a trajectory, an action, a character or an attitude (e.g.: 2 hands drawing the form of the referent; hand or head moving in some direction to represent the trajectory of the referent; 2 hands or body mimicking an action), or which symbolises, by metaphor or metonymy, an abstract idea (e.g.: hand or head gesture pointing to a spot that locates a virtual character or object; hand or head movement towards the left or the right to symbolise the past or the future; gesture metaphors for abstract concepts).

Performative » gesture which allows the gestural realisation of a non assertive speech act (e.g.: head nod as a "yes" answer, head shake as a "no" answer), or which reinforces or modifies the illocutionary value of a non assertive speech act (e.g.: vigorous head nod accompanying a "yes" answer).

Framing » gesture occurring during assertive speech acts (during the telling of an event, or commenting an aspect of the story, or explaining) and which expresses an emotional or mental state of the speaker (e.g. face showing amusement to express the comical side of an event; shrugging or facial expression of doubt to express incertitude of what is being asserted).

Discursive » gesture which aids in structuring speech and discourse by the accentuation or highlighting of certain linguistic units (e.g. beat gesture accompanying a certain word; repeated beats accompanying stressed syllables), or which marks discourse cohesion by linking clauses or discourse units (e.g. pointing gesture with an anaphoric function, e.g. pointing to a spot to refer to a character or an object previously referred to and assigned to this spot; brief hand gesture or beat accompanying a connective).

Interactive » gesture accompanied by gaze towards the interlocutor to express that the speaker requires or verifies his attention, or shows that he has reached the end of his speech turn or his narrative, or towards the speaker to show his own attention (e.g. nodding head while interlocutor speaks).

Word Searching » hand gesture or facial expression which indicates that the speaker is searching for a word or expression (e.g. frowning, staring above, tapping fingers while searching for words).

3.3 Definition of the Relation of Gesture to Corresponding Speech

The third stage consisted in giving a definition of the relation of the gesture to corresponding speech. The gesture-speech relation has proved a relevant issue in studying infant gestures during the transition to two-word speech (Butcher & Goldin-Meadow, 2000; Volterra, Caselli, Capirci & Pizzuto, 2005). For instance, the production of certain gesture + word combinations (complementary or supplementary combinations) predicts the onset of syntax acquisition whereas other combinations (redundant combinations) do not. However, with older children (6 years and above) and adults, these combinations are joined by other gesture-speech relations (Martin, 1999; Colletta, 2004). The coders had to choose between:

Reinforces » the information brought by the gesture is identical to the linguistic information it is in relation with (e.g. head nod accompanying a yes answer; face expressing ignorance while saying "I don't know"). This annotation does not concern the representational gestures, because we consider that information brought by the representational gesture, due to its imagistic properties, always says more than the linguistic information, as per McNeill (1992) or Kendon (2004). See <Integrates>.

Complements » the information provided by the gesture brings a necessary complement to the incomplete linguistic information provided by the verbal message: the gesture disambiguates the message, as in the case of deixis (e.g. pointing gesture accompanying a location adverb like « here », « there »; pointing gesture aiming at identifying an object not explicitly named).

Supplements » the information brought by the gesture adds a supplementary signification to the linguistic information, like in the case of framing gestures and certain performative gestures (e.g. vigorous shaking of head accompanying a no answer; face showing amusement signs to express a comical side of an event; shrugging or showing a mimic of doubt to express incertitude of what has been asserted).

Integrates » the information provided by the gesture does not add supplementary information to the verbal message, but makes it more precise, thanks to the imagistic properties of gesture. For instance, drawing a trajectory provides information on the location of the characters or objects we refer to, drawing the shape of an object may at the same time give information on its dimensions.

Contradicts » the information provided by the gesture is not only different from the linguistic information in which it is linked but contradicts it, as in the case of certain framing and performative gestures as in ironic expressions.

Substitutes » the information provided by the gesture replaces linguistic information, as in the case of certain performative and interactive gestures (e.g. the speaker nods as a yes answer, shakes head as a no answer, shrugs to express his ignorance of the information required), such as emblems or quotable gestures (Brookes, 2001).

3.4 Indication of the Temporal Placement of the Gesture in Relation to the Corresponding Speech

The fourth stage indicated the temporal placement of the gesture stroke in relation to the corresponding speech:

Synchronous » the stroke begins at the same time as the corresponding speech segment, whether it is a syllable, a word or a group of words.

Anticipates » the stroke begins before the corresponding speech segment; the speaker starts the gesture while delivering linguistic information prior to the one corresponding to it.

Follows » the stroke begins after the corresponding speech segment: the speaker begins the gesture after having finished speaking, or while delivering a linguistic information posterior to the one corresponding to it.

3.5 Gesture Form

Kipp, Neff & Albrecht (2006) mention two distinct ways to describe gesture form: "gesture form is captured by either a free-form written account or by gestural categories which describe one prototypical form of the gesture". In our work, as we focus on gesture function and gesture-speech relation, we relied on basic linguistic descriptions of the body movements.

The coder gave a brief linguistic description of each annotated gesture stroke, sticking to its most salient points:

- body part of movement: head, chest, shoulders, 2 hands, left hand, right hand, index, eyebrows, mouth, etc.
- if there is a trajectory: direction of the movement (towards the top, bottom, left, right, front, back, etc.)

- if there is a hand shape: the form of the hand (flat, cutting, closed in a punch-like form, curved, palm up, palm down, fingers pinched, fingers in a circle, etc.)
- the gesture itself: head nod, beat, circular gesture, rapid or not, repeated or not, etc.
For example: "Raises right hand to the front right, palm open, facing upwards", "Right hand opens and closes rapidly mimicking the beak of a bird".

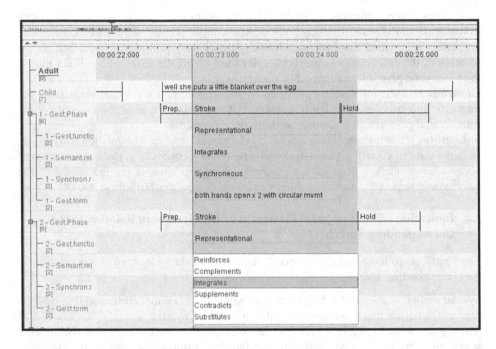

Fig. 3. Annotation of the gesture level

4   A 3-Coder Validation Method for the Gesture Annotation

In most cases, the validation of the gestural annotation is based on the comparison of the annotations done by two independent coders (Kita & Özyürek, 2003) and even more rarely, on re-creating gestures by an animated agent (Kipp, Neff & Albrecht, 2006). These methods are useful to test the validity of an annotation scheme, but they do not allow checking and stabilising the analysis of a corpus at the end of an annotation procedure. Indeed, in our case, it was not only a question of testing a gestural annotation grid, but it was also a question of validating the annotation of a multimodal corpus (gestures + speech) before using the results of the annotation in statistical analyses.

As a consequence, the last step of the analysis covered two objectives:

- Firstly, to finalise the gestural annotation from choices made by both coders and decide in case of disagreement;
- Secondly, to calculate the inter-reliability of agreement between all the coders.

The validation phase only applied to the first three parameters (identification of a gesture unit, function and relation to speech), as our goal was to check whether they vary as a function of age and culture. It did not apply to the fifth parameter because gesture form was written in free form and therefore the coders could see the same gesture differently, which will prove useful in a more detailed and qualitative analysis. Nor did it apply to the fourth parameter (temporal placement), which will prove useful too in such an analysis.

In order to achieve the validation task, a third independent coder had to perform two tasks. Firstly, he had to check all the annotations and choose the annotation he deemed to be the correct one in order to stabilise the data and to allow for statistical analysis. In the event of agreement between the two coders, he simply maintained what had been annotated. In the event of disagreement, he arbitrated by selecting the annotation that he observed to be valid. His choice then appeared on three new tracks, one for gesture identification, one for gesture function and one for gesture-speech relation (see fig.4). This first part of the validation was a necessary step to obtain basic data for quantitative analysis.

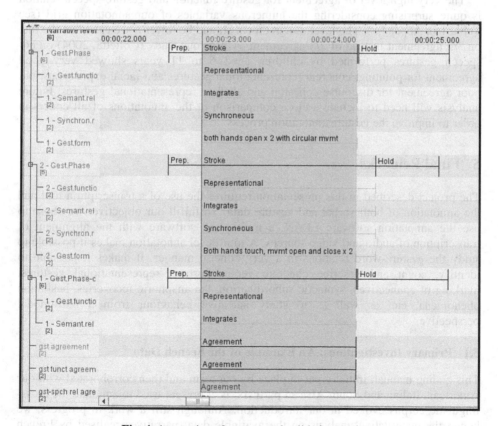

Fig. 4. Annotation of gesture and validation tracks

The second part of the validation task was achieved once the third coder annotates "agreement" when at least two coders of the three agreed on the presence of a gesture, its function, and its relation to speech, and "disagreement" on the contrary (see fig.4). This last step of validation allowed a measure of inter-reliability amongst the coders. We then calculated:

- Inter-reliability for the identification of gestures: number of agreement / number of gesture strokes per file.
- Inter-reliability for the identification of gesture function: number of agreement / number of gesture strokes per file.
- Inter-reliability for the identification of gesture-speech relation: number of agreement / number of gesture strokes per file.

To date, our results on the 120 French narratives indicated very high rate of agreement (Colletta, Pellenq & Guidetti, submitted). Using the above mentioned method, i.e. "2/3 agreement", there was 90% agreement for the gesture-identification, 94% for the gesture function, and 92% for the gesture-speech relation.

The very high level of agreement for gesture function and gesture-speech relation is quite surprising considering the numerous variables of our annotation grid (see Table 1 in Appendix). The level of agreement should be lower if we calculate the rate on 3/3 agreement instead of 2/3 agreement. A previous study (Colletta, 2004) on co-speech gestures performed by children aged 6 to 11 years showed very good agreement for pointing, concrete representational gestures and facial expressions, but poor agreement for discourse cohesion and abstract representational gestures. Future analysis will need to include a close comparison of the annotations of all coders in order to improve the gesture annotation process.

5 Final Remarks

The project described in this presentation requires the use of a transcription tool and the annotation of both verbal and gesture data. To fulfill our objective, we chose to use the annotation software ELAN, a multi-track software with the alignment of transcription of audio and video sources. A multilevel annotation makes it possible to study the gesture-word relations in a very concise manner. It makes it possible to identify, count and describe concrete versus abstract representational gestures, marking of connectives, syntactic subordination, the anaphoric recoveries, hesitation phenomena, etc. as well as to study narrative behaviour from a multimodal perspective.

5.1 Primary Investigations: An Example of the French Data

This coding manual, initially put in place by our team and then corroborated with our American, Italian and South African partners, is at present used to annotate the cross-linguistic corpus evoked in our introduction. Although still a work in progress, we began the quantitative analysis on the available data: narratives realised by French children and adults. As we can see tables 2 and 3, we were able to observe the following information:

- The length of narratives, measured by the number of clauses and words
- The degree of syntactic complexity, measured by the number of subordination cues
- Discourse cohesion measured by the number of connectors
- Their pragmatic content measured by the manner of their narrative clauses and non-narrative clauses (explanations, interpretations, commentaries)
- The gestural realisation measured by the number of gestures (strokes), and amongst these, the number of representational and non –representational gestures.

Table 2. Means (S.D.) of language measures for each age group

Age group		Clauses	Words	Connectors	Anaphors	Narrative clauses
Adults	m	37.18	215.61	28.66	39.00	24.42
	sd	13.49	75.63	12.43	14.92	9.61
9-10yrs	m	44.33	247.19	40.23	53.35	37.63
	sd	21.82	116.59	21.94	26.81	17.92
5-6yrs	m	26.02	157.51	27.73	28.17	22.59
	sd	14.23	80.41	15.49	17.95	13.42

Table 3. Means (S.D.) of language and gesture measures for each age group

Age group		Subordina-tion cues	Non-narrative clauses	Gesture strokes	Representation gestures	Other gestures
Adults	m	11.13	12.84	28.58	14.05	12.34
	sd	5.89	6.10	21.07	14.55	9.31
9-10yrs	m	6.60	6.53	21.35	12.81	6.00
	sd	4.46	6.04	27.92	18.58	8.86
5-6yrs	m	2.54	3.10	7.07	3.78	1.24
	sd	2.23	2.93	7.42	6.14	1.80

Without going into detail of the results, which can be read on (Colletta, Pellenq and Guidetti, submitted), we present some of the first findings from this developmental study

1. A strong age effect on the length of narratives with an inversed V shape: 10-years-old children give more detailed accounts than 6-years-olds' whereas adults tend to summarise the narrative frame
2. A strong and linear age effect on syntactic complexity, pragmatics and gesture: 6-years-old's narratives contain significantly less subordinate clauses, non-narrative clauses and co-speech gestures than 10-years-old's, and 10-years-old's narratives contain significantly less than adult's

To summarise these first results, older children perform longer and more detailed narratives than younger ones, whereas adults tend to give summarised accounts. However, adults significantly use more syntactic complexity cues, add more comments while narrating, and gesture more than the 2 groups of children. They also use more non-representational gestures (discourse cohesion and framing gestures) than the 2 groups of children. There is a developmental shift towards commenting the narrated events (by words or gesture) and marking discourse cohesion with gestures, and our results support the notion that gesture and narrative production co-develop with age.

5.2 Discussion

Yet, some technical issues need to be enhanced: the gesture annotation can be more precise if one dissociates the body parts: head, face, hand(s), and whole body. This would avoid the fact that for the same complex gesture involving several body parts, several coders code different aspects of the same behaviour. Moreover, this is painstaking, particularly for adult gestures, where the same gesture can perform two, even three functions simultaneously, which means that the values given in the drop-down menus should, in the future, include this multi-function feature.

The coding manual remains to be adapted for the isiZulu language (Kunene & Colletta, 2008). The close comparison of the three coders' gesture annotations will allow us to better understand the link between the diverse gesture functions as well as their link to specific gesture-speech relations... in the aim of improving our coding manual.

Aknowledgments. This research was conducted and financed by the French Agence Nationale de la Recherche. The authors thank their partners on the ANR Multimodality Project NT05-1_42974: Olga Capirci (CNR di Roma), Carla Cristilli (Università degli Studi di Napoli "L'Orientale"), Michèle Guidetti (université Toulouse II Le Mirail), Susan Goldin-Meadow and Susan Levine (University of Chicago). The authors also thank the HSRC of South Africa & Heather Brooks and for the financing of the isiZulu data collection.

References

1. Beattie, G., Shovelton, H.: When size really matters: How a single semantic feature is represented in the speech and gesture modalities. Gesture 6(1), 63–84 (2006)
2. Berman, R.A., Slobin, D.I.: Relating events in narrative: A cross-linguistic developmental study. Lawrence Erlbaum Associates, Hillsdale (1994)
3. Brookes, H.: O clever 'He's streetwise'. When gestures become quotable: the case of the clever gesture. Gesture 1, 167–184 (2001)
4. Butcher, C., Goldin-Meadow, S.: Gesture and the transition from one- to two-word speech: When hand and mouth come together. In: McNeill, D. (ed.) Language and gesture, pp. 235–257. Cambridge University Press, Cambridge (2000)
5. Brugman, H., Russel, A.: Annotating Multi-media / Multi-modal resources with ELAN. In: 4th International Conference on Language Resources and Language Evolution (LREC 2004), Lisbon, May 26-28 (2004)
6. Calbris, G.: Multicanalité de la communication et multifonctionnalité du geste. In: Perrot, J. (ed.) Polyphonie pour Yvan Fonagy, Paris, L'Harmattan (1997)
7. Calbris, G.: L'expression gestuelle de la pensée d'un homme politique. Paris, Editions du CNRS (2003)

8. Capirci, O., Iverson, J.M., Pizzuto, E., Volterra, V.: Gesture and words during the transition to two-word speech. Journal of Child Language 23, 645–673 (1996)
9. Colletta, J.-M.: Le développement de la parole chez l'enfant âgé de 6 à 11 ans. Corps, langage et cognition. Hayen, Mardaga (2004)
10. Colletta, J.-M.: Comparative analysis of children's narratives at different ages: A multimodal approach (in press)
11. Colletta, J.-M., Pellenq, C.: Les coverbaux de l'explication chez l'enfant âgé de 3 à 11 ans. In: Actes du 2e Congrès de l'ISGS: Interacting bodies, corps en interaction, Lyon, June 15-18 (2005), CDRom Proceedings (2007)
12. Colletta, J.-M., Pellenq, C.: The development of multimodal explanations in French children. In: Nippold, M., Scott, C. (eds.) Expository Discourse Development and Disorders: International Perspectives (in press)
13. Colletta, J.-M., Pellenq, C., Guidetti, M.: Age-related changes in co-speech gesture and narrative. Evidence form French children and adults (submitted)
14. Cosnier, J.: Etude de la mimogestualité. In: Pléty, R. (ed.) Ethologie des communications humaines: aide-mémoire méthodologique, pp. 103–115. ARCI et Presses Universitaires de Lyon, Lyon (1993)
15. Diessel, H.: The acquisition of complex sentences. Cambridge University Press, Cambridge (2004)
16. Ech Chafai, N., Pelachaud, C., Pelé, D.: Analysis of gesture expressivity modulations from cartoons animations. In: LREC 2006 Workshop on "Multimodal Corpora", Genova, Italy, May 27 (2006)
17. Fayol, M.: Des idées au texte. Psychologie cognitive de la production verbale, orale et écrite. Paris, P.U.F. (1997)
18. Fayol, M.: Comprendre et produire des textes écrits: l'exemple du récit. In: Kail, M., Fayol, M. (eds.) L'acquisition du langage, T.2: Le langage en développement. Au-delà de trois ans, pp. 183–213. Paris, P.U.F. (2000)
19. Goldin-Meadow, S.: Hearing gesture. How our hands help us think. Harvard University Press, Cambridge (2003)
20. Goldin-Meadow, S.: Talking and thinking with our hands. Current Directions in Psychological Science 15, 34–39 (2006)
21. Guidetti, M.: Yes or no? How young French children combine gestures and speech to agree and refuse. Journal of Child Language 32(4), 911–924 (2005)
22. Hickmann, M.: Children's discourse: person, space and time across languages. Cambridge University Press, Cambridge (2003)
23. Jisa, H.: Growing into academic French. In: Berman, R. (ed.) Language Development across Childhood and Adolescence, Trends in Language Acquisition Research, vol. 3, pp. 135–161. John Benjamins, Amsterdam (2004)
24. Jisa, H., Kern, S.: Relative clauses in French children's narrative texts. Journal of Child Language 25, 623–652 (1998)
25. Kendon, A.: Some relationships between body motion and speech. In: Siegman, A.W., Pope, B. (eds.) Studies in dyadic communication, pp. 177–210. Pergamon Press, Elmsford (1972)
26. Kendon, A.: Gesticulation and speech, two aspects of the process of utterance. In: Key, M.R. (ed.) The relationship of verbal and nonverbal communication, pp. 207–227. The Hague, Mouton (1980)
27. Kendon, A.: Gesture. Visible action as utterance. Cambridge University Press, Cambridge (2004)

28. Kendon, A.: Reflections on the Development of Gestural Competence. In: Conference, ANR Multimodality Project, Université Stendhal, Grenoble (July 2006)
29. Kipp, M., Neff, M., Albrecht, I.: An Annotation Scheme for Conversational Gestures: How to economically capture timing and form. In: Proceedings of the Workshop on Multimodal Corpora (LREC 2006), pp. 24–27 (2006)
30. Kipp, M., Neff, M., Kipp, K.H., Albrecht, I.: Towards Natural Gesture Synthesis: Evaluating gesture units in a data-driven approach to gesture synthesis. In: Pelachaud, C., Martin, J.-C., André, E., Chollet, G., Karpouzis, K., Pelé, D. (eds.) IVA 2007. LNCS (LNAI), vol. 4722, pp. 15–28. Springer, Heidelberg (2007)
31. Kita, S.: Language and gesture interface: A study of spontaneous gestures and Japanese mimetics. Unpublished doctoral dissertation. University of Chicago (1993)
32. Kita, S.: Jesuchaa: Kangaeru karada [Gesture: The body that thinks]. Kanebo Shobo, Tokyo (2002)
33. Kita, S., Özyürek, A.: What does cross-linguistic variation in semantic coordination of speech and gesture reveal?: Evidence for an interface representation of spatial thinking and speaking. Journal of Memory and Language 48, 16–32 (2003)
34. Kita, S., Özyürek, A.: How does spoken language shape iconic gestures. In: Duncan, S.D., Cassell, J., Levy, E.T. (eds.) Gesture and the dynamic dimension of language. Essays in honor of David McNeill, pp. 67–74. John Benjamins, Amsterdam (2007)
35. Kopp, S., Krenn, B., Marsella, S., Marshall, A.N., Pelachaud, C., Pirker, H., Thórisson, K.R., Vilhjálmsson, H.: Towards a Common Framework for Multimodal Generation: The Behavior Markup Language. In: Gratch, J., Young, M., Aylett, R.S., Ballin, D., Olivier, P. (eds.) IVA 2006. LNCS (LNAI), vol. 4133, pp. 205–217. Springer, Heidelberg (2006)
36. Kunene, R., Colletta, J.-M.: A Cross-linguistic annotation model for children and adults oral language and spontaneous gestures. In: Workshop on Speech and Face to Face communication, Grenoble, France, October 27-29 (2008)
37. Le Chenadec, G., Maffiolo, V., Chateau, N.: Analysis of the multimodal behavior of users in HCI: the expert viewpoint of close relations. In: 4th Joint Workshop on Multimodal Interaction and Related Machine Learning Algorithms, Brno, Czech Republic, June 28-30 (2007)
38. Le Chenadec, G., Maffiolo, V., Chateau, N., Colletta, J.M.: Creation of a Corpus of Multimodal Spontaneous Expressions of Emotions in Human-Interaction. In: LREC 2006, Genoa, Italy (2006)
39. Martin, J.C.: TYCOON: six primitive types of cooperation for observing, evaluating and specifying cooperations. In: AAAI Fall 1999. Symposium on Psychological Models of Communication in Collaborative Systems, November 5-7 (1999); Sea Crest Conference Center on Cape Cod, North Falmouth, Massachusetts, USA (1999)
40. McNeill, D.: Hand and mind. What gestures reveal about thought. University of Chicago Press, Chicago (1992)
41. McNeill, D.: Gesture and thought. University of Chicago Press, Chicago (2005)
42. McNeill, D., Quek, F., McCullough, K.E., Duncan, S., Furuyama, N., Bryll, R., Ma, X.F., Ansari, R.: Catchments, prosody and discourse. Gesture 1(1), 9–33 (2001)
43. Özcaliskan, S., Goldin-Meadow, S.: How gesture helps children construct language. In: Clark, E.V., Kelly, B.F. (eds.) Constructions in Acquisition, pp. 31–58. CSLI Publications, Palo Alto (2006)
44. Özyürek, A., Kita, S., Allen, S., Furman, R., Brown, A.: How does linguistic framing influence co-speech gestures? Insights from cross-linguistic differences and similarities. Gesture 5(1/2), 216–241 (2005)

45. Scherer, K.R.: Les fonctions des signes non verbaux dans la conversation. In: Cosnier, J., Brossard, A. (eds.) La communication non verbale, pp. 71–100. Neuchâtel, Delachaux et Niestlé (1984)
46. Slobin, D.I.: From « thought and language » to « thinking for speaking ». In: Gumperz, J.J., Levinson, S.C. (eds.) Rethinking linguistic relativity, pp. 70–96. Cambridge University Press, Cambridge (1996)
47. Talmy, L.: Lexicalisation patterns: semantic structures in lexical forms. In: Language typology and syntactic description. Grammatical categories and the lexicon, vol. 3, pp. 57–149. Cambridge University Press, Cambridge (1985)
48. Vilhjalmsson, H., Cantelmo, N., Cassell, J., Chafai, E.N., Kipp, M., Kopp, S., Mancini, M., Marsella, S., Marshall, A.N., Pelachaud, C., Ruttkay, Z., Thórisson, K.R., van Welbergen, H., van der Werf, R.J.: The Behavior Markup Language: Recent Developments and Challenges. In: Pelachaud, C., Martin, J.-C., André, E., Chollet, G., Karpouzis, K., Pelé, D. (eds.) IVA 2007. LNCS (LNAI), vol. 4722, pp. 99–111. Springer, Heidelberg (2007)
49. Volterra, V., Caselli, M.C., Capirci, O., Pizzuto, E.: Gesture and the emergence and development of language. In: Tomasello, M., Slobin, D. (eds.) Beyond Nature-Nurture. Essays in Honor of Elizabeth Bates, pp. 3–40. Lawrence Erlbaum Associates, Mahwah (2005)
50. de Weck, G.: La cohésion dans les textes d'enfants. Etude du développement des processus anaphoriques. Neuchâtel, Delachaux et Niestlé (1991)
51. Weinrich, H.: Grammaire textuelle du français. Paris, Didier/Hatier (1989)

Appendix

Table 1. The complete annotation grid

CHILD		child's speech and gesture
Speech turns		*segmentation of child's speech in speech turns*
Clauses		*segmentation of child's speech in clauses*
	Types of clauses	Independent / Main / Name compl. / Verb compl. Sentence compl. / Adjective compl. / Adverb compl. Focalised name compl./ Factitive / Infinitive nominal sentence
	Words	*segmentation of child's speech in words*
	Synt.complex.clues	Preposition Relative pronoun Subordinating conjunction Coordinating conjunction
	Disc.coherence.clues	Name / Verb / Adjective / Determiner Adverb / Connective / Relative pronoun Pronoun / Zéro anaphora
Narrative	child's speech segmented in clauses	
Macro-unit	A B C D E F G	In the nest From nest to bed The hatching "Imprinting" Damage How to calm the baby bird Back to the nest
Micro-unit	A1 A2 A3 ...	The mother knits The mother looks at the egg The mother knits ...
Pragmatic acts	Narrates Comments Explains	
Narrative level	Foreground Background	
Gest.phase		Prep Stroke Hold Return Chain
Gest.function		Deictic Representational Performative Framing Discursive Interactive Word searching
Semant. relation		Reinforces Complements Integrates Supplements Contradicts Substitutes
Synchron. relation		Anticipates Synchronous Follows
Gest.form		*description of the gesture features*

Gesture, Gaze and Persuasive Strategies in Political Discourse

Isabella Poggi[1] and Laura Vincze[2]

[1] Dipartimento. di Scienze dell'Educazione
Università Roma Tre
Via del Castro Pretorio 20, 00185 Roma
poggi@uniroma3.it
[2] Dipartimento di Linguistica
Università di Pisa
Via Santa Maria 85, 56126 Pisa
l.vincze@ling.unipi.it

Abstract. The paper investigates the use of gesture and gaze in political discourse, and presents an annotation scheme for the analysis of their persuasive import. A model in terms of goals and beliefs is illustrated, according to which persuasion is a case of social influence pursued through communication in which the persuader aims to influence the persuadee to pursue some goal while leaving him free to adopt it or not, and arguing how that goal is in the persuadee's interest. Two studies are reported on electoral debates of three politicians in Italy and France (Achille Occhetto, Romano Prodi and Ségolène Royal), and an annotation scheme is presented through which the gesture and gaze items produced in some fragments of political discourse were analyzed as to their signal and their literal and indirect meanings, and classified in terms of the persuasive strategies they pursue, *logos*, *ethos* or *pathos*. The results of the two studies are presented, showing that the pattern of persuasive strategies found in the meanings of gesture and gaze of each politician is coherent with either the persuasive structure of the specific fragment analyzed or with the politician's general political strategy.

Keywords: persuasion, persuasive strategies, gesture, gaze, facial expression.

1 The Rhetorical Body

The importance of body behaviour in persuasive discourse has been acknowledged back since the ancient Roman treatises of Rhetoric, by Cicero [1] and Quintilian [2] as an indispensable part of "Actio" (discourse delivery), in that gesture, gaze and head movements fulfil various communicative functions, often of use in the economy of persuasive discourse. By gestures and other body movements we can summon, promise, exhort, incite, approve, express apology or supplication, display emotions (regret, anger, indignation, adoration), depict or point at objects.

In recent literature, from Atkinson [3] on, several studies have overviewed aspects of the body's relevance in political communication: see the use of pauses facial expression and other body behaviours [4], [5] or the use of intonation to quell the

M. Kipp et al. (Eds.): Multimodal Corpora, LNAI 5509, pp. 73–92, 2009.
© Springer-Verlag Berlin Heidelberg 2009

applause [6]. More recently [7], by relying on the assumption that the audience applauds when persuasive attempts succeed, take applause as a cue to find out, through automatic analysis, persuasive words and sentences in a corpus of political speeches. Other studies concerning the detection of deceptive behaviours, like [8] and [9,] can provide hints as to which nonverbal behaviours are ineffective or even prevent persuasion. For example, self-manipulation, talking faster, averting eyes have a negative effect on persuasion in that they are felt as – and may be in fact – a cue to deception.

Two studies directly concerned with the impact of gestural communication on political discourse are [10] and [11]. The former analyses the gestures of Lionel Jospin as a way to understand the intimate expression of his political thought: for example, the metaphors exploited by his manual behaviour – whether he uses the left or right hand, and the hand shape exploited – can express abstract notions like effort, objective, decision, balance, priority, private or public stance. Yet, they also fulfil discourse functions: they can delimit or stress, enumerate or explicate the topics of discourse. Streeck [11], in analysing the gestural behaviour of the Democratic candidates during the political campaign of 2004 in USA, shows how important bodily behaviour may be in political persuasion. As to the transmission of factual information he observes how the tempo of body movements and their relation to speech rhythm provide information about discourse structure, distinguishing background from foreground information. Further, in spite of his not crediting a specific meaning to gestures, he seems to attribute them some persuasive (or counter-persuasive) effect: for instance, he reminds how the defeat of Howard Dean might have been due to the frequency of his "finger wag": a "hierarchical act" that might have given an impression of presumption and contempt toward the audience. Finally, among the gestures analysed by Kendon [12] some that may have a persuasive effect are the "ring" gestures, that bear a meaning of 'making precise' or 'clarifying', and are used every time this clarification is important "in gaining the agreement, the conviction or the understanding of the interlocutor" (p. 241).

The importance of facial expression and co-verbal gesture in conveying information that is effective in persuasion has been shown at length in the studies above; but also gaze, within facial behaviour, is relevant in this connection. Both face and gaze, in fact, may be used with persuasive functions, not only as an accompaniment of speech, but also while one is not holding the turn and is playing the role of the silent interlocutor. For example, in Italian political talk shows, during a politician's turn often the cameras record the facial expressions of his opponents, which are sometimes very communicative and may have a counter-persuasive role.

In this work we investigate the persuasive functions of gesture and gaze. Starting from a model of persuasion based on the notions of goal and belief (Sect.2), we present an annotation scheme for the analysis of the macro-structure of persuasive discourse in terms of its hierarchy of goals (Sect.3), a hypothesis on how to assess the persuasive import of gesture and gaze in multimodal persuasion (4 and 5), and an annotation scheme for the transcription, analysis and classification of gesture and gaze in persuasive political discourse (6 – 8). After analysing gesture and gaze items in some fragments of political discourse, we finally argue how the annotation schemes presented allow to compute and analyse the quantity and quality of persuasive gesture and gaze in a discourse, finding different patterns of persuasive body behaviour in different politicians, and showing how they are coherent with the persuasive structure of a politician's discourse and his or her political strategy.

2 A Model of Persuasion

According to a model of mind, social interaction and communication in terms of goals and beliefs [13], [14], [15], persuasion is an act aimed at social influence. Social influence, as defined by [14] is the fact that an Agent A causes an increase or decrease in the likeliness for another Agent B to pursue some goal GA Influence may occur even inadvertently: I wear a dress and a girl who admires me buys one like mine. But often people have the goal – even a conscious goal – of influencing others . In this case, to have B more likely pursue a goal GA, A must raise the value that GA may have for B, and does so through having B believe that pursuing GA is a means for B to achieve some other goal GB that B already has, and considers valuable (goal hooking) [16]. In some cases, even having someone feel some emotion is a way to influence him, since emotions are states with a high motivating power – they trigger goals [17]. Given this definition of social influence, there are many ways to influence others, ranging from education to threat, promise, manipulation, and the use of force. Among these, persuasion is an action aimed at social influence through conviction: that is, A aims at having B pursue the proposed goal GA thanks to the fact that B is convinced – i.e., he believes with a high degree of certainty – that GA is a means to GB. Moreover, as an act of influence, persuasion shares some features with a particular kind of speech act: advice. In fact, *suadeo* in Latin means "I give advice". And like advice [18], persuasion is characterised by the following features:

1) A pursues a goal of social influence through communication, that is, not only he tries to induce GA in B, but also makes clear to B he wants to do so,
2) A leaves B free of either pursuing the goal GA proposed by A or not, in this differing from threat, for example; and finally,
3) A aims to convince B that GA is in the interest of B. In fact, to persuade B to have GA as a goal of his, A must convince B, that is, induce B to believe with a high degree of certainty, that GA is worth pursuing – it is a goal of high value – since it is a sub-goal to some goal GB that B has.

To persuade B, A can make use [16] of the three strategies already highlighted by Aristotle [19]: *logos* (in our terms, the logical arguments that support the desirability of GA and the link between GA and GB); *pathos* (the extent to which A, while mentioning the pursuit of goal GA, can induce in B emotions or the goal of feeling or not feeling them); and *ethos* (A's intellectual credibility – his having the skills necessary for goal choice and planning, that we may call "ethos-competence", and his moral reliability – the fact that he does not want to hurt, to cheat, or to act in his own concern – that we call *"ethos-benevolence"*).

To persuade others we produce communicative acts by exploiting different modalities – written text, graphic advertisement, words, intonation, gestures, gaze, facial expression, posture, body movements: we thus make multimodal persuasive discourses, that is, complex communicative plans for achieving communicative goals. Any discourse, whether persuasive or not, can be analysed as a hierarchy of goals: a communicative plan in which each single communicative act (either verbal or non verbal) aims at a specific goal. Moreover, each goal may also aim at one or more supergoals: further goals for which the first goal is a means, but that, different from the first goal, which can be understood from the literal meaning of the communicative act, by definition are not explicitly stated but must be caught through inference by the Addressee. For example, if I say *"Are you going home?"* my literal goal is to ask you if you are going home, but through this I may aim at the supergoal of asking for a lift. So, two or more communicative acts may have a common super-goal: saying *"I am here with this face"* plus saying *"this is the face of an honest person"* may aim at the supergoal of implying "I am an honest person". A discourse (both a unimodal and a multimodal one) is a sequence of communicative acts that all share a common supergoal. For example, in a pre-election discourse, all the sentences, gestures, face and body movements aim at one and the same common supergoal: "I want you to vote for me". They do so by making up a persuasive multimodal discourse, in which each signal with its direct and indirect meanings, that is, through its literal and intermediate supergoals, pursues a *logos*, *ethos* or *pathos* strategy. Thus, all signals in a persuasive discourse are planned as aiming at the global persuasive message, even if not all of them, of course, are planned at the same level of awareness. While verbal signals are generally planned in a conscious way, gestures, facial expressions, gaze and body posture may be planned and produced at a lower level of awareness. But this does not imply that they do not make part of the global communicative plan, nor that the Sender does not have a (more or less aware) goal of communicating the meanings they bear. This is witnessed by the fact that, apart from cases of ambivalence or deception, the whole multimodal message is generally coherent with its global meaning [15], that is "distributed" across modalities. Of course, in delivering a speech, it is easier for words to be planned accurately than it is for gestures. Even if well trained, we cannot plan every gesture we produce: gestures, and even more facial expressions, gaze, body postures, are planned at a lower level of awareness than words. Nonetheless, words and gestures together make part of a global multimodal communicative plan and the Sender has a (more or less aware) goal of communicating the meanings they bear.

3 Annotating the Structure of a Persuasive Discourse

Let us now provide an example of how a persuasive discourse can be analysed in terms of a hierarchy of goals.

Figure 1 shows the analysis of a fragment of one minute drawn from a TV interview to Ségolène Royal before the French Presidential elections in 2007, held in the studios of the French channel France 2, after the first round of the elections, when she came second with 25,87% after Nicolas Sarkozy. In the political show "A vous de juger", Arlette Chabot interviews Mrs. Royal about her political vision and projects for France. Here is the fragment.

"Voilà, je n'ai aucune revanche à prendre, je n'ai aucune revendication, je n'ai pas d'enjeu personnel dans cette affaire, je ne suis liée à aucune puissance d'argent, je n'ai personne à placer, je ne suis prisonnière d'aucun dogme, et au même temps je sens que les Français ont envie d'un changement extrêmement profond. Et mon projet c'est eux, ce n'est pas moi, mon

projet. Mon projet ce sont les Français et aujourd'hui le changement que j'incarne. Le changement, le vrai changement c'est moi. Donc là il y a aujourd'hui un choix très clair entre soi continuer la politique qui vient de montrer son inefficacité. Certaines choses ont été réussies, tout n'est pas caricaturé, par exemple le pouvoir sortant a réussi la lutte contre la sécurité routière, par exemple, mais beaucoup de choses ont été dégradées dans le pays, Arlette Chabot, beaucoup de choses... Et quand Nicolas Sarkozy refuse le débat, c'est parce qu'il ne veut pas être mis devant le bilan."

(Here I am, I have no revenge to take, I have no claiming, no personal stake in this affair, I'm not bond to any financial power, I have no one to place, I'm not prisoner of any dogma, and at the same time I feel that the French desire an extremely profound change. And my project is them, my project is not myself. My project is the French and the change I embody today. The change, the real change, is me. So today there is a very clear choice on whether continuing the politics that has just shown its inefficacy. Some things were well done, not everything is caricaturized, for instance the party in charge came out successful of the fight for security in driving. But a lot of things have been degraded in the country, Arlette Chabot, a lot of things... And when Nicolas Sarkozy refuses this debate it is because he doesn't want to confront the balance).

Following [13], to represent the hierarchy of goals of a discourse you have to segment the fragment under analysis into its speech acts (written in italics in Fig. 1), then you write down their literal goals and super-goals (i.e., the inferences each communicative act aims to induce, numbered as G1, G2 etc.), and you single out the final goal of the fragment, while using arrows to represent the means-end relations between goals.

In this fragment, Royal explains to the electors that she has no revenge to take (Speech Act 1), any personal claiming or advantage in becoming president (2, 3, 5), nor is she bond to any financial power (4), thus implying (G7) that she does not work in her own interest; the only reason why she runs for President is for the sake of the French who wish for a change (SAs 7 and 9, that aim at G9, and 8 that aims at G8). By implying G7 and G8 she aims at demonstrating that she is altruistic (G6). At the same time, indirectly acknowledging (through SA 11) the good things done by her opponent (G10), she implies that she is fair (G5), with fairness and altruism bearing on an image of benevolence (G2), whose projection makes part of an *ethos* strategy. Meanwhile SAs 6 ("I'm not prisoner of any dogma"), and 9 ("I am the change"), that implies G9, provide an image of flexibility, novelty, intelligence (G3): the competence side of the ethos strategy. Moreover, through SAs 10 and 12 she implies G11 ("Sarkozy is incapable to run France"), while through 13 and 14 she indirectly communicates G12 ("he is a coward"). So, symmetrically with the positive evaluations of competence and benevolence she implied about herself (G2 and G3), she now provides two negative evaluations (G11 and G12) of her opponent both on the competential and on the moral side. Further, that Sarkozy does not want to confront the balance of what he did (14) implies that the balance of what the political right side has done is negative (G13), so it is necessary to vote for the change (9), for the left (G4), for Royal (G1). The chaining of events and consequences from 14 to G13 and from G13 to G4 may be seen as a *logos* strategy. Only the *pathos* strategy does not show so much in this fragment of discourse.

In her persuasive structure, Royal identifies the desire of the French for an extremely deep change (SA7) and she hooks her own goal of being elected to that

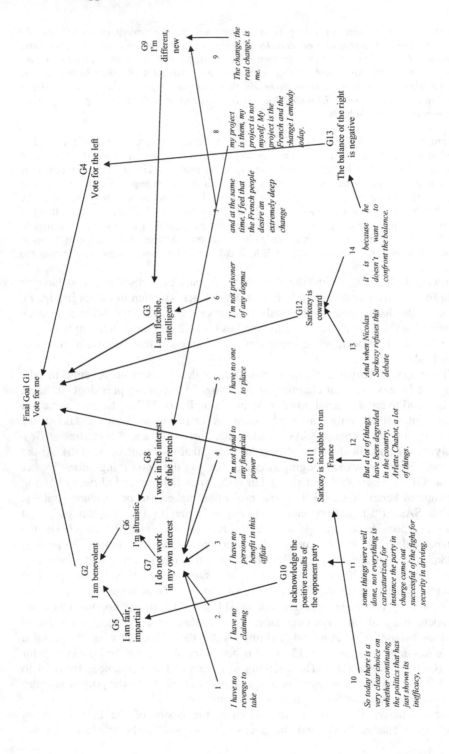

Fig. 1. The persuasive strategy of Ségolène Royal's political discourse

goal, by communicating, through inference or explicit words (SAs 8 and 9) that *she* is the change: so voting for her (G1) is the means to their goal of change.

As can be seen in Fig. 1, the analysis of a persuasive discourse in terms of its hierarchy of goals allows: 1. to show the links between the goals proposed by the Persuader and the goals s/he attributes to the Persuadee, 2. to specify which parts of the persuasive act, respectively, pursue the strategies of *logos*, *ethos* and *pathos*, and 3. to discern if they do so in a direct or in an indirect – inferential – way.

4 Multimodal Communication in Persuasion

In face-to-face communication and in visual media, also bodily signals take part in the whole hierarchy of goals of discourse. We make multimodal discourses, where even gesture, gaze, facial expression and posture may each have their role in pursuing our persuasive goals. To account for how they do so it is necessary to distinguish a literal vs. an indirect meaning not only for words but for all kinds of signals. Since not only words, but all bodily codified signals – like symbolic gestures, gaze items, facial expressions – can be viewed as forming a "lexicon", a list of signal-meaning pairs written in long term memory, by "literal" meaning we refer to that represented in the lexicon as the codified meaning of a signal, while the indirect meaning is meaning that can be inferred – and that the Sender has the supergoal that the Addressee infers – from the literal meaning of one or more verbal or bodily signals. For example, in begging – a persuasive communicative act aimed at getting help from someone – the beggar may 1. *stare* at a passer-by (thus meaning "I am addressing you"), with 2. *oblique eyebrows*, ("I am sad, helpless"), 3. *head* slightly *bent down* ("I am asking for your empathy"), and 4. *cupped hand with palm up* ("I am ready to take [what you give me]"). The literal meanings of these bodily communicative acts all aim at the common supergoal (at having the interlocutor infer the indirect meaning) of begging; and among them, oblique eyebrows and bent head aim at a pathos strategy. How multimodal persuasive fragments, taken from everyday communication, political discourse and entertainment can be analysed is shown in Poggi [15].

In this work, we wonder what are the functions that gesture and gaze can fulfil in persuasive discourse, and how their work can be annotated.

Actually, if gesture and face can have a function in persuasive discourse, we wonder, more specifically: do some gestures, facial expressions, items of gaze exist that are in themselves "persuasive", i.e., that have the effect of persuading people?

Some authors [7], [20], [21], [22], [23] claim that the persuasive effects of gestures depends on their type, whether they are iconic, deictic, symbolic, or adaptors of different types. In particular, a low level of persuasiveness is attributed to discourse accompanied by many self-adaptors. In our view, though, it is not so much what *type* of gesture you use in a speech that is persuasive, but what is the *meaning* it conveys. Finding that a politician is less persuasive if he makes many adaptors probably depends on the fact that most adaptors are used out of a need for self-reassurance. Thus, either they convey a message like "I am feeling insecure", or they, by inducing the impression that the Speaker is embarrassed, may let infer a suspicion of deception. In both cases they fail to inspire trust in the audience.

But again, also in the hypothesis that the persuasive effect of body movements depends on their meaning, we should wonder: are there some gestures, or facial expressions, or items of gaze, whose meaning can be defined "persuasive"?

5 Persuasion in Gesture and Gaze

In a previous work [24] it was found out that, except for very few cases, like gestures whose meaning is "I incite you" or so, there do not exist gestures that one can call "persuasive" per se. Rather, some gestures have a persuasive import since they convey some of the information required in the persuasive structure of discourse. But, what are the types of information that make a discourse persuasive?

According to the model presented, some types of information that are typically conveyed in persuasion, and that make a discourse a persuasive discourse, are those linked to the scenario of persuasion: a goal proposed by a Sender, its being important and good for the Addressee's goals, and the certainty of this mean-end relationship, but also the Addressee's emotions and his or her trust in the Sender. Thus, the meanings relevant to persuasion – the types of information a persuasive discourse must convey, through whatever modality – are the following:

1. *Importance*. If something is important, to obtain it will be a high value goal that you want to pursue. And gestures that convey the meaning "important" mention the high value of a proposed goal, to convince the Addressee to pursue it. This meaning is typically borne by gestures that convey performatives of incitation or request for attention, or other gestures like Kendon's [25] *"finger bunch"*, that convey a notion of importance as their very meaning; but expressing "importance" is also the goal of *beats*, since every beat stresses a part of a sentence or discourse, thus communicating "this is the important part of the discourse I want you to pay attention to". Finally, this can also be the goal of irregularity or discontinuity in the gesture movement: an effective way to capture attention.

2. *Certainty*. To persuade you I must convince you, that is, cause you to have beliefs with a high degree of certainty, about what goals to pursue (their value, importance) and how to pursue them (means-end relationship). To induce certainty in you, I may need to show self-confident and certain about what I am saying. This is why gestures that convey high certainty, like Kendon's [12] *"ring"*, may be persuasive.

3. *Evaluation*. Expressing a positive evaluation of some object or event implies that it is a useful means to some goal; thus, to bring about that event or to obtain that object becomes desirable, a goal to be pursued. In the marketplace, to convince someone to buy a food, the grocer's *"cheek screw"* (rotating the tip of the index finger on cheek to mean "good", "tasty"), would be a good example of persuasive gesture.

4. *Sender's benevolence*. In persuasion not only the evaluation of the means to achieve goals, but also the evaluation of the Persuader is important: his *ethos*. If I am benevolent toward you – I take care of your goals – you can trust me, so if I tell you a goal is worthwhile you should pursue it. A gesture driven by the *ethos* strategy of showing one's moral reliability is one quite frequent in political communication: *putting one's hand on one's breast* to mean "I am noble, I am fair" [26].

5. *Sender's competence*. Trust implies not only benevolence but also competence. If I am an expert in the field I am talking about, if I am intelligent, efficient, you might join with me and pursue the goals I propose. In a fragment of a political debate the Italian politician Silvio Berlusconi, in talking of quite technical things concerning taxes, uses his *right hand curve open, with palm to left, rotating rightward twice*, meaning that he · is passing over these technicalities, possibly difficult for the audience; but at the same time his *relaxed movement* lets you infer that he is smart because he is talking of such difficult things easily, and unconstrained. This aims at providing an image of competence.

6. *Emotion*. Emotions trigger goals. So A can express an emotion to affect B by contagion and thus induce him to pursue or not to pursue some goal. In talking about his country, for example, Romano Prodi, *moving his forearm with short and jerky movements of high power and velocity*, conveys the pride of being Italian to induce the goal of voting for him.

These are the meanings that, when found in a discourse, give it a persuasive import. Among these types of information, Emotion (n.6) typically makes part of a *pathos* strategy; the Sender's *benevolence* and *competence* (n.5 and 4), but also *certainty* (n. 2), are clearly *ethos* information; while the elements of *importance* and *evaluation* (n. 1 and 3) are generally conveyed through a *logos* strategy. Nonetheless, these categories can merge with each other: for example, expressing an emotion about some possible action or goal may imply it is an important goal for me, and should be so for you. In this case, at a first level there is a *pathos* strategy – the goal of inducing an emotion, but this pathos is aimed at demonstrating the importance of the proposed goal, thus conveying a *logos* strategy at the indirect level.

In order to classify gestures in terms of the three strategies, we first categorise them on the basis of the taxonomy of meanings presented in [15]. According to this taxonomy, gestures – as all other communicative signals – can be classified as conveying Information on the World, on the Sender's Mind or on the Sender's Identity. The gestures on the World inform on concrete or abstract events and entities, such as persons, objects, actions, quantifiers, properties of objects or persons, relations among them, etc. But they can communicate Information on the Sender's Mind as well: some for example inform on the cognitive status of beliefs in the Sender's Mind and on the degree of certainty of the mentioned beliefs. To the same category belong gestures which inform on the Sender's goals (gestures which communicate a performative), or those which inform on the Sender's emotions The third category contains gestures which convey information on the Sender's Identity and a positive image of self.

We applied same taxonomy to gaze items as well.

On the basis of these hypotheses both gesture and gaze can be analysed as to their persuasive import in a discourse.

6 Persuasive Gesture

We analysed some fragments of political discourse in Italian and French elections.

An annotation scheme (see Table 1) was constructed to assess the persuasive import of gestures. In the 9 columns we write, respectively:

1) the number of the gesture under analysis and its time in the video;
2) the speech parallel to the gesture under analysis;
3) a description of the gesture in terms of its parameters [15]: handshape, location, orientation and movement, and for the movement the parameters of expressivity [27]: temporal extent, spatial extent, fluidity, power and repetition;
4) the literal meaning of the gesture. A gesture, as any communicative signal, by definition means something, that is, it corresponds to some meaning; this meaning can be either codified, as in a lexicon, or created on the spot but yet comprehensible by others, and then in any case shared. As such, any gesture may be paraphrased in words. (For examples of signal-meaning pairs in gestures, see [15]. This verbal paraphrase is written down in col. 4;
5) a classification of the meaning written in col.4, according to the semantic taxonomy proposed by [15], that distinguishes meanings as providing information on the World (events, their actors and objects, time and space relations between them), the Sender's Identity (sex, age, socio-cultural roots, personality), or the Sender's Mind (beliefs, goals and emotions);
6) on the basis of the semantic classification in Column 5), the gesture is classified as to whether it has a persuasive function, and if so, in terms of the persuasive strategy pursued: whether it conveys information bearing on *logos*, *pathos*, *ethos benevolence*, or *ethos competence*;
7) 8) and 9). Columns 7), 8) and 9) contain, for possible indirect meanings of the gesture, the same analysis of cols. 4), 5) and 6).

The gestures analysed were taken from the political debates of Achille Occhetto and Romano Prodi, both candidates of the Centre-leftists against Silvio Berlusconi, during the Italian elections in 1994 and 2006, respectively. Some fragments were analysed as to their global meaning and their persuasive structure, and the gestures performed during discourse were annotated by two independent coders, previously trained in the annotation of multimodal data.

Table 1 contains the annotation of the fragment below and shows how the elements of persuasiveness listed above can be found in the gestures under analysis.

Si è detto recentemente con ironia: "Ma guarda Prodi fa il discorso con la CGIL e con la Confindustria". Sì, faccio il discorso con la CGIL e la Confindustria.
(Recently people ironically said: "Ok look Prodi is talking to both trade unions and factory owners". Ya I talk to trade unions and factory owners).

At line 1, Prodi quotes an ironic objection to his political action in order to counter-object to it. While saying "*Si è detto recentemente con ironia*" ("recently people ironically said"), *his hands, with palms up a bit oblique, open outward*: an iconic gesture referring to something open, public; a way to open a new topic in your discourse, like when the curtain opens on the stage: a metadiscursive gesture, but with no indirect meaning and no persuasive import. Then (line 2), while saying "*ma guarda Prodi fa il discorso con la CGIL e con la Confindustria*" ("Oh look, Prodi is talking to both trade unions and factory owners"), *he puts his left hand on his hip*, and at the same time, with his *chest erected, he shakes his shoulders* (first left shoulder forward and right backward, then the reverse). His *hand on hip* bears the meaning of someone taking the stance of a judge, the *erected chest* shows self-confidence, almost,

Table 1. The persuasive import of gestures

1. Time	2. Speech	3. Gesture description	4. Literal meaning	5. Meaning type	6. Persuasive import	7. Indir. meaning	8. Meaning type	9. Persuasive import
1 0.00.1	*"Si è detto recentemente con ironia"* Recently people ironically said	hands palms up oblique open outward Sp.ext: +1 Fluid: +1 Power: -1 Temp.ext: 0 Rep.: 0	Open, public, I show, I exhibit,	ISM Metadiscursive				
2 0.00.6	*"Ma guarda Prodi fa il discorso con la CGIL e con la confindustria"* Ok look Prodi is talking to both trade unions and factory owners	Left arm near body, hand on Hip + Shoulder shaking Sp.ext: 0 Fluid: + 1 Power: - 1 Temp.ext: 0 Rep.: 0	I am mimickin g those who ironically judge by looking down to us	ISM Metadiscursive		I want you to laugh about them	ISM Performative	PERS (Pathos)
3 0.00.8	*Sì, faccio il discorso con la CGIL e la cofindustria* Ya I talk to trade unions and factory owners	Left arm near body, hand on hip, Bowing rhythmically Sp.ext: + 1 Fluid: - 0.5 Power: + 0.5 Temp.ext: + 1 Rep.: 4	I defy you	ISM Performative		I am self-confident in doing so	ISM Certainty	PERS (Ethos Competence)

Legend: IW: Information on the World.

a self attribution of superiority, and the *shoulder shaking* shows that he is gloating for the other being judged and ridiculed. This whole movement is a way to mimic the ones who uttered the quoted sentence, while making fun of them. Actually, he is somehow meta-ironizing: he is being ironic about others' irony, by ridiculing their attitude of superiority through exaggeration. Irony in fact is often brought about through hyperbole [28]. This gesture has a persuasive import in that ridiculing aims to bring about an emotion of amusement in the audience, thus exploiting a *pathos* strategy in order to elicit a negative evaluation of the ridiculed people. And by inducing a negative evaluation of the opponents, Prodi intends to lead the audience to prefer him. Then he says (line 3): *"sì faccio il discorso con la cigielle e la confindustria"* ("Yes I am talking to trade unions and factory owners"), again with *left hand on hip*, but with *bust bowing* five times rhythmically, simultaneously with the stressed syllables in the concomitant sentence. The *bust bow*, somehow similar to an ample nod, means: "I acknowledge that what you say is true", while the *hand on hip* claims self-confidence. But acknowledging that an accusation or a criticism is true while showing confidence means that you accept it as a neutral or even positive statement, devoid of any negative evaluation: thus the combination of the two movements means "I will really do what they accuse me of", conveying a meaning of defiance, hence giving the impression of an even higher self-confidence.

Table 2. shows the patterns of persuasive strategies pursued by Occhetto and Prodi in some fragments of the debates analysed. For each fragment, within the gestures performed we computed the number of communicative units conveyed, since in a single gesture the various parameters may convey more than one meaning; then within these we computed the number of persuasive units, distinguished into *logos*, *pathos*, *ethos competence* and *ethos benevolence*.

Table 2. Persuasive strategies in gestures

	Occhetto		Prodi	
Length	30"		1'32"	
Gestures	14		27	
Communicative units	24		49	
Persuasive units	20		34	
	n.	%	n.	%
Logos	1	5	8	23
Pathos	6	30	4	12
Ethos competence	9	45	17	50
Ethos benevolence	4	20	5	15

Occhetto makes a higher percentage of persuasive gestures than Prodi out of the total of communicative gestures (Occhetto 20 out of 24, 83%, Prodi 34 out of 49, 69%), but this is also due to the fact that Prodi sometimes uses iconic gestures, that convey Information on the World and have no persuasive import except for some in expressivity. Moreover, Occhetto relies much more on *pathos* than on *logos* gestures (30% vs. 5%); Prodi uses the two strategies in a more balanced way, but with a preference for *logos* (23% vs. 12%). In both, the majority of gestures (65%) pursue an *ethos* strategy, and both tend to project an image of competence more than one of benevolence, but this preference for competence holds more for Prodi (50% vs. 15%) than for Occhetto (45% vs. 20%).

These differences can be accounted for both by specific aspects of the fragments analysed, and by the different political origins of the two politicians. On the former side, in the fragment under analysis Occhetto is attacking his opponent Berlusconi from an ethical point of view, and therefore he aims to project an ethically valuable image of himself, while Prodi is describing his program and thus he wants to project the image of one who is able to carry it on effectively. On the side of the different political origins, Prodi is a centre-leftist coming from a former catholic party (the Christian Democrats), while Occhetto is a communist, and Berlusconi still makes appeal to the old prejudice that the Communists "eat the kids"! Hence, Occhetto in fact has a higher need than Prodi to show his image of benevolence a discourse.

7 Persuasion in Gaze

If gesture is so important in conveying information that is effective in persuasion, also gaze could be relevant in this connection. Yet, not so much literature has been devoted to the persuasive impact of facial expression and gaze in persuasion. So in this case we analysed the discourse of Prodi and the interview to Ségolène Royal to investigate the persuasive use of gaze in political discourse. The fragments were analysed by two independent expert coders.

Also in this study the hypothesis was that the persuasive import of gaze, just as for words and gestures, depends on the meanings it conveys. Therefore, to assess how persuasive the gaze displayed in a discourse might be, you have to assess its meaning. For the analysis of gaze in the fragments of Royal's and Prodi's discourse we used an annotation scheme similar to that used for gestures. Table 3 shows the analysis of two gaze items in Royal's discourse.

In example 1, while talking of the top managers who spoil the enterprises, like Mr. Forgeat (Col.2), Royal *looks at the Interviewer*, Arlette Chabot, with a *fixed gaze* (col.3) which means "I am severe, I do not let you avert your gaze" (4): information about Royal's personality, her being serious and determined (5), aimed at a strategy of Ethos competence (6), and possibly to indirectly conveying that she is one who struggles against injustice (7): again information on her personality (8), bearing on the moral side of *ethos, benevolence* (9). Then Royal, leaning her head on the left, *looks at the Interviewer obliquely and with half-closed eyelids*, an expression of anger and indignation: information about her emotion, which she possibly wants to induce in the audience, thus pursuing a *pathos* strategy.

In example 13, she refers to a proposal made by Sarkozy that the unemployed people should be induced to choose a job out of no more than two, and lest they do so, they should lose their unemployment subsidy. Royal argues that this imposed choice can only be acceptable if the conditions of the two jobs are not very punitive. So, while saying *il faut accepter cet emploi* ("you have to accept this job"), she *looks down, first rightward then leftward*, as if looking at two things before deciding, thus referring to the choice between the two jobs. This is an iconic use of gaze, providing Information on the World, namely an action of choice, by mimicking it. After that, she *raises her eyebrows while keeping her eyelids in the défault position*: one more iconic gaze that means "order", mimicking the expression of someone who orders the unemployed to make his choice. By these two gaze items Royal is playing the roles of

Table 3. The persuasive import of gaze

1. Time	2. Speech	3. Gaze description	4. Literal meaning	5. Meaning type	6. Persuasive import	7. Indir. meaning	8. Meaning type	9. Persuasive import
1 48.10	*Et aux hauts dirigeants qui abîment l'entreprise en faillite comme M. Forgeat* And as to the top managers who spoil the enterprises, like Mr. Forgeat	*Fixed gaze to the Int.* *Looks at Interviewer leaning head leftward, from down to up, with half-closed eyelids*	I'm severe, I feel anger and indignation	ISI Personality ISM Emotion	ETHOS Competence	I struggle against injustice I ask you to feel indignation	ISI Personality ISM Performative	ETHOS Benevolence PATHOS
13 49.10	*Non, là, il faut... il faut accepter cet emploi,* No, you have.... You have to accept this job	*She looks down, first rright then to left* *Eyebrows raised, Eyelids défault*	Choice, choose a job I order you (to choose one)	IW Action ISM Performative		I am ridiculing S.'s proposal His proposal is too punitive	ISM Emotion ISM Negative Evaluation of opponent	PATHOS LOGOS

Legend: IW: Information on the World; ISM = Information on the Sender's Mind; ISI = Information on the Sender's Identity.

both, the unemployed person and the job proposer, thus enacting the scene of Sarkozy's proposal. On the basis of the following argumentation, in which Royal is very critic about it, we can interpret her enactment as a parody, a way to make fun of Sarkozy's proposal, thus conveying a negative evaluation of her opponent through a *pathos* strategy.

On the basis of this qualitative analysis, a quantitative analysis was finally carried on. Out of the fragments analysed of Prodi's and Royal's speeches, we finally selected a sample of 20 items of gaze per each politician, and computed their persuasive functions. Table 4 and Figures 2 and 3 show the different distribution of gaze communication across the four different strategies: *logos, pathos, ethos competence* and *ethos benevolence*.

Table 4. Persuasive strategies in gaze

	Prodi		Royal	
Length	53"		1'20"	
Gaze items	20		20	
Communicative units	25		25	
Persuasive units	16		22	
	n.	%	n.	%
Logos	4	25	12	54
Pathos	2	13	3	14
Ethos competence	10	62	6	27
Ethos benevolence	0	0	1	5

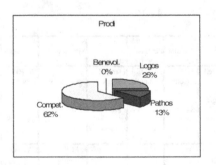
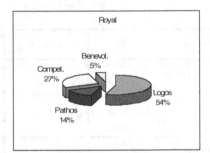

Fig. 2. Persuasive strategies in Prodi's gaze   **Fig. 3.** Persuasive strategies in Royal's gaze

From the analysis of Prodi's and Royal's gaze it results that the two differ as to the persuasive strategies of their gaze. Prodi's most frequent strategy (62%) is to show his competence to elicit the electors' trust, while he does not aim at showing his benevolence. He uses a *logos* strategy in 25% of his gaze, and pathos in 13%. Quite striking, instead, the frequency of *logos* strategy in Royal's gaze (54%) and then the appeal to her own competence (27%) which, however, does not rule out benevolence (5%). Finally, the *pathos* strategy is used slightly more than in Prodi's discourse (14% as opposed to 13%).

The high incidence of the competence strategy and total lack of the benevolence strategy in Prodi's gaze is coherent with his need to enhance more his image of skill and political intelligence than that of an honest and altruistic person. Between Prodi and his opponent Berlusconi, the latter generally has the image of one who deals with politics more for the sake of his own financial interests than for the Italians. On the other hand, the propaganda of the right would often ridicule Prodi by comparing him to a "mortadella" (a salted meat typical of his hometown, Bologna): a fat, cheap, popular, not luxurious food, evoking someone who is over-soft, not so charismatic, skilled and determined. As for the high incidence of the *logos* strategy in Royal's gaze, two tentative explanations could be the goal to contrast stereotypes of feminine irrationality, or the French *esprit de géométrie*.

What these analyses show is how coherent is the use of gaze with the whole of an Orator's argumentation and persuasive plan.

8 Body Side and Political Side

As we mentioned, the body may be used in persuasive discourse at different levels of awareness, but also when some body behaviour is not completely aware we can still leave it open the hypothesis that the Speaker does have a specific goal of using that movement as a subgoal of his discourse plan, and possibly of his persuasive strategy.

An intriguing example of this may be the use of hands and head movements to indicate two opposed parties and political stances. While analysing Royal's debate, we fell in with a curious use of the location of her hands that systematically matches the abstract location of left and right in the political sense. A such use of hands has been observed already by Calbris [10] concerning Jospin's gestures : "The Left in politics is situated at the locutor's left. Jospin refers to the Left by systematically exploiting his left hand. Every allusion to the left government, such as the Left's objectives, the Left's political programme, are represented by the left hand. [...] In general way, the Leftist government is mentally situated on the left." (p. 67, our translation).

We can see the same phenomena in the interview of Ségolène Royal, where she very consistently uses her right hand while speaking of the right, the rich, the speculation, while she uses her left hand while mentioning the poor, the workers, or the middle class.

We annotated this meaningful use of hands through the scheme in Table 5. Here, column 1 contain the sentence under analysis, while in the subsequent six columns, respectively, you write whether Royal moves her right (col. 2-4) or her left hand (5-7), and whether toward right, or left or to the centre.

From a quantitative point of view (see Table 6), in a fragment of 4'6'' Ségolène Royal moves her right hand 40 times and her left hand 6 times. Her right hand moves to the right 25 times, 14 to the centre, and only once to left, while the left hand always moves to the left.

Table 5. Body side and political side

Speech		Right Hand			Left Hand		
		RH on right	RH in center	RH on left	LH on right	LH in center	LH on left
46.28	There are too many rich people on one side	X					
	and too many poor people on the other						X
46.44	But when I hear the candidate of the Right		X				
	saying that he is going to make a "tax shield"	X X X					
	for the rich people	X					
	But where is that money going?						
	In the real estate,						
	in the real estate speculation						
47.17	It's going into the real estate speculation,	X					
	that is, the middle class						X
	has more and more difficulties to	X					X
	buy a house,						
	because there is speculation						
47.47	Because if the private income is more rewarding than work, how do you want to motivate people to work, how do you want to motivate the small enterprises,	X					X
	if they earn more money by real estate speculation, *then by cre*ating,	X	X				X
	by crea*ting*		X				
	by creating		X				
	the industrial activities which France needs?						

Table 6. Right and left hand location

	To Right	To centre	To left	TOT.
Right Hand	25	14	1	40
Left Hand			6	6

From a qualitative point of view, the right hand moving to the right in 24 cases out of 25 is concomitant with sentences mentioning *Sarkozy, the right, rich people,* people *earning money.* When the right hand moves to the centre, in front of the Speaker, 8 times out of 14 the concomitant sentences concern Royal's personal stance: in all of them she speaks in first person and mentions her own desires, opinions, feelings. As Calbris [10] noticed, concerning Jospin, "The private person expresses himself through the right hand and the public personality through the left hand." (p. 68). It is the same for Royal: she moves her right hand when expressing her personal stance, in correspondence of the following statements:

Ben, moi je veut changer ça, je veut changer ce désordre de choses (I want to change this, I want to change this disorder of things)

Je suis pour respecter le gens, je ne suis pas pour dresser les Français les uns contre les autres (I'm for respecting people, I'm not for raising the French one against another)

Je vois beacoup de gens qui n'ont pas de travail (I see many people who don't have a job

C'est une mauvaise façon de parler des êtres humains (I think this is a bad way of speaking about human beings)

Finally, when the right hand moves to the left, like when the left hand is moving, the concomitant sentences concern *the poor, the working class, the middle class*:

Il y a trop de riches d'un côté et trop de riches d'un autre (There are too many rich people on one side and too many poor people on the other).

Les catégories moyennes ont de plus en plus mal à se loger (The middle class has more and more difficulties to buy a house);

Les chômeurs cherchent un travail. Il y a comme dans toute catégorie des gens qui essaient d'en profiter. Mais pas plus chez les chômeurs que chez les autres. (Unemployed people are looking for a job. There are among them, as among all categories, some people who try to take advantage of it. But there aren't more so among the unemployed than among other people).

A similar device of referring to the different political parties, left and right, through body movements, has also been found in a study on head movements in Italian politicians [29]. During a pre-electoral debate versus Prodi in 2006, Silvio Berlusconi, the candidate of the right, while talking of his stance about a brutal crime of murderers who kidnapped and then killed a one year child, is saying: *"Vorrei anche aggiungere che noi abbiamo portato critiche alla magistratura"* (I further would like to add that we criticized the Magistracy). While uttering the word *"we"* his *head points to the right*, and immediately after, while uttering the word *"Magistracy"*, it *points downward leftward*. This is coherent, first with his being a member of the right, second with Berlusconi's stance that the Magistracy, that he always complains is persecuting him, is manoeuvred by the left, and that all judges are leftists.

Do these body behaviours have a persuasive import? They might in fact, in at least two senses. First, in the process of persuasion, a first step is for the Persuader to get access to the Persuadee's mind: to be understood. In this sense, hands and head may contribute to the comprehensibility of political discourse by continuously indicating whether the Speaker is talking of the left or the right. Moreover, always reminding the audience what party is one talking about can have a subtly evaluative import, thus being persuasive in a more strict sense. In any case, though, these light or strong persuasive goals must be conceived of at a low level of awareness.

Another hypothesis, though, might be put forward. Among gesture scholars [30], [31], [32], [33], [12], [34], [35], [36], [15], some point at the communicative function of gestures, which provide referential and discourse information by adding to, replacing, contradicting words; others stress its cognitive function by considering them a device to help the speaker's thinking and lexical retrieval; others finally maintain they serve both cognitive and communicative functions.

In our case, one could make the hypothesis that Royal is accompanying her words *right* and *left* with her right and left hands mainly to help herself retrieve the corresponding images, concepts or words. In this case the gesture would have primarily a cognitive, not a communicative and persuasive function.

This hypothesis is made somewhat plausible by contrasting Royal's behaviour with that of an Italian politician, Gianni De Michelis, as observed in a previous work [15]. While talking of Boris Eltsin's politics, De Michelis says:

Sara' meno condizionato da destra e' meno condizionato da destra ma e' più condizionato da sinistra anzi e' molto più condizionato da sinistra (It may be less conditioned by the right; it is less conditioned by the right but it is more conditioned by the left, actually it is much more conditioned by the left).

While uttering the word *"right"* he pushes his right hand to the left, which, to the audience facing him, means "right", thus taking up the specular point of view of the audience. This was taken, in that work [15], as an evidence of how sophisticated the communicative competence of this politician is, exhibiting a clear representation of the audience's viewpoint, even at the perceptual level. This is a case where hand movements clearly do have a communicative goal: they are conceived right in view of the listeners' comprehension. While it might not be so in the case of Ségolène Royal, who uses her right hand – seen by the audience as the left – to accompany words and concepts referred to the right, and her left hand for the left.

9 Conclusion

This work presents an approach to multimodal persuasive discourse in terms of the communicative goals pursued by the Persuader's words, gesture and gaze. Starting from a model of persuasion in terms of goals and beliefs, we have proposed two kinds of annotation schemes, devoted to analyse the macro- and micro-structure of multimodal discourse, respectively: on the one side, the hierarchy of goals of the persuasive verbal discourse, on the other, the persuasive import of single gesture and gaze items. By applying these schemes to the analysis of political discourse in different politicians, we have seen that the pattern of persuasive strategies in their gesture and gaze is quite coherent both with the specific context of their discourse and with their political line and political style: that is, the goals pursued at the micro level are consistent with those at the macro level. Actually, our approach by definition looks at the goals of the Orator more than at the effects on the Audience, and when people's goals are at stake you can but guess them: goals are internal, invisible representations. But the reciprocal consistency of the results at the macro and micro levels may credit reliability to our results and confirm the descriptive adequacy of our annotation schemes.

References

1. Cicero, M.T.: De Oratore (55 B.C.)
2. Quintilianus, M.F.: Institutio Oratoria. Le Monnier, Firenze (95)
3. Atkinson, M.: Our Master's Voices. The Language and Body Language of Politics. Methuen, London (1984)
4. Frey, S.: Die Macht des Bildes. Der Einfluss der nonverbalen Kommunikation auf Kultur und Politik. Huber, Bern (1998)

5. Bucy, E.P., Bradley, S.D.: Presidential Expressions and Viewer Emotion: Counter Empathic Responses to Televised Leader Displays. Social Science Information 43(1), 59–94 (2004)
6. Bull, P.E.: The Use of Hand Gestures in Political Speeches: Some Case Studies. Journal of Language and Social Psychology 5, 102–118 (1986)
7. Guerini, M., Strapparava, C., Stock, O.: CORPS: A corpus of tagged Political Speeches for Persuasive Communication Processing. Journal of Information Technology and Politics 5(1), 19–32 (2008)
8. Ekman, P.: Telling lies. Norton, New York (1985)
9. De Paulo, B.M., Lindsay, J.J., Malone, B.E., Muhlenbruck, L., Charlton, K., Cooper, H.: Cues to deception. Psychological Bulletin 129, 74–118 (2003)
10. Calbris, G.: L'expression Gestuelle de la Pensée d'un Homme Politique. Paris, Ed. du CNRS (2003)
11. Streeck, J.: Gesture in Political Communication. A Case Study of the Democratic Presidential Candidates during thwe 2004 Primary Campaign. To be published in Research on Language and Social Interaction (forth.)
12. Kendon, A.: Gesture. Visible Action as Utterance. Cambridge University Press, Cambridge (2004)
13. Parisi, D., Castelfranchi, C.: Discourse as a hierarchy of goals. Working Papers. 54–55 Urbino: Centro Internazionale di Semiotica e Linguistica (1975)
14. Conte, R., Castelfranchi, C.: Cognitive and Social Action. University College, London (1995)
15. Poggi, I.: Mind, Hands, Face and Body. A Goal and Belief View of Multimodal Communication. Weidler, Berlin (2007)
16. Poggi, I.: The Goals of Persuasion. Pragmatics and Cognition 13, 298–335 (2005)
17. Miceli, M., de Rosis, F., Poggi, I.: Emotional and non emotional persuasion. Applied Artificial Intelligence: an International Journal 20, 849–879 (2006)
18. Poggi, I., Castelfranchi, C.: Dare consigli. In: Humphris, C. (ed.) (a cura di) Atti del 2o Seminario Internazionale per Insegnanti di Lingua. Bollettino DILIT, vol. 3, pp. 29–49 (1990)
19. Aristotle: Retorica. Bari, Laterza (1973)
20. Argentin, G., Ghiglione, R., Dorna, A.: La gestualité et ses effets dans le discours politique. Psychologie Française 35, 153–161 (1990)
21. Burgoon, J.K., Birk, T., Pfau, M.: Nonverbal behaviors, persuasion, and credibility. Human Communication Research 17, 140–169 (1990)
22. Henley, N.M.: Body politics: Power, sex, and nonverbal behavior. Prentice-Hall, Englewood Cliffs (1977)
23. Moore, H.E., Porter, N.K.: Leadership and nonverbal behaviours of Hispanic females across school equity environments. Psychology of Women Quarterly 12, 147–163 (1988)
24. Poggi, I., Pelachaud, C.: Persuasive gestures and the expressivity of ECAs. In: Wachsmuth, I., Lenzen, M., Knoblich, G. (eds.) Embodied Communication in Humans and Machines, pp. 391–424. Oxford University Press, Oxford (2008)
25. Kendon, A.: Gestures as Illocutionary and Discourse Structure Markers in Southern Italian Conversation. Journal of Pragmatics 23, 247–279 (1995)
26. Serenari, M.: Examples from the Berlin Dictionary of Everyday Gestures. In: Rector, M., Poggi, I., Trigo, N. (eds.) Gestures. Meaning and Use, pp. 111–117. Edicoes Universidade Fernando Pessoa, Porto (2003)

27. Hartmann, B., Mancini, M., Pelachaud, C.: Formational Parameters and Adaptive Prototype Instantiation for MPEG-4 Compliant Gesture Synthesis. In: Computer Animation 2002, pp. 111–119 (2002)
28. Attardo, S., Eisterhold, J., Hay, J., Poggi, I.: Multimodal markers of irony and sarcasm. Humour. International Journal of Humour Research 16(2), 243–260 (2003)
29. Cirmi, C.: Il testonario: segnali e significato dei movimenti della testa. Unpublished Degree Thesis, Università Roma Tre (2007)
30. Rimé, B.: The elimination of visible behaviour from social interactions: Effects on verbal, nonverbal and interpersonal variables. European Journal of Social Psychology 12, 113–129 (1982)
31. Krauss, R.M., Dushay, R.A., Chen, Y., Rauscher, F.: The communicative value of conversational hand gestures. Journal of Experimental Social Psychology 31, 533–552 (1995)
32. Krauss, R.M., Chen, Y., Gottesman, R.F.: Lexical gestures and lexical access: a process model. In: McNeill, D. (ed.) Language and gesture. Cambridge University Press, Cambridge (2000)
33. McNeill, D.: Gesture and Thought. University of Chicago Press, Chicago (2005)
34. Alibali, M.W., Kita, S., Young, A.: Gesture and the process of speech production: We think, therefore we gesture. Language and Cognitive Processes 15, 593–613 (2000)
35. Alibali, M.W., Heath, D.C., Myers, H.J.: Effects of visibility between speaker and listener on gesture production: Some gestures are meant to be seen. Journal of Memory and Language 44, 169–188 (2001)
36. Melinger, A., Kita, S.: Conceptualization load triggers gesture production. Language and Cognitive Processes 22(4), 473–500 (2007)

Unsupervised Clustering in Multimodal Multiparty Meeting Analysis

Yosuke Matsusaka[1], Yasuhiro Katagiri[2], Masato Ishizaki[3], and Mika Enomoto[4]

[1] National Institute of Advanced Industrial Science and Technology,
1-1-1 Umezono, Tsukuba, Ibaraki, Japan
[2] Future University Hakodate, 116-2 Kamedanakano, Hakodate, Hokkaido, Japan
[3] The University of Tokyo, 7-3-1 Hongo, Bunkyo-ku, Tokyo, Japan
[4] Tokyo University of Technology, 1404 Katakura, Hachioji, Tokyo, Japan

1   Introduction

Nonverbal signals such as gazes, head nods, facial expressions, and bodily gestures play significant roles in organizing human interactions. Their significance is even more emphasized in multiparty settings, since many interaction organization behaviors, for example, turn-taking and participation role assignment, are realized nonverbally. Several projects have been involved in collecting multimodal corpora [3,4] for multiparty dialogues, to develop techniques for meeting event recognitions from nonverbal as well as verbal signals (e.g., [11,2]).

The task of annotating nonverbal signals exchanged in conversational interactions poses both theoretical and practical challenges for the development of multimodal corpora. Many projects rely on both manual annotation and automatic signal processing in corpus building. Some projects apply different methods to different types of signals to facilitate the efficient construction of corpora through the division of labor [9]. Others treat manual annotations as ideal values in the process of validating their signal processing methods [7].

In this paper, we propose a method of assisted annotation for nonverbal signals exchanged in conversations by combining statistical and qualitative analyses in corpus building. We have been developing a corpus of multiparty conversations to develop a comprehensive model of conversational structures in consensus-building discussion meetings. One of the objectives of this study is to investigate the roles and contributions of participants' nonverbal signals in the process of arriving at a mutual consensus. For this purpose, we adopt a bottom-up strategy of assisted annotation, in which we interactively apply unsupervised clustering techniques to raw signal data to obtain initial candidate labeling, which is then evaluated in terms of its effectiveness in the qualitative analysis of interaction events, as well as selective validation against manually coded labelings. We also describe the methodologies and tools we use for the process of assisted annotation.

2   Challenges in Multimodal Meeting Analysis

Unlike in the case of conventional unimodal analyses of spoken dialogues, wherein one has to deal with only limited channels of information (e.g., speech and transcripts) for

M. Kipp et al. (Eds.): Multimodal Corpora, LNAI 5509, pp. 93–108, 2009.
© Springer-Verlag Berlin Heidelberg 2009

a pair of participants, multimodal meeting analyses require one to deal with a wider variety of information channels, for example, gaze direction, nodding, facial expressions, and gestures, and that too, for a number of participants. Dealing with a larger number of signal types and participants gives rise to theoretical and practical challenges.

First, for most nonverbal behaviors, we still lack clear and explicit definitions, particularly with regard to the functional categorization of the behaviors. To maintain consistency both across annotations and annotators, we need to prepare a "coding scheme," that is, a set of clear and explicit definitions for the types of behaviors corresponding to annotation labels. Unlike spoken dialogue cases, for which there already exist well-developed coding schemes, such as ToBI, that we can rely on when we produce annotations, for nonverbal behaviors, such a coding scheme still needs to be developed. In multimodal behavior analysis, coding scheme development amounts to theory development, and multimodal analysis tends to become an experimental process that defines the coding scheme, applies it to the data, and assesses the quality of its outcome, and all these processes together result in the formation of an iterative analysis unit that possibly leads to the revision of the coding scheme.

Second, in the case of nonverbal behaviors, the amount of annotations that have to be dealt with is significantly larger than in the case of spoken dialogues. This increase in the amount of annotations in the case of spoken dialogues is naturally caused, in part, by the increase in the number of information channels in multimodal analyses. But the number of annotations for each of the channels itself gets larger. For example, when we manually transcribe data from a speech channel, the number of annotations is on the order of one annotation/s or one word/sec. We do not have to monitor every single frame of speech data because the speech stream does not change too quickly. We can thus speed up the annotation process by skipping frames. In contrast, when we manually annotate gaze direction, we have to monitor every frame without skipping frames, because gaze has a very high change frequency. Thus, the number of annotations we need to produce will increase the number of video frames in the data, for example, the number of annotations will be on the order of 30 annotations/s. Therefore, manual annotation is highly labor intensive and often takes a very long time.

3   Nonverbal Signals in Consensus-Building Discussion Meetings

Face-to-face conversation is the most effective means for a group of people to reach an agreement, be it with regard to a joint action plan for a work group or a purchase contract in a commercial transaction. In a multiparty conversation between three or more participants, the participants negotiate by producing, understanding, and expressing approval or disapproval about a number of proposals until they reach an agreement. Typical exchanges would consist of an assertion or proposal put forth by one participant, followed by a variety of listener responses, including assessments, discussions, and counter-proposals from other participants. These responses often take the form of nonverbal expressions as well as explicit linguistic utterances.

Backchannels, nodding, and gazing could be considered as listener responses expressing a positive assessment or support for a proposal. On the other hand, the lack of backchannels, gaze aversions, and talking to other participants could be seen as expressing a negative assessment or disapproval. A listener can also indicate readiness and the intention to take a turn by bodily movements and gazing. The speaker, observing these listener responses, will, in turn, adjust his utterance production accordingly.

Given the experimental nature of nonverbal signal annotations, it is almost mandatory to rely on some form of automation to obtain a comprehensive picture of this intricate interaction process. Several researches have focused on creating a tool to assist in efficient hand annotation (e.g., [5]). Researches have also introduced machine learning and automatic recognition techniques to speed up multimodal corpus building processes (e.g., [7]). We believe, however, that these approaches still fail to provide us with an adequate environment for supporting efficient and reliable multimodal annotation processes. As discussed above, manual annotation in multimodal analysis is labor intensive even with the use of efficient tools. We cannot avoid performing manual annotation even when applying automatic recognition techniques, because certain amounts of training data have to be prepared beforehand manually to build an automatic recognizer, using machine learning algorithms. Moreover, the amounts of such training data that are usually required are not insignificant.

In this paper, we propose a method of assisted annotation to solve these problems. Assisted annotation is a semi-automatic nonverbal signal annotation process supported by three types of tools to extract and symbolize multimodal human behaviors. We first introduce our image processing tool that enables the automatic extraction of parametric features from videos of human behaviors. Second, we introduce an unsupervised clustering algorithm that enables the extraction of category candidates to be used in the symbol-based analysis of multimodal human behaviors. Third, we introduce an interactive visualization tool that enables the quick tuning and optimization of clustering parameters. By combining these tools, we can begin our analysis without any predefined coding scheme, which, we argue, facilitates easier and quicker connections with higher level qualitative analysis and the efficient development of a coding scheme.

In the following sections, we will present the tools we use for assisted annotation for the extraction and symbolization of multimodal human behaviors, and show that with these tools, quantitative analysis of our multimodal multiparty conversation data can be conducted efficiently. We will also present examples of qualitative analysis utilizing assisted annotation to elucidate listener responses in multiparty consensus-building conversations. We will argue that the automatic extraction of categories combined with suitable interactive visualization is an effective and efficient way to capture the structure and processes of multiparty multimodal conversation interactions.

4 Meeting Analysis

4.1 Data

We have been collecting Japanese conversational data obtained from multiparty design tasks, which are a type of collaborative problem solving task where participants are asked to come up with a design plan. Different from ordinary problem solving tasks, the design goal in these tasks is only partially specified, as a result of which participants need to jointly determine the plan's evaluative criteria during discussion.

Fig. 1. Recording device: AIST-MARC and recording scene

Some details regarding the data collection are as follows:

Number of participants: A group of six people participated in each session.
Conversation setting: Participants were seated face-to-face around a round table.
Task setting: Participants were asked to write an idea proposal for new cell phone service features in the near future.
Role setting: No predetermined roles were imposed. None of the members had professional knowledge about the topic.
Information media: Each participant was provided with a sheet of paper to write down ideas. No computers were provided.

We used the AIST-MARC system [1], shown in Figure 1, and six supportive cameras to record the conversation. A sample meeting scene is shown in Figure 1.

The participants were recruited from among graduate students majoring in information sciences. The data we examined in this paper consisted of 30-min conversations engaged in by five males and one female. Even though we did not assign any roles to the participants, a chairperson and a clerk were spontaneously elected by the participants at the beginning of the session.

4.2   Video-Based Motion Extraction Algorithm

To obtain a classification of the nonverbal responses used to build a multimodal corpus, we first applied the image processing algorithm shown in Figure 2 to extract head directions and head motions.

For the extraction of head directions, we first detected the face positions using "haar" features and cascaded a classifier-based algorithm [13]. Then, based on the texture of the detected area, we used a head direction estimation algorithm [8].

For the extraction of head motions, the optical flow was calculated from the differences between the images of the current and previous frames that represent the moving amplitude and the direction of the pixels of each image between the time frames. We

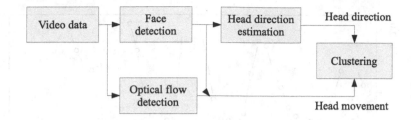

Fig. 2. Image processing algorithm

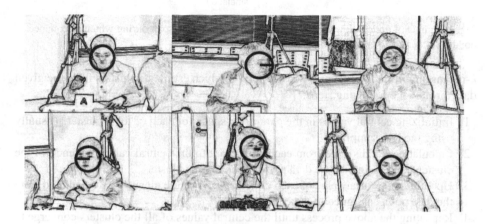

Fig. 3. Sample scene with image processing results: the circles represent detected face areas, and the lines in the circles represent head directions

used a gradient method to calculate the optical flow from the video stream. The motion of the entire head was defined as the mean amplitude and the direction over the detected face area.

Figure 3 shows a sample scene and the results of the application of the face direction estimation algorithm.

4.3 Unsupervised Clustering Algorithm

Human behaviors in conversation should exhibit regular patterns that can be observed as clusters in the space of relevant parameters such as the head direction and head motion parameters that are calculated in Section 4.2.

Nodding behavior manifests itself as a vertical movement of the head (Figure 4). Figure 5 shows a scatter plot of various instances of head movement behaviors. The X-axis indicates the amplitude of vertical head movement, and the Y-axis indicates the frequency of the zerocross of vertical head movement.

By applying unsupervised clustering to the above parameters, we expect to obtain clustered patterns of behaviors in conversational organization. In this paper, we use the

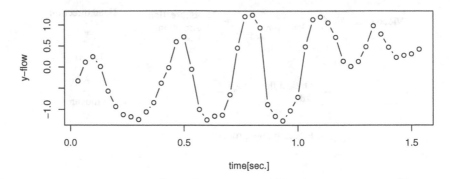

Fig. 4. Sample of optical flow in x direction plotted in the time span during which a sequence of nodding occurred

k-means algorithm for unsupervised clustering, which estimates clusters from the given data through the following steps:

1. Initializing central values in the parameter space for each of the *k* clusters (usually using random sampling)
2. Calculating the distance from each data point to the central values for each of the clusters, and assigning the data point to the closest cluster
3. Updating the central value of each cluster, based on the mean value calculated from the data points assigned to the cluster
4. Repeating the above process until the central values of all the clusters converge to a set of stable values.

The letters in Figure 5 represent clusters calculated using the *k*-means algorithm. Cluster A represents the quick and strong nod group; Cluster B represents the small and slow nod group; and Cluster C represents the deep nod group.

We noted that the use of unsupervised clustering enabled us to classify nods in a more elaborate manner, as opposed to the case in most previous conversation studies, wherein nods were treated only in terms of the binary distinction between occurrence and non-occurrence. Once the finer categories are confirmed to play different functional roles in conversational organization, they will become a legitimate candidate for inclusion in the "coding scheme." The clustering technique can also be applied to nonverbal behaviors other than nodding.

To apply unsupervised clustering, we first have to decide on the feature space in which to run the clustering. Depending on the feature space that is selected, we may or may not be able to obtain a set of meaningful categories that are suitable for understanding the processes in conversational organization. In conventional manual annotation, the task of analysts is to scan through all parts of the video data to make categorization judgments for all the instances of human behaviors. In our method of assisted annotation, the task of the analysts is to design a feature space sufficient for initializing the categorization process, and the rest of the task is performed by a computer. To facilitate this process of "semi-automatic coding," we developed a GUI to support the feature space design. The implementation of the tool is described in the next section.

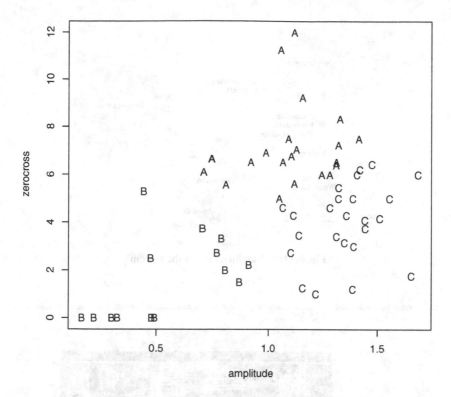

Fig. 5. Scatter plot and clusters of head behaviors in a feature space: the X-axis indicates the amplitude of optical flow in the vertical direction (depth of nodding). The Y-axis indicates the frequency of zerocross normalized by the duration of the behavior (speed of nodding). The letters correspond to the data points for each of the head behaviors. The different letters represent clusters estimated automatically using the k-means algorithm. Cluster A represents the quick and strong nodding group. Cluster B represents the small and slow nodding group. Cluster C represents the deep nodding group.

4.4 GUI for Semi-automatic Coding

The overall architecture of the system for semi-automatic coding is shown in Figure 6. The system consists of a web server, a GNU-R server, and a web browser user interface.

The web browser user interface is shown in Figure 7. It is implemented using Wireit javascript library[1] , and runs on a standard web browser. Users can design a feature space for clustering by connecting the functional blocks by dragging the wires.

Once the user has decided on the feature space in which to run the clustering, he/she sends a request to the web server. The javascript running on the web browser user interface sends requests to the web server along with configuration parameters. Configuration parameters consist of options given to each functional block and the connection between each of the blocks. Figure 8 shows an example of the configuration parameters.

---

[1] http://javascript.neyric.com/wireit/

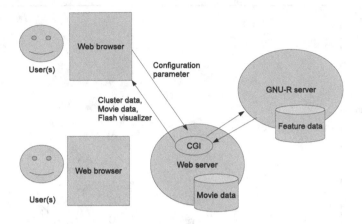

Fig. 6. Overall architecture of the system

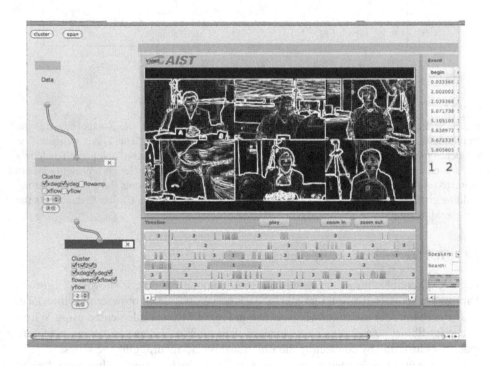

Fig. 7. The user interface: the left part displays the wired functional blocks for the feature space design. The right part is the visualization panel with the time line, which displays the synchronized video (top) and the assigned category labels obtained by clustering (bottom).

```
I1 <- data(NA, "");
I2 <- cluster(I1, "data", c("xflow", "yflow"), 3);
I3 <- span(I2, "cluster", c("xflow", "flowamp"), 1, 1);
savexml(I3);
```

```xml
<?xml version="1.0" encoding="UTF-8" ?>
<madl>
<body>
    <audio seq = "1" delay = "0s">
        <utt id="7" speaker="S4" begin="4.250000s" end="12.500000s">
            <rectext>1</rectext>
        </utt>
        <utt id="12" speaker="S5" begin="13.250000s" end="19.250000s">
            <rectext>2</rectext>
        </utt>
        <utt id="39" speaker="S4" begin="24.750000s" end="63.750000s">
            <rectext>1</rectext>
        </utt>
        <utt id="59" speaker="S4" begin="68.750000s" end="93.500000s">
            <rectext>1</rectext>
        </utt>
...
```

Fig. 8. Example of configuration parameters and a clustered result: configuration parameters from the GUI are encoded in GNU-R command form and sent to the CGI (top). Clustered results are encoded in XML and returned from CGI to GUI (bottom).

When the web server receives a request for data clustering, a CGI script takes a configuration parameter from the user interface as input, and invokes GNU-R. The feature parameters for head motion are stored in the GNU-R process, which runs continuously in the background as a server. This configuration was adopted to reduce the response time of the CGI script by avoiding repetitive data loading. The clustering functions implemented in GNU-R compute clusters in the user-specified feature space, and return the clustered result back to the user through the web server CGI script. A detailed explanation of each clustering function will be provided in the next section.

The clustered result returned by the CGI script is displayed in the visualization panel on the user interface. The visualization panel is implemented in Flash. It displays the occurrences of categorized events on the time line, in synchronization with the movie.

The response time of the system depends on the length of the movie and the number of connected functional blocks. The system is capable of sending a clustered result back to the user within a few seconds on a 2GHz Pentium PC, when the video is up to an hour in length. The visualization panel update takes place as soon as the update button for functional block has been clicked, as the request to the web server is made by AJAX call.

4.5   Functional Blocks for Feature Space Design

Four types of functional blocks are provided for analysts to interactively explore possibilities for clustering.

Input block: Specifies raw feature data (Outputs: X-degree, X-flow, Y-flow, flow amplitude feature)

Output block: Contains visualization panel

Cluster block: Applies k-means clustering (Options: # of centroids, feature selection, Outputs: cluster id)

Span block: Calculates statistics of selected time span (Options: feature selection, span selection (using upstream cluster id), calculated feature (zerocross & amplitude); Outputs: respective zerocross and amplitude of selected features)

The input block specifies the source of raw feature data. The output block contains the visualization panel. The output block is updated when one of the update buttons on each of the functional blocks is clicked. The cluster block considers the number of centroids and feature selection as options. Feature selection items are dynamically generated when the block is connected to the upstream block. The span block calculates zerocross and amplitude in the selected time span. The zerocross value is automatically normalized by the length of the time span. The span is specified by the cluster id calculated in the upstream block.

Figure 9 shows an example of a sequence of interaction steps when a user is designing a feature space for clustering by using the interface.

4.6   Quantitative Analysis

To analyze the conversational structures in the data from the consensus-building discussion meeting that we collected as part of our project, we investigate the following two configurations of cascaded functional blocks.

Configuration 1. Classifies the amplitude of the optical flow into three classes and, excluding the smallest amplitude class, classifies the direction of the face into three classes.

Configuration 2. Decomposes the optical flow into horizontal and vertical amplitude and classifies these data, which have two-dimensional features, into four classes.

Table 1 shows the central value and the size of each cluster generated by configuration 1. The central value represents the mean of the (normalized) feature of the data in each cluster. Cluster #1 is classified as having the smallest amplitude in step 1 and corresponds to an almost motionless state since the central value of the cluster is approximately 0. This cluster constitutes 80% of the data; that is, participants displayed movement only 20% of the time during the course of the conversation. Clusters #2~#4 represent the forward, left, and right directions of face, respectively. The distributions

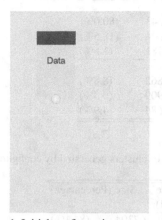

1. Initial configuration.

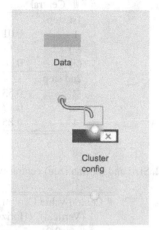

2. Connecting a cluster block to the input (raw data) block.

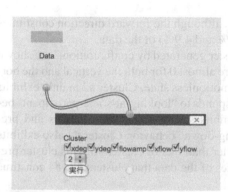

3. Configuration parameters for the cluster block are displayed (items change dynamically dependent on the configurations of upstream blocks).

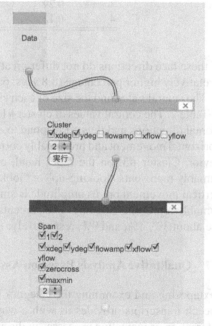

4. Cascading the existing blocks to other functional blocks.

Fig. 9. Usage of the user interface

Table 1. Size and (normalized) central value of clusters generated by configuration 1

# Central value		Size (Percentage)	
1st step			
1	0.01	254543	(80.0%)
(2)	0.13	58674	(18.5%)
(3)	0.36	4781	(1.5%)
2nd step			
2	0.53	27862	(8.8%)
3	0.17	19909	(6.3%)
4	0.85	15684	(4.9%)

Table 2. Size and (normalized) central value of clusters generated by configuration 2

#	Central value (Vertical)	Central value (Horizontal)	Size (Percentage)	
1	0.01	0.01	267304	(84.1%)
2	0.07	0.25	9356	(2.9%)
3	0.29	0.07	13539	(4.3%)
4	0.12	0.04	27799	(8.7%)

of these face directions do not differ greatly, although the forward direction constitutes a relatively higher percentage (8.8% vs. 6.3% and 4.9%) of the data.

The central value and the size of each cluster generated by configuration 2 are shown in Table 2. The central values of cluster #1 are almost 0 for both the vertical and the horizontal directions and thus correspond to a motionless state. Cluster #2 mainly exhibits horizontal movement and presumably corresponds to "looking-at-some-participant" behavior. Cluster #3, on the other hand, exhibits strong vertical movements and presumably represents "looking-up" or "looking-down" behavior. Cluster #4 also exhibits vertical movement but its amplitude is smaller than that of cluster #3. This cluster presumably represents nodding. The percentages of the data that clusters #2~#4 constitue are about 3%, 4%, and 9%, respectively.

4.7   Qualitative Analysis Based on Assisted Annotations

Juxtaposing and examining the category labels obtained from assisted annotation and speech transcripts provides us with a way to obtain an in-depth understanding of the interaction organization processes in discussion meetings.

Conversational Engagement. Figure 10 shows an excerpt from the data. Each row in the figure represents speech contents and nonverbal behaviors displayed by each of the six participants (A~F) on between the 170th and 195th s. Nonverbal behavior annotations were obtained by configuration 2 in 4.6. From the transcript, we can observe that the main speaker changes from D to C in this scene on around the 187th s. The following facts can be observed from the figure:

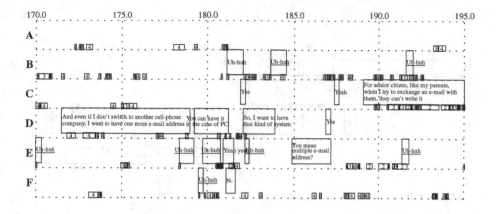

Fig. 10. Nonverbal responses and conversational engagement: the underlined utterances indicate backchannels

- Speech utterances, including verbal backchannels, are frequently produced by listeners except by the clerk A.
- Utterances by the main speakers, D and C, are often accompanied by their own nonverbal behaviors.
- Nonverbal responses given by B, E, and F are produced even without their accompanying verbal responses.
- After D relinquishes his role as the main speaker and gives it to C, he does not produce any nonverbal behaviors.

These observations are in accordance with our expectation that the production of nonverbal behaviors is backed by the participants' interest in the topic as well as by their high level of conversational engagement. The inspection of the video of the corresponding scene revealed that the two main speakers, namely, D and C, and chairperson E played dominant roles as speaker and addressee and exhibited frequent nonverbal responses (nodding and gazing). B and F were active side participants, who produced both verbal and nonverbal responses. We also observed that once D relinquished his turn, he looked down at the table and displayed a disinterested attitude toward the conversation.

Listener Responses to Proposals. Figure 11 shows another excerpt in which a number of listener responses followed a proposal. In this scene, C produced a proposal based on his idea about insurance service on the 1074th 1078th s. After the proposal, B, D, and F produced many nonverbal responses from category 4 (nodding); however, E produced almost no nonverbal responses. The inspection of the video revealed that B, D, and F expressed either strong support or follow-up responses to C's proposal, whereas E failed to grasp the idea's merit and directed the following question to C: "Are there currently any services like that?" These observations are also in accordance with our expectation that the production (or the lack) of nonverbal responses reflects participants' positive (or negative) attitudes toward the salient topic of the ongoing conversation.

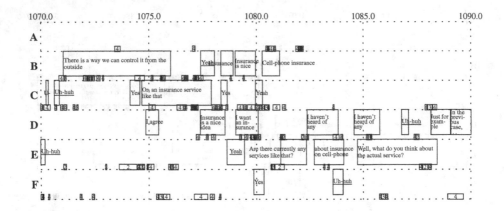

Fig. 11. Listener's response after a proposal

An examination of these excerpts demonstrates that unsupervised annotations provide characterizations of nonverbal behaviors that are functionally coherent with our interpretation of conversational organization processes and suggests that our method of assisted annotation can be used to obtain a starting point in the development of nonverbal behavior coding schemes.

5   Related Researches on the Application of Unsupervised Clustering Techniques

With regard to the application of unsupervised clustering techniques to human behavior analysis, there exists some research related to the topic discussed in this paper.

There are some studies that aimed to use unsupervised clustering to automatically find key points in the video. For example, Lee et al. [6] used the hierarchical clustering technique to cluster chunks of video into similar categories and sub-categories and added an interactive GUI to help users to choose the chunk of their interest.

Corina et al. [10] used a SOM (self-organizing map) to visualize the relations and similarity among trajectory patterns of agents in a virtual environment. Wang et al. [14] used HMM to model human gestures and used hierarchical clustering to visualize the relations and similarity among the patterns of agents. Turaga et al. [12] used the ARMA model to model video events and used unsupervised clustering for the analysis.

As we have described in this paper, our main contribution was developing the interactive GUI, using which we can decide the feature space in which to run the clustering. In the future, we would like to implement a greater variety of modeling and unsupervised clustering algorithms in the form of functional blocks that are user-friendly.

6   Conclusion

In this paper, we presented an initial attempt to apply unsupervised clustering techniques in multimodal corpora construction to extract, from video images, categories of bodily movements that are significant in organizing multiparty interactions. We proposed a bottom-up method of assisted annotation, in which unsupervised clustering is interactively applied to raw signal data to obtain a candidate for a coding scheme for nonverbal signals. We used this method to analyze our multiparty design conversation data, and we identified different types of head movements in the conversation. A qualitative examination of excerpts demonstrated that head movement annotations obtained through assisted annotation were effective in revealing the functions of both verbal and nonverbal listener responses, with respect to displaying listener engagement and support, in organizing the course of consensus building.

By combining statistical and qualitative analyses, assisted annotation enabled us to quickly obtain a clear picture of the interrelationships between types of nonverbal behaviors and to pursue ideas on their interaction organization functions. We believe that assisted annotation provides us with a promising methodology to obtain data-driven coding schemes in multimodal multiparty corpus development.

Acknowledgments

The work reported in this paper was partially supported by the Japan Society for the Promotion of Science Grants-in-aid for Scientific Research (A) 18200007 and (B) 18300052.

References

1. Asano, F., Ogata, J.: Detection and separation of speech events in meeting recordings. In: Proc. Interspeech, pp. 2586–2589 (2006)
2. Ba, S., Odobez, J.-M.: A study on visual focus of attention recognition from head pose in a meeting room. In: Renals, S., Bengio, S., Fiscus, J.G. (eds.) MLMI 2006. LNCS, vol. 4299, pp. 75–87. Springer, Heidelberg (2006)
3. Carletta, J., Ashby, S., Bourban, S., Flynn, M., Guillemot, M., Hain, T., Kadlec, J., Karaiskos, V., Kraaij, W., Kronenthal, M., Lathoud, G., Lincoln, M., Lisowska, A., McCowan, I., Post, W., Reidsma, D., Wellner, P.: The ami meeting corpus: A pre-announcement. In: Renals, S., Bengio, S. (eds.) MLMI 2005. LNCS, vol. 3869, pp. 28–39. Springer, Heidelberg (2006)
4. Chen, L., Travis Rose, R., Qiao, Y., Kimbara, I., Parrill, F., Welji, H., Han, T.X., Tu, J., Huang, Z., Harper, M., Quek, F., Xiong, Y., McNeill, D., Tuttle, R., Huang, T.: Vace multimodal meeting corpus. In: Renals, S., Bengio, S. (eds.) MLMI 2005. LNCS, vol. 3869, pp. 40–51. Springer, Heidelberg (2006)
5. Kipp, M.: Gesture Generation by Imitation: From Human Behavior to Computer Character Animation. Dissertation.com, Boca Raton, FL (2004)
6. Lee, S., Hayes, M.H.: An application for interactive video abstraction. In: IEEE International Conference on Acoustics Speech and Signal Processing, vol. 5, pp. 17–21 (2004)
7. Martin, J.-C., Caridakis, G., Devillers, L., Karpouzis, K., Abrilian, S.: Manual annotation and automatic image processing of multimodal emotional behaviours: Validating the annotation of TV interviews. In: Proc. LREC 2006, pp. 1127–1132 (2006)
8. Matsusaka, Y.: Recognition of 3 party conversation using prosody and gaze. In: Proc. Interspeech, pp. 1205–1208 (2005)
9. Pianesi, F., Zancanaro, M., Leonardi, C.: Multimodal annotated corpora of consensus decision making meetings. In: LREC 2006 Workshop on Multimodal Corpora, pp. 6–9 (2006)

10. Sas, C., O' Hare, G., Reilly, R.: Virtual environment trajectory analysis: a basis for navigational assistance and scene adaptivity. Future Generation Computer Systems 21, 1157–1166 (2005)
11. Stiefelhagen, R., Yang, J., Waibel, A.: Modeling focus of attention for meeting indexing based on multiple cues. IEEE Transactions on Neural Networks 13(4), 923–938 (2002)
12. Turaga, P.K., Veeraraghavan, A., Chellappa, R.: From videos to verbs: Miningvideos for events using a cascade of dynamical systems. In: Proc. of IEEE Computer Society Conf. on Computer Vision and Pattern Recognition (2007)
13. Viola, P., Jones, M.J.: Robust real-time face detection. International Journal of Computer Vision 57(2), 137–154 (2004)
14. Wang, T., Shum, H., Xu, Y., Zheng, N.: Unsupervised analysis of human gestures. In: Shum, H.-Y., Liao, M., Chang, S.-F. (eds.) PCM 2001. LNCS, vol. 2195, pp. 174–181. Springer, Heidelberg (2001)

Multimodal Corpora Annotation: Validation Methods to Assess Coding Scheme Reliability

Federica Cavicchio and Massimo Poesio

CIMeC Università di Trento, Corso Bettini 31, 38068 Rovereto (Tn), Italy
{federica.cavicchio,massimo.poesio}@unitn.it

Abstract. Many multimodal corpora have been collected and annotated in the last years. Unfortunately, in many cases most of the multimodal coding schemes have been shown not to be reliable. This poor reliability may be caused either by the nature of multimodal data or by the nature of statistic methods to assess reliability. In this paper we will review the statistical measures currently used to assess agreement on multimodal corpora annotation. We will also propose alternative statistical methods to the well known kappa statistics.

Keywords: multimodal corpora annotation, corpora validation, kappa statistics, Unbiased hit rate.

1 Introduction

In the last years the growing interest of the scientific community toward multimodality has resulted in an increasing number of multimodal corpora collected. These corpora have been recorded in several languages and have being elicited with different methodologies: acted (such as for emotion corpora), task oriented, multiparty dialogs [6], corpora elicited with scripts or storytelling (see for example [29] for gestures; [8] for emotions) and ecological corpora such as [1]. Among the goals of collection and analysis of corpora there is shading light on crucial aspects of speech production. Some of the main research questions are how language and gesture correlate with each other [21] and how emotion expression modifies speech [26] and gesture [33]. Moreover, great efforts have been done to analyze multimodal aspects of irony [34], persuasion [32], [17] or motivation [39].

Multimodal coding schemes are mainly focused on dialogues (dialogue acts, topic segmentation, and also emotion and attention) including also task roles and "emotional area" roles (such as EMOTV annotation scheme [1]) and the relationship between gesture and speech (as FORM [27], [28], CoGEST [18] and [21] annotation schemes). The Multimodal Score [26] is strictly focused on communicative goals of prosody, facial movements and posture analysis. Other multimodal schemes such as MUMIN [2], [3], analyze turn management, gesture and face movements as well.

The collection of such a large amount of multimodal data has also raised the question of coding scheme reliability. The aim of testing coding scheme reliability is to assess whether it is able to capture in some way observable reality allowing some generalizations. From the mid Nineties, in Natural Language Processing (NLP) and

M. Kipp et al. (Eds.): Multimodal Corpora, LNAI 5509, pp. 109–121, 2009.

Computational Linguistics (CL) studies, kappa has begun to be applied to validate coding scheme reliability. Basically, the kappa statistic is a statistical method to assess agreement among a group of observers, currently applied to assess agreement on corpora annotation. In multimodal communication (henceforth MMC) it is very important assessing the coding scheme reliability too. Thus, in order to validate some multimodal coding schemes, kappa has been used. However, up to now many multimodal coding schemes have a low kappa score [6]; [12]; [31], [36]. This could be due to the nature of multimodal data. In fact, some authors [10] argued that annotation of mental and emotional states of mind is a very demanding task. The analysis of non verbal features requires a different, sometimes complicated, approach as MMC is multichannel and multilayer [10]. Even the corpus elicitation method becomes an independent variable to take into account. Multimodal corpora can be acted, task oriented or ecologically recorded. Acted corpora are mainly focus on facial displays of emotions recording. As emotive facial expressions are produced by expert or semi expert actors, it is taken for granted that they are a "gold" standard to study facial display of emotions. This is not completely true, as for example each actor production should be validated assessing the real closeness to the "standard" emotion representation which the group of annotators has in mind. Task oriented corpora, such as map task and multiparty dialogues, are mainly focused on face to face verbal (and non verbal) interactions. Thus, these kinds of corpora are specifically produced to analyze linguistic features such as turn management and feedback but sometimes non verbal behavior (such as gaze, gesture and even emotion displays) is analyzed as well. Ecological corpora are usually recorded from TV shows, news and interviews and have a wide range of verbal and nonverbal features. It is up to the researcher the ability of developing coding schemes to annotate such a variety of verbal and nonverbal features.

The low annotation agreement which affects multimodal corpora validation could also be due to the nature of the kappa statistics. In fact, the assumption underlining the use of kappa as reliability measure is that coding scheme categories are mutually exclusive and equally distinct one another. This is clearly difficult to be obtained in MMC as communication channels (i.e. voice, face movements, gestures and posture) are deeply interconnected one another and contribute (case by case with different weight) to the final meaning of the multimodal "sentence".

In the following, we review in section 2 the methodologies currently used to validate multimodal corpora. Then, in section 3 we propose an alternative method, unbiased hit rate, which is commonly applied in non verbal behavior studies. These studies deal with categorical judgments and validation of nonverbal behavior such as gaze, gesture and emotions, which are the main focus of investigation in most MMC coding schemes as well.

2   Agreement Studies in Multimodal Corpora Annotation: Percent Agreement, Kappa and Alpha

In multimodal annotation many different methods have been proposed to study the reliability of nonverbal behavior. Usually these methods are borrowed from CL such as pairwise agreement [25] [22] and percent agreement [30]. In pairwise agreement a third coder is asked to finalize the annotation made by two independent coders ([22],

[32], [11], [12]), deciding in case of disagreement. Percent agreement is calculated as the number of items identified with the same label by two or more independent coders. The total amount is then divided by the total number of labels identified. In many annotation schemes [2], [3], [9], [21] [27], [28]) percent agreement has been used as validation method. But neither pairwise agreement nor percent agreement are corrected for agreement due by chance and assure reliability and generalization of annotated results. In 1993 Wagner [40] claimed validation processes based on percent agreement and hit rate to be meaningless. In fact, suppose to annotate 100 items (stimuli) with 3 category labels: neutral, pleasant and unpleasant (see table 1). The items are pre-selected and categorized by the experimenter: 45 of them are pleasant, 30 neutral and 25 unpleasant ([40], p. 4). The experimenter asks to an annotator to attribute one of the three categories (neutral, pleasant, unpleasant) to each of the 100 items. In table 1 we report the fictitious ratings of one annotator on the 100 emotional items:

Table 1. Fictitious ratings of one annotator on 100 emotive items

Items	Annotator Ratings			
	Pleasant	Neutral	Unpleasant	Total
Pleasant	36	9	0	45
Neutral	6	6	18	30
Unpleasant	14	5	6	25
Total	56	20	24	100

Overall, 48 items match with the category attributed by the experimenter. The agreement scores are .800 for pleasant, .200 for neutral and .240 for unpleasant. Thus, pleasant items seem to be very recognizable. But we can't be sure that these scores are more than we could expect by chance. Consequences expected from inappropriate measure of performance or failing to correct chance rates are not easily predictable at all. In particular, Wagner notices that inaccuracies will be risky for data interpretation when:

1. accuracy rates are low in comparison to chance agreement so that there is a greater proportional error on (true) chances frequencies;
2. variation in ratings is very high (so that, again, proportional error is greater on true chances frequencies);
3. high number of observations, that have as a result an increasing in errors due to incorrect estimation of binomial and chi squared distributions.

Conditions 1 and 2 frequently occur in studies on emotions expressions. For example, when accuracy rate is high (as with emotional expressions produced by actors) choosing an unsuitable chance level would lead to totally different reliability results. As regard error number 3, it might be avoided taking care that the number of items to be annotated is not greater than the number of annotators whatever the unit of analysis is. Some attempts to solve this type of error has been made in studies on facial expressions of embarrassment [19] and in facial expressions of contempt [14], focusing only on one particular response category and comparing its use for different items. Although sophisticated, those types of procedure clearly are not general and suitable for all type of nonverbal rating studies.

Following Wagner, for a widest application in nonverbal behavior, a measure must fulfill 4 properties ([40] p. 10):

1. it should be insensitive to annotators' bias;
2. it should be insensitive to differences in the presented items of different type;
3. it should allow separate analysis of accuracy for each item type;
4. It should allow comparison of performance between studies even with different numbers of categories.

The first two requirements are due to correct raw hit frequencies, the third and fourth assure generalization and reliability of results.

Carletta ([7], p. 252) suggested to apply kappa to measure agreement in corpora annotation. The kappa coefficient (K) measures pairwise agreement among two coders making category judgments, correcting for expected chance agreement:

$$K= \frac{P(A)-P(E)}{1-P(E)}$$

where P(A) is the proportion of times the coders agree and P(E) is the proportion of times we expect them to agree by chance. For more than two coders chance agreement is calculated as the agreement expected on the basis of a single distribution, reflecting the combined judgments of all coders [15]. Thus, expected agreement is measured as the overall proportion of items assigned to a category k by all coders n. Two important problems are present in kappa studies: 1) annotator bias, underlining the need of increasing the number of annotators when annotators' marginal distributions are widely divergent [5]; 2) the prevalence problem, which concerns the difficulty in reaching significant agreement values when most of the items falls under one category. For the latter problem, Artstein and Poesio [4] argued that, as reliability is the ability to distinguish between categories, in case of skewed data (which means that a category is very common with respect to the others) we must focus on agreement on rare categories whether these are the category of interest. Thus, in these cases agreement test on rare categories turns to be the significant one.

Another debated point on agreement studies is the interpretation of kappa scores. There is a general lack of consensus on how interpret those values. Some authors [3], [7] consider as reliable values between .67 and .8, others as a "rule-of-thumb" accept as reliable only scoring rate over .8 [23], [24]. Some attempts have been made to apply kappa to nonverbal or emotion annotation but with little success. Usually, for emotions, gesture and gaze annotation kappa score is quite low. As an example, in the MUMIN coding scheme, gaze direction and head have scored respectively .54 and .20 [3]. In the AMI meetings corpus annotation, Carletta [6] has reported a kappa score of .54 referred to the so-called "socio-emotional area", comprising emotions and other non verbal features, such as gaze direction; Pianesi et al. [31] in "socio-emotional area" have scores ranging from .40 to .60. In emotion annotation, Douglas-Cowie et al. [12] have kappa scores ranging from .37 to .54 for emotion annotation in three different conditions: audio, visual and audiovisual. It should be noted that most of the multimodal corpora henceforth cited are recorded from TV shows, interviews or storytelling. As most of them are not task oriented the coders have to face with a large variety of nonverbal behavior and linguistics features. It should be noted that the assumption underlining CL corpora annotation is that coding scheme categories are mutually exclusive and equally distinct one another. This is often not the case of MMC coding schemes. As a consequence multimodal coding schemes turn to be too general or too narrow in categorization to annotate MMC. So far, what is clear is that it seems inappropriate to propose a general cut off point, especially for multimodal annotation, as very little literature on multimodal scheme validation has been reported up to now.

Another interesting coefficient for corpora validation is α [23]; [24]. α is a weighted measure which calculates the expected agreement by looking at the overall distribution of judgments without telling which coder has produced these judgments. It can be applied to multiple coders' agreement study and allows for different magnitudes of disagreement. Moreover, α is useful to assess chance agreement when categories are not clearly distinguished one another. At the beginning it emerged in content analysis but now is widely applied when two or more methods of processing data are applied to the same set of items, such as in anaphoric relation annotation. It is calculated as:

$$\alpha = 1 - \frac{D_o}{D_e}$$

where D_o is the observed disagreement and D_e is the expected disagreement when the coding is due to chance. It should be noted that for the same data set is it possible having very different α scores as a result of different chosen boundaries (too narrow or too wide) and the consequent distance metrics. In MMC annotation, α has been applied as a reliability measure only by Reidsma et al. [36]. They use α to validate "addressing" annotation in AMI multimodal corpus. AMI corpus is made up of multiparty dialogues on problem solving task. The addressing to one speaker is annotated not only linguistically (as for example, when one of the participants asks to another to clarify his/her point or is addressing to the group) but also with the focus of attention, primarily passing through gaze direction. They found an α score of .57 and .87 which seems not completely reliable. As pointed out by Artstein and Poesio [4], it should be noted that α score interpretation is sometimes even more problematic than kappa score. As α is a weighted measure, its score interpretation is unpredictable with the kappa "rule-of-thumbs". This is because we can report very different scores for the very same experiment. New task and distance-metric specific interpretation methods should be assessed. Apart from this difficulty, α seems a promising reliability measure for multimodal data annotation. In fact, as the nature of multimodal data usually leads to overlapping categories annotation, α can help in estimating data reliability.

To try getting rid of problem due to agreement score interpretation, recently Reidsma and Carletta [35] propose to rely on machine learning alone to generalize computational linguistics data. They show how highly reliable annotated data can give as a result patterns difficult to be generalized, whereas poorly reliable data can be successfully generalized when disagreement does not have learnable patterns. They conclude that agreement coefficients seem not to be suitable indicators of success in machine learning. However, it should be noted that the aim of annotation is not only producing set of data to be implemented in machine learning studies but to assess if they can capture some kind of reality. Even if disagreement patterns would lead to generalization, it is not automatic that this generalization will be meaningful. Instead, poor agreement in annotated data should lead researchers to rethink at categorization typologies they are using in their coding scheme or to ask themselves which is the nature of the data they are facing with. As the decision whether a coding scheme is reliable is a qualitative one, than we still have to rely on coding agreement. Having this in mind, for example in [8] emotion annotation categories have been selected to be clearly separated each other. Lower and upper face configurations are annotated following mouth and eyebrows shape alone. In this way annotators do not directly take into account aspects such as valence and arousal which can give overlapping of two dimensions over a single category. Finally, as in multimodal annotation field very few kappa and α studies are still reported, it seems very necessary that researches report clearly the method they apply to validate their annotation (e. g. the number of coders, if they code independently or not, if their coding relies only manually etc.).

3 Measuring Category Judgment Performance in Nonverbal Communication Studies: Hit Rate, Index of Accuracy and Unbiased Hit Rate

In the previous section we discuss the kappa-like statistics and their use for multimodal data validation. Particularly, two main problems have been raised: 1) the non-disjoint of judgments of multimodal data may be difficult to be captured by kappa and 2) the (generalized) difficulty to interpret kappa scores.

In this section we will focus on measures currently used to assess data reliability in nonverbal behavior and nonverbal communication studies. These studies mainly deal with emotion recognition [16], cultural differences in emotion expression and gesture regulation [20] which are hot topics in multimodal annotation as well. Usually, in nonverbal behavior studies the experimenter selects two or more labels from discrete categories (such as, for example, emotion categories or gesture typology) that have to be assigned to a group of stimuli by a group of judges. Items (which are, for example, emotional faces to be annotated) are pre-annotated by the experimenter. The aim of the experimenter is finding out if his/her labeling is the same of the annotators'. To do so, hit rate (H), calculated as the proportion of stimuli identified with the same labels of the experimenter, is usually used [42]. H calculation is very similar to percentage agreement. In fact, given data in table 1, as 48 items match with the category attributed by the experimenter, H is .800 for pleasant, .200 for neutral and .240 for unpleasant. Again, chance agreement is not taken into account in H calculation. Therefore, Wagner [40] proposed two alternative statistics to be applied: they are index of accuracy (IA) and Unbiased Hit Rate (Hu).

In the following we sketch these two statistical measures currently used in nonverbal behavior studies in which chance probability is taken into account.

3.1 Index of Accuracy (IA)

A measure which takes into account misses or false alarms is index of accuracy (IA). IA is calculated as the difference between the probability of a hit p(H) and chance probability p(C) (which is calculated as the proportion of all ratings of that response category). The difference is then divided by p(C) [40]:

$$IA = \frac{p(H)-p(C)}{p(C)}$$

which can also be written as:

$$IA = \frac{p(H)}{p(C)} - 1$$

The resulting index of accuracy is the extent to which rating performance is to be expected better or worse than chance. Using values in table 1, for pleasant items p(H) is 36/45 and p(C) is 56/100, thus IA is calculated as (36/45-56/100)/(56/100)=.429, for neutral p(H) is 6/30 and p(C) is 20/100, so IA is (6/30-20/100)/(20/100)= .000. Finally, for unpleasant items p(H) is 6/25 and p(C) is 24/100, so IA is (6/25-24/100)/(24/100)=.000. Thus, with this analysis we find out that neutral and unpleasant stimuli recognition are rated by the annotators below chance level with respect to the labels attributed by the experimenter. However, this measure is not suitable for certain type of stimuli. In particular, IA fails in recognition of rarely used categories. Moreover, as IA depends on the size of chance probability, it does not allow comparison between different studies or even different categorical classes.

An example of how IA is applied is in [41]. Wagner and Smith investigated the effect of expression of positive and negative emotions under social conditions. Pairs of friends and pairs of strangers were unobtrusively videotaped while they viewed and rated (individually) a number of emotional stimulus slides. In a second time, a group of separate annotators try to code from videotapes the emotions reported by each subject. IA was performed to assess the latter ratings reliability. Expressions were more correctly identified for participants videotaped with friends than for those recorded with strangers. These results support the hypothesis that the degree to which emotions are expressed depends on the role of an accompanying person. Unfortunately, as this result rely entirely on p(C) size (that is to say on number of ratings and the number of the response categories) it is impossible to compare this study with others having a different number of emotion categories. Thus, IA does not fulfill the fourth property suggested by Wagner for a widest application of a measure in nonverbal behavior categorization (see par. 2).

3.2 Unbiased Hit Rate (Hu)

An interesting measure to overcome chance agreement and allowing comparison between different studies is unbiased hit rate (Hu). This measure has been proposed by Wagner [40] to analyze agreement on non verbal behavior. As explained before, hit rate takes account only of ratings. In order to take into account annotator rating performance, Hu is proposed. It includes false alarms and annotator biases.

Hu is obtained multiplying together the conditional probabilities of a hit p(H) and the differential accuracy p(A) (the latter is the conditional probabilities that the category selected by the annotator matches the same one chosen for that very same item by the experimenter):

$$Hu= p(H) \times p(A)$$

When none of the items is identified by the annotator and none of the selected category matches the experimenter ones, Hu has a value of 0. When an item is always identified by an annotator and the chosen category always matches the experimenter ones, Hu value is 1. Given data in table 1, for pleasant items Hu is (36x36)/(45x56)=.514, for neutral Hu is (6x6)/(30x20)= .060 and for unpleasant Hu is (6x6)/(25x24)=.060. Hu is insensitive to biases, to proportion of different types of items to be rated and to the number of the used categories. In addition, this measure can capture not only sensitivity but also how specific a categorization task is carried out, resulting more precise in estimating annotators' performance.

As for kappa, Hu score must be tested for significance (in contrast, as Krippendorff pointed out in [23], [24], α does not require to be tested for significance). Thus, once Hu is computed for each annotator and each category, a within-subject ANOVA and a pair t-test must be performed on Hu results to check if raters selected a category higher than chance. As Hu is a proportion, it must be arcsin transformed to perform an ANOVA and a T-test. The within-subject ANOVA should be conducted with each category as within-subject and the arcsin Hu value for each annotator as dependent variable. Furthermore, pair t-tests are conducted between arcsin Hu and chance probability for each annotation category (i. e. for every emotion category such as pleasant, unpleasant and neutral). The aim is to find out if the selection of categories by the group of annotators is above chance. Chance scores are obtained by multiplying together the two condition probabilities of both item and annotator performance into a joint probability p(c). p(c) will check per each annotator if the stimulus is correctly identified and the selected category is correctly used. Given data in table 1, the chance proportion for item/annotation combination is (.45x.56)=.252 for pleasant, (.30x.20)=.060 for neutral and (.25x.24)=.060 for unpleasant. It should be noticed that the chance values for neutral and unpleasant categories are the same as the Hu values. The performance of a group of annotators may be compared with chance by pairing observed values of Hu with corresponding values of p(c). If both within-subject ANOVA and pair t-test have significant p-values than the selection of the intended category will be above chance level.

In the following we will summarize an application of Hu to validate a corpus of emotive faces, the *Karolinska Directed Emotional Faces* [18]. The 490 acted affective facial pictures belonging to the six basic emotions (angry, fearful, disgusted, happy, sad, and surprised) plus the neutral expression have been validated using Hu. After the ratings, Hu values per each emotion ranged from .29 to .89. This means that some emotive facial displays are really near to the annotators' representation of the corresponding emotion while others are not. Then, an arcsin transformation of Hu score per annotator for each emotion has been separately performed. To validate Hu performance, a within-subject ANOVA has been conducted, with emotion categories

Table 2. Pros and Cons of some corpora validation measures

	Pros	Cons
kappa	- It is corrected by chance agreement; - it allows comparisons among different coding schemes and different annotation conditions; - it has been widely used in literature for natural and task driven corpus.	- It needs a consistent number of annotators to avoid annotator's bias; - difficult in reaching significant agreement values for skewed data; - interpretation of kappa scores is not so straightforward.
α	- It is useful to assess chance agreement and disagreement patterns when categories are not clearly distinguished one another, such as in natural multimodal corpora.	- The interpretation of its score values is sometimes even more problematic than with kappa; - up to know it has been applied only once in multimodal corpora validation.
Machine Learning Techniques	- Highly reliable annotated data can give patterns difficult to be generalized. On the contrary, poorly reliable data can be successfully generalized when disagreement does not have learnable patterns.	- The aim of annotation is not only producing a set of data to be implemented in machine learning but also to assess if they can capture some kind of reality; - poor agreement should lead to rethink at categorization typologies used in the coding scheme.
IA	- It takes into account misses or false alarms; - it does not have agreement coefficients or cut off points to rely on to assess reliability.	- It does not take into account annotator's bias - it fails in recognition of rarely used categories; - it depends on the size of chance probability, therefore it does not allow comparison between different studies or different categorical classes
Hu	- It takes into account chance agreement and the annotator rating performance (bias); - it does not rely on agreement scores difficult to be interpreted or cut off points.	- It is only suitable for corpora in which item values are pre-selected by the experimenter such as emotion or gesture corpora and, more generally, in all elicited or task oriented corpora.

as within-subject variable and Hu values as dependent variable. Results reveal a main effect of emotion with respect to subject (p<.0001). To check if annotators rated each emotion higher than chance, chance proportions have been calculated per annotator for each emotion. A paired t-test has been performed between arcsin Hu and chance scores for each emotion. As results are significant (p<.0001), then emotion ratings is far above chance. Another recent study using Hu to validate a corpus of sign language gestures and emotions is [19].

4   Conclusions

In multimodal corpora annotation several methods have been used to calculate agreement among coders and to assess coding schemes reliability. In some of them the kappa statistic has been applied. As kappa is suitable only for clearly separate categories, in this paper we propose to start assessing multimodal data reliability with the kappa-like statistics such as α, or with alternative statistics, such as Hu. Multimodal corpora are collected with different modalities: they can be acted, task oriented, or ecological. On the basis of the data typology and the categories of the annotation coding scheme, it is important choosing which validation statistics we could or could not perform. Hu is a good validation method when the researcher is facing with data produced in a structured or semistructured frame, such as facial emotive corpora or task oriented corpora. In these types of corpora, items to be annotated can be pre-selected by the researcher on the basis of quantitative data such as psychophysiological index [8]. Ecological data are quite difficult to pre-select, therefore a statistic such as α seems more suitable for ecological multimodal corpora.

Kappa agreement score interpretation is a widely debated point. Recently, Reidsma and Carletta [35] have proposed to rely on machine learning techniques to generalize annotated data. It should be noted that in multimodal corpora annotation the final aim is often assessing if a given annotation scheme is able to capture some kind of data validity. Thus, the main focus is not generalizing learnable patterns but also testing multimodal models of communication. The advantage of Hu is that it does not rely on agreement scoring. Moreover, it is insensitive to annotators' bias and chance agreement. For all these reasons, Hu seems particularly suitable to annotate acted and task oriented multimodal corpora.

In table 2 we sum up pros and cons of the reliability measures and methods we have dealt with. One of the main goals of the authors is making an overview of the available methods and measures to validate multimodal corpora. Our wish is helping multimodal community having an informed choice on validation coefficients and their interpretation and fostering multimodal annotation reliability studies.

References

1. Abrilian, S., Buisine, S., Devillers, L., Martin, J.-C.: EmoTV: Annotation of Real-life Emotions for the Specification of Multimodal Affective Interfaces. In: Proceedings of International HCI (2005)
2. Allwood, J., Cerrato, L., Jokinen, K., Navarretta, C., Paggio, P.: The MUMIN coding scheme for the annotation of feedback, turn management and sequencing phenomena. Language Resources and Evaluation 41(3-4), 273–287 (2007)

3. Allwood, J., Cerrato, L., Jokinen, K., Navarretta, C., Paggio, P.: A Coding Scheme for the Annotation of Feedback, Turn Management and Sequencing Phenomena. In: Martin, J.-C., Kühnlein, P., Paggio, P., Stiefelhagen, R., Pianesi, F. (eds.) Multimodal Corpora: From Multimodal Behavior Theories to Usable Models, pp. 38–42 (2006)
4. Artstein, R., Poesio, M.: Inter-Coder Agreement for Computational Linguistics. Computational Linguistics 34, 555–596 (2008)
5. Artstein, R., Poesio, M.: Bias decreases in proportion to the number of annotators. In: Proceedings of FG-MoL (2005)
6. Carletta, J.: Unleashing the killer corpus: experiences in creating the multi-everything AMI Meeting Corpus. Language Resources and Evaluation 41, 181–190 (2007)
7. Carletta, J.: Assessing agreement on classification tasks: The kappa statistic. Computational Linguistics 22, 249–254 (1996)
8. Cavicchio, F., Poesio, M.: Annotation of Emotion in Dialogue: The Emotion in Cooperation in Perception. In: André, E., Dybkjær, L., Minker, W., Neumann, H., Pieraccini, R., Weber, M. (eds.) PIT 2008. LNCS (LNAI), vol. 5078, pp. 233–239. Springer, Heidelberg (2008)
9. Cerrato, L.: A coding scheme for the annotation of feedback phenomena in conversational speech. In: Martin, J.-C., Os, E.D., Kühnlein, P., Boves, L., Paggio, P., Catizone, R. (eds.) Proceedings of Workshop Multimodal Corpora: Models of Human Behavior for the Specification and Evaluation of Multimodal Input and Output Interfaces, pp. 25–28 (2004)
10. Colletta, J.-M., Kunene, R., Venouil, A., Tcherkassof, A.: Double Level Analysis of the Multimodal Expressions of Emotions in Human-machine Interaction. In: Martin, J.-C., Patrizia, P., Kipp, M., Heylen, D. (eds.) Multimodal Corpora: From Models of Natural Interaction to Systems and Applications, pp. 5–11 (2008)
11. Colletta, J.-M., Kunene, R.N., Venouil, A., Kaufmann, V., Simon, J.-P.: Multitrack Annotation of Child Language and Gestures. In: Kipp, M., Martin, J.-C., Paggio, P., Heylen, D. (eds.) Multimodal Corpora: From Models of Natural Interaction to Systems and Applications, 2008. LNCS (LNAI), vol. 5509, pp. 54–72. Springer, Heidelberg (2009)
12. Douglas-Cowie, E., Devillers, L., Martin, J.-C., Cowie, R., Savvidou, S., Abrilian, S., Cox, C.: Multimodal Databases of Everyday Emotion: Facing up to Complexity. In: Interspeech 2005, Lisbon, Portugal, September 4-8, pp. 813–816 (2005)
13. Dybkjær, L., Bernsen, N.O.: Recommendations for Natural Interactivity and Multimodal Annotation Schemes. In: Martin, J.-C., Os, E.D., Kühnlein, P., Boves, L., Paggio, P., Catizone, R. (eds.) Proceedings of Workshop Multimodal Corpora: Models of Human Behavior For The Specification And Evaluation of Multimodal Input And Output Interfaces, pp. 5–8 (2004)
14. Ekman, P., Friesen, W.V.: A new pan-cultural facial expression of emotion. Motivation and emotion 10, 159–168 (1986)
15. Fleiss, J.L.: Measuring nominal scale agreement among many raters. Psychological Bulletin 76, 378–382 (1971)
16. Goeleven, E., De Raedt, R., Leyman, L., Verschuere, B.: The Karolinska Directed Emotional Faces: A validation study. Cognition and Emotion 22, 1094–1118 (2008)
17. Guerini, M., Stock, O., Zancanaro, M.: A Taxonomy of Strategies for Multimodal Persuasive Message Generation. Applied Artificial Intelligence 21(2), 99–136 (2007)
18. Gut, U., Looks, K., Thies, A., Gibbon, D.: CoGesT–Conversational Gesture Transcription System. Version 1.0. Technical report. Bielefeld University (2003)
19. Hall, J.A., Levin, S.: Affect and verbal-nonverbal discrepancy in schizophrenic and non-schizophrenic family communication. British Journal of Psychiatry 137, 78–92 (1980)

20. Hietanen, J.K., Leppänen, J.M., Lehtonen, U.: Perception of Emotions in the Hand Movement Quality of Finnish Sign Language. Journal of Nonverbal Behavior 28, 53–64 (2004)
21. Kipp, M., Neff, M., Albrecht, I.: An Annotation Scheme for Conversational Gestures: How to economically capture timing and form. In: Martin, J.-C., Kühnlein, P., Paggio, P., Stiefelhagen, R., Pianesi, F. (eds.) Multimodal Corpora: From Multimodal Behavior Theories to Usable Models, pp. 24–28 (2006)
22. Kowtko, J.C., Isard, S.D., Doherty, G.M.: Conversational games within dialogue. Technical Report HCRC/RP-31, Human Communication Research Centre, University of Edinburgh (1992)
23. Krippendorff, K.: Reliability in content analysis: Some common misconceptions and recommendations. Human Communication Research 30, 411–433 (2004)
24. Krippendorff, K.: Content Analysis: An introduction to its Methodology. Sage Publications, Thousand Oaks (1980)
25. Litman, D., Hirschberg, J.: Disambiguating cue phrases in text and speech. In: Proceedings of the Thirteenth International Conference on Computational Linguistics, pp. 51–256 (1990)
26. Magno Caldognetto, E., Poggi, I., Cosi, P., Cavicchio, F., Merola, G.: Multimodal Score: an Anvil Based Annotation Scheme for Multimodal Audio-Video Analysis. In: Martin, J.-C., Os, E.D., Kühnlein, P., Boves, L., Paggio, P., Catizone, R. (eds.) Proceedings of Workshop "Multimodal Corpora: Models of Human Behavior For The Specification And Evaluation of Multimodal Input And Output Interfaces", pp. 29–33 (2004)
27. Martel, C., Osborn, C., Friedman, J., Howard, P.: The FORM Gesture Annotation System. In: Maybury, M., Martin, J.-C. (eds.) Proceedings of Multimodal Resources and Multimodal Systems Evaluation Workshop, pp. 10–15 (2002)
28. Martell, C., Kroll, J.: Using FORM Gesture Data to Predict Phase Labels. In: Martin, J.-C., Kühnlein, P., Paggio, P., Stiefelhagen, R., Pianesi, F. (eds.) Multimodal Corpora: From Multimodal Behavior Theories to Usable Models, pp. 29–32 (2006)
29. McNeill, D.: Hand and mind: What the hands reveal about thought. University of Chicago Press, Chicago (1992)
30. Passonneau, R.J., Litman, D.: Intention-based segmentation: human reliability and correlation with linguistic cues. In: Proceedings of the 31st Annual Meeting of the ACL, pp. 148–155 (1993)
31. Pianesi, F., Leonardi, C., Zancanaro, M.: Multimodal Annotated Corpora of Consensus Decision Making Meetings. In: Martin, J.-C., Kühnlein, P., Paggio, P., Stiefelhagen, R., Pianesi, F. (eds.) Multimodal Corpora: From Multimodal Behavior Theories to Usable Models, pp. 6–9 (2006)
32. Poggi, I., Vincze, L.: The Persuasive Impact of Gesture and Gaze. In: Kipp, M., Martin, J.-C., Paggio, P., Heylen, D. (eds.) Multimodal Corpora: From Models of Natural Interaction to Systems and Applications, 2008. LNCS (LNAI), vol. 5509, pp. 73–92. Springer, Heidelberg (2009)
33. Poggi, I.: Mind, hands, face and body. A goal and belief view of multimodal communication. Weidler Buchverlag, Berlin (2007)
34. Poggi, I., Cavicchio, F., Magno Caldognetto, E.: Irony in a judicial debate: analyzing the subtleties of irony while testing the subtleties of an annotation scheme. Language Resources and Evaluation 41(3-4), 215–232 (2007)
35. Reidsma, D., Carletta, J.: Reliability Measurement without Limits. Computational Linguistics 34, 319–326 (2008)

36. Reidsma, D., Heylen, D., op den Akker, R.: On the Contextual Analysis of Agreement Scores. In: Kipp, M., Martin, J.-C., Paggio, P., Heylen, D. (eds.) Multimodal Corpora: From Models of Natural Interaction to Systems and Applications, 2008. LNCS (LNAI), vol. 5509, pp. 122–137. Springer, Heidelberg (2009)

37. Scott, W.A.: Reliability of content analysis: The case of nominal scale coding. Public Opinion Quarterly 19, 321–325 (1955)

38. Siegel, S., Castellan Jr., N.J.: Nonparametric Statistics for the Behavioral Sciences, 2nd edn. McGraw-Hill, New York (1988)

39. Sosnovsky, S., Brusilovsky, P., Lee, D.H., Zadorozhny, V., Zhou, X.: Re-assessing the Value of Adaptive Navigation Support in E-Learning Context. In: Nejdl, W., Kay, J., Pu, P., Herder, E. (eds.) AH 2008. LNCS, vol. 5149, pp. 193–203. Springer, Heidelberg (2008)

40. Wagner, H.L.: On measuring performance in category judgment studies on nonverbal behavior. Journal of Non-verbal Behavior 17, 3–28 (1993)

41. Wagner, H.L., Smith, J.: Facial Expressions in the Presence of Friends or Strangers. Journal of Nonverbal Behavior 15, 201–214 (1991)

42. Woodworth, R.S.: Experimental Psychology, 1st edn. Henry Holt, New York (1938)

On the Contextual Analysis of Agreement Scores

Dennis Reidsma*, Dirk Heylen, and Rieks op den Akker

Human Media Interaction, University of Twente,
P.O. Box 217, 7500 AE Enschede, The Netherlands
{dennisr,heylen,infrieks}@ewi.utwente.nl
http://hmi.ewi.utwente.nl/

Abstract. This paper explores the relation between agreement, data quality and machine learning, using the AMI corpus. The paper describes a novel approach that uses contextual information from other modalities to determine a *more reliable subset* of data, for annotations that have a low overall agreement.

Keywords: reliability, annotation, corpus, multimodal context.

1 Introduction

Researchers working with annotated multimodal corpora often find that annotations of many interesting phenomena can only be produced with a relatively low level of agreement. Sometimes this problem can be solved by spending more (time consuming) effort on defining the annotation scheme and training the annotators. Sometimes however, this is not possible, because of a lack of resources, or because the phenomenon is simply too difficult to annotate with a higher level of agreement. When one wants to use the annotated data for machine learning purposes, low agreement means lower quality training data, lower machine learning performance and less generalizable results.

Beigman Klebanov and Shamir [2006] argued that, if data has been annotated with a very low level of inter-annotator agreement, one could improve the quality of (parts of) the data by finding out whether one can pinpoint a *subset* of the data that has been annotated with a higher level of inter-annotator agreement. This more reliable subset can then be used for training and testing of machine learning, with a higher confidence in the validity of the results (see also the discussion in Reidsma and Carletta [2008]).

The approach of Beigman Klebanov and Shamir [2006] works as follows. In order to find the more reliable subset, they proposed an approach in which *all* data is annotated multiple times. They used annotations from 20 separate annotators

---

* The authors would like to thank the developers of the AMI annotation schemes and the AMI annotators for all their hard work, as well as Nataša Jovanović for many discussions about addressing. This work is supported by the European IST Programme Project AMIDA (FP6-033812). This article only reflects the authors' views and funding agencies are not liable for any use that may be made of the information contained herein.

M. Kipp et al. (Eds.): Multimodal Corpora, LNAI 5509, pp. 122–137, 2009.

on a data set annotated for lexical cohesion. Given these annotations they induced random *pseudo-annotators* from each annotator. Each pseudo-annotator marked up the data with the same distributions as the actual annotator, but chose the items at random. Given these pseudo-annotators, they calculated the probabilities that a certain item would be marked with a certain label by more than N of the random pseudo-annotators. They found that, for items that were marked with a specific label by at least 13 out of the 20 human annotators, the label could not have been the result of random annotation processes, with an overall confidence of 99%. For a different data set, concerning markup of metaphors in text annotated by only 9 annotators, they showed that an item needed to be marked by at least 4 out of the 9 annotators to make it sufficiently improbable that the assignment of that particular label to that particular item was the result of random coding behavior [Beigman Klebanov et al., 2008]. The particular proportion (here: 13 out of 20 or 4 out of 9) may depend on factors such as the number and distribution of class labels and the pairwise agreement between annotators. By taking the subset of only those items that were marked the same by at least that proportion of annotators, they obtain a subset of the data that has a higher reliability. Machine learning results obtained on this subset will potentially be more valid. Note, though, that the resulting classifiers are no longer qualified to render a judgement on all items: they have been trained only on the 'more reliable subset', and therefore are only qualified to render a judgement on items that belong in this same subset.

A major drawback of the method described above is, firstly, that it requires all training and test data to be multiply annotated — without exception. This requires an investment that otherwise might be spent on annotating more content, or different content, or on feature selection and classification experiments, and so forth. An important drawback to this approach appears when the classifier, trained and tested on such a subset, is applied to unseen data. This data has not been annotated by humans, so it is unknown *a priori* whether specific new instances would belong to the domain in which the classifier is qualified to render a judgement, that is, the reliable subset of data for which the classifier was trained and tested. The problem is, in other words, that the performance of the classifier as observed *on the reliable subset* in the testing phase is not necessarily a valid indicator of the performance of the classifier on the new, unseen data, as the classifier will assign a label to *all instances* in the new data. The problem would be solved if it were possible to deduce for new, unseen instances (from the same domain) whether they should belong to this more reliable subset.

This paper investigates whether this solution can be achieved, for the case of addressee detection on dialog acts in the AMI corpus, by taking the *multimodal context* of utterances into account. Naturally, the approach still relies on a certain amount of multiply annotated data. However, in contrast to the method described above, only a limited part of the data needs to be annotated more than once, and it is possible for new, unseen data to determine whether it falls in the subset of data for which the classifier was trained, without requiring a large number of human judgements on this new data first. The approach set out in this paper might be used for other data sets as well, using in-depth analyses of the contextual agreement and disagreement patterns in annotations to gain more insight in the quality and usability of (subsets of) the data.

The paper is structured as follows. Section 2 introduces the AMI corpus, of which the addressee annotations were used for this paper. Section 3 concerns the basic inter-annotator agreement for the addressee annotations. Section 4 considers the relevance of the multimodal context of utterances to the level of inter-annotator agreement with which they are annotated. In Section 5 it is shown that the multimodal context of utterances can indeed be used to determine a more reliable subset of the annotations. Finally, the paper ends with a discussion and conclusions.

2   The AMI Corpus

The data used for this study was taken from the hand annotated face-to-face conversations from the 100 hour AMI meeting corpus. This corpus has been described before in other publications [Carletta, 2007; Carletta et al., 2006]. In this section a brief overview of the relevant annotations is given.

The corpus consists of 100 hours of recorded meetings. Of these recordings, 65 hours are of meetings that follow a guided scenario [Post et al., 2004]. In the scenario-based meetings, design project groups of four players have the task to design a new TV remote control. Group members have roles: project manager (PM), industrial designer (ID), user interface design (UD), and marketing expert (ME). Every group has four meetings (20-40 minutes each), dedicated to a sub-task. Most of the time the participants sit around a table. During the meetings, as well as between the meetings, participants will get new information about things such as market trends or changed design requirements, via mail. This process is coordinated by a scenario controller program. The whole scenario setup was designed to provide an optimal balance between control over the meeting variables and the freedom to have natural meetings with realistic behavior from the participants [Post et al., 2004].

All meetings were recorded in meeting rooms full of audio and video recording devices (see Figure 1) so that close facial views and overview video, as well as high quality audio, is available. Speech was transcribed manually, and words were time-aligned. The corpus has several layers of annotation for a large number of modalities, among which dialog acts, topics, hand gestures, head gestures, subjectivity, visual focus of attention (FOA), decision points, and summaries. The corpus uses the Nite XML Toolkit (NXT) data format as reference storage format, making it very easy to extend the corpus with new annotations either by importing data created in other formats or by using one of the many flexible annotation tools that it comes with [Carletta et al., 2005, 2003; Reidsma et al., 2005a,b]. Of these annotations, the dialog act, addressee and Focus of Attention annotations are presented in more detail in the rest of this section.

Fig. 1. A still image of the meeting recording room in Edinburgh

2.1   The AMI Dialog Act Annotations

The AMI dialog act annotation schema concerns the segmenting and labeling of the transcripts into dialog acts. The *segmentation* guidelines are centered around the speaker's intention, with a few rules that describe how the annotators should deal with the different situations they are likely to encounter. The rules are summarized below; more details can be found in the annotation manual [AMI Consortium, 2005].

- The *first* rule is: *each segment should contain a single speaker intention.*
- The *second* rule is that *all segments only contain transcription from a single speaker*. This rule allows dialog act segmentation to be carried out on the speech of one speaker.
- The *third* rule is that *everything in the transcription is covered in a dialog act segment, with nothing left over.*
- Finally, in case of doubt, annotators were instructed *to use two segments, instead of one.*

The guidelines for *labeling* dialog acts again center around the speaker's intention — as expressed in an utterance — to, for example, exchange information, contribute to the social structure of the group, carry out an action, get something clarified, or express an attitude towards something or someone. The schema contains fifteen types of dialog acts: eleven proper dialog acts, three 'Quasi-acts' (BACKCHANNEL, STALL, and FRAGMENT) and the 'bucket' class OTHER. The 'proper dialog acts' represent certain speaker's intentions. The 'Quasi-acts' are not proper dialog acts at all, but are present in the annotation schema to account for something in the transcript that does not really convey a speaker's intention. Furthermore, although the class OTHER *does* actually represent a speaker intention ('any intention not covered by the rest of the label set'), it is present as a 'bucket' class rather than a real part of the label set, and therefore it has also been included in the group 'quasi acts' for all analyses presented in this paper. The term 'proper dialog act' will apply to the labels not taken as 'quasi-acts'.

Most of the scenario data in the AMI corpus has been annotated for dialog acts, resulting in over 100,000 utterances. Details on the distribution of class labels, and the level of inter-annotator agreement obtained on meeting IS1003d, annotated by four annotators, can be found elsewhere [Reidsma, 2008, page 44].

2.2   The AMI Addressee Annotations

A part of the AMI corpus is also annotated with addressee information [Jovanović et al., 2006; Jovanović, 2007]. In that subset, all proper dialog acts were assigned a label indicating who the speaker addressed his speech to (was talking to). In the type of meetings considered in the AMI project, most of the time the speaker addresses the whole group, but sometimes his dialog act is addressed to some particular individual. This can be, for example, because he wants to know that individual's opinion, or is presenting information that is particularly relevant for that individual. The basis of the concept of addressing underlying the AMI addressee annotation schema originates from Goffman [Goffman, 1981]. The addressee is the participant *"oriented to by the speaker in a manner to suggest that his words are particularly for them, and that some answer is therefore anticipated from them, more so than from the other ratified participants"*. Sub-group addressing hardly occurs, at least in the meetings that make up the AMI corpus, and was not included in the schema. Thus, dialog acts are either addressed to the group (*G-addressed*) or to an individual (*I-addressed*). Annotators could also use the label UNKNOWN when they were unsure about the intended addressee of an utterance.

The AMI addressee annotation schema was applied to a subset of 14 meetings from the corpus[1], containing 9987 dialog acts in total. In total, three annotators contributed to the addressee/dialog act annotations of those 14 meetings. For every one of those 14 meetings, the addressee annotation was performed by the annotator who also performed the dialog annotation of that particular meeting. Table 1 shows the label distribution in the 14 meetings annotated with addressee information. In addition, one meeting (meeting IS1003d) was annotated with dialog act and addressee labels four times, by four independent annotators (DHA, S95, VKAR, and MA). The resulting annotations on this meeting were used as reliability data, to determine the level of inter-annotator agreement. Table 2 presents Krippendorff's α for multiple annotators for the dialog acts annotated with addressee, for all annotators and once for each of the single annotators left

---

[1] This concerns the meetings ES2008a, TS3500a, IS1000a, IS1001a, IS1001b, IS1001c, IS1003b, IS1003d, IS1006b, IS1006d, IS1008a, IS1008b, IS1008c, and IS1008d.

Table 1. The distribution of labels in the part of the AMI corpus annotated with the addressee annotation schema

Type		Number of utterances	Frequency
Quasi-acts (no addressee)		3397	34.0%
I-addressed			
	A	804	8.1
	B	598	6.0
	C	638	6.4
	D	703	7.0
	Total	2743	27.5%
G-addressed		3104	31.1%
Unknown		743	7.4%
Total		9987	100.0%

Table 2. Overview of the multi-annotator α values for addressee annotation, for the group of all four annotators and for each of the single annotators left out of the group once. The number of agreed segments for each group is given as N.

Group	N	α
All	120	0.38
Without VKAR	213	0.36
Without MA	157	0.39
Without S95	162	0.37
Without DHA	198	0.53

out of the calculation. A more detailed analysis of these annotations is presented in later sections.

2.3 The AMI Focus of Attention Annotations

A subset of meetings in the AMI corpus were also annotated with visual Focus of Attention (FOA) information, which annotators had to derive by watching the head, body and gaze of the participant [Ba and Odobez, 2006]. FOA forms an important cue for, among other things, addressing behavior. The FOA annotation contains, for every participant in the meeting, at all times throughout the meeting, whom or what he is looking at. This annotation schema was applied to the same subset of 14 meetings that was used for addressee annotation (but by other annotators). The FOA annotation was done with a very high level of agreement and with very high precision: changes are marked in the middle of eye movement between old and new target with α agreement between annotators ranging from 0.84 to 0.95 [Jovanović, 2007, page 80][2].

---

[2] These results were obtained on the AMI corpus, with a label set of 8 possible targets. Voit and Stiefelhagen [2008a] report a reliability of $\kappa = 0.70$ for a label set of 36 possible FOA targets.

3   Basic Agreement and Class Maps for Addressee

The inter-annotator agreement for the AMI addressee annotations was given in Section 2.2. Recall that the value of Krippendorff's multi-annotator α was 0.44. This indicates a quite low level of agreement: it falls into the range usually reported on highly subjective annotation tasks. Before the contextual dependencies for the inter-annotator agreement are discussed in the next section, some more information about the basic agreement analysis is given here. Table 3 presents the pairwise agreement values expressed in Krippendorff's multi-annotator α [1980]. Table 4 shows an example of a confusion matrix for the addressee annotation, representative of the other confusion matrices. The values in the confusion matrix suggest that it is not so much problematic to decide *which* individual was addressed as it is to distinguish between I-addressed utterances versus utterances that are G-addressed or labeled UNKNOWN. In the remainder of this section, inter-annotator agreement is discussed for two derived versions of the label set, namely for the annotation without the label UNKNOWN and for the class map in which the annotation is reduced to the binary distinction I-addressed/G-addressed. Note that all results presented in the remainder of this paper concern only proper dialog acts and are based upon a pairwise comparison of agreed segments, as in the table below (the agreed segments of a pair of annotators are those segments for which the two annotators assigned axactly the same start and end boundaries).

Table 3. Pairwise agreement (Krippendorff's α) for addressee annotations by four annotators, on agreed segments annotated as proper dialog act

	MA	VKAR	DHA	S95
MA	.	0.57	0.32	0.46
VKAR		.	0.36	0.50
DHA			.	0.31
S95				.

Table 4. Confusion matrix for annotators VKAR and MA for the addressee labels of agreed segments in meeting IS1003d. Krippendorff's α is 0.57 for this matrix.

	A	B	C	D	G	U	Σ
A	46				26	2	74
B	1	25			12	1	39
C		−	38	1	10	1	50
D				63	16	4	83
G	7	5	9	10	155	5	191
U	16	1	4	4	15	2	42
Σ	70	31	51	78	234	15	479

3.1 Reliability for the Addressee Label Unknown

The annotators indicated whether an utterance was addressed to a particular person or to the whole group. They could also use the label UNKNOWN, if they could not decide who was being addressed. All four annotators used this label at some point in their annotation of meeting IS1003d. Given the annotation guidelines, there might have been two reasons why an annotator would use the label UNKNOWN. Firstly, the utterance may have been ambiguously or unclearly addressed, making it impossible to choose a single label like the annotation task requires. The reason for assigning the label UNKNOWN then lies within the content. A certain amount of inter-annotator agreement for this label could be expected, and the applicability of the label could be learnable and worth learning. Secondly, the utterance may have been unambiguously addressed, but nevertheless the annotator may have been uncertain about his own judgement, for example because he was tired, or did not understand what was being said. In that case, the reason for assigning the label UNKNOWN lies completely with the annotator, rather than with the content. This second type of uncertainty would *not* cause the label UNKNOWN to exhibit a large inter-annotator agreement, and would by far be less interesting to learn to classify.

The question to be answered here is then: does the uncertainty in the addressee annotation, expressed by the annotator assigning the label UNKNOWN, reflect an attribute of the content, or rather an attribute of the specific annotator who assigned the label at a certain point? Inspection of the confusion matrices shows a clear answer to this question. The matrix displayed in Table 4 is certainly representative in this respect. Inter-annotator agreement on the applicability of the label is virtually non-existent for each and every pair of annotators. This means that the occurrence of the label UNKNOWN in the corpus does not seem to give any useful information about the annotated content at all.

For this reason, it was decided to remove all UNKNOWN labels from the corpus before proceeding with further analysis. That is, for all segments that an annotator labeled UNKNOWN, the label was removed, and the segment was taken as if the annotator had not labeled it with addressee at all — reducing the number of segments available for the analyses presented later in this paper by one, for

Table 5. Inter-annotator agreement for all proper dialog acts versus only the dialog acts not annotated with the UNKNOWN addressee label

	Inc. UNKNOWN	Excl. UNKNOWN
MA vs VKAR	0.57	0.67
DHA vs S95	0.31	0.47
S95 vs VKAR	0.50	0.63
DHA vs VKAR	0.36	0.47
MA vs S95	0.46	0.59
DHA vs MA	0.32	0.43

Table 6. Pairwise α agreement for the unmapped label set (left) and for the class mapping $(A, B, C, D) => S$ (right), both after removing the label UNKNOWN from the data set

	Normal label set (excl. UNKNOWN)	Class map $(A, B, C, D) => S$ (excl. UNKNOWN)
MA vs VKAR	0.67	0.55
DHA vs S95	0.47	0.37
S95 vs VKAR	0.63	0.52
DHA vs VKAR	0.47	0.37
MA vs S95	0.59	0.46
DHA vs MA	0.43	0.32

that annotator, but leaving the number of segments available from the other annotators unaffected.

The effect of this data set reduction on the inter-annotator agreement on the remaining segments is shown in Table 5. This table presents the α values for the addressee annotations computed on all proper dialog acts versus the α values calculated after removing all UNKNOWN labels from the corpus. The increase in level of inter-annotator agreement ranges from 0.10 to 0.16. This does not only hold for the overall data set reported in this table, but also for each and every contextual subset of the data set reported later in this paper.

3.2 Class Map: Group/A/B/C/D vs Group/Single

The second label that really contributed to the disagreement, according to the confusion matrix of Table 4, is the GROUP label. However, in large contrast to the label UNKNOWN discussed above, the majority of its occurrences are actually agreed upon by at least some of the annotators. From the confusion matrices it can nevertheless be seen that annotators cannot make the global distinction between G-addressed and I-addressed utterances with a high level of agreement: there is a lot of confusion between the label G on the one hand and A, B, C and D on the other hand. If annotators see an utterance as I-addressed they subsequently do not have much trouble determining who of the single participants was addressed: there is hardly any confusion between the individual addressee labels A, B, C and D.

This observation is quantified using a class mapping of the addressee annotation in which the individual addressee labels A, B, C and D are all mapped onto the label S. Table 6 shows pairwise α agreement for this class mapping, next to the values obtained for the full label set excluding only the label UNKNOWN (see also the previous section). Clearly, agreement on who of the participants was addressed individually is a major factor in the overall agreement.

4   The Multimodal Context of Utterances

The remainder of this paper concerns multimodal contextual agreement. To a large extent multimodal behavior is a holistic phenomenon, in the sense that the contribution of a specific behavior to the meaning of an utterance needs to be decided upon in the context of other behaviors that coincide, precede or follow. A nod, for instance, may contribute to a conversation in different ways when it is performed by someone speaking or listening, when it is accompanied by a smile, or when it is a nod in a series of more than one. When we judge what is happening in conversational scenes, our judgements become more accurate when we know more about the context in which the actions have taken place. The occurrences of gaze, eye-contact, speech, facial expressions, gestures, and the setting determine our interpretation of events and help us to disambiguate otherwise ambiguous activities.

Annotators, who are requested to label certain communicative events, be it topic, focus of attention, addressing information or dialog acts, get cues from both the audio and the video stream. Some cues are more important than others: some may be crucial for correct interpretation whereas others may become important only in particular cases. The reliability of annotations may crucially depend on the presence or absence of certain features, even if these features are not mentioned in the annotator instructions. Using or not using the video and audio while annotating may therefore have a large impact on the agreement achieved for certain annotations. Also, one annotator may be more sensitive to one cue rather than to another. This means that the agreement between annotators may depend on particular variations in the multimodal input.

Within the AMI corpus, one of the more obvious annotations to which this bears relevance is the combination of addressee and visual focus of attention (FOA) annotations. Visual focus of attention of speakers and listeners is an important cue in multimodal addressing behavior. The combination of these two layers will therefore be used in an attempt to determine a more reliable subset of the corpus.

5   Finding More Reliable Subsets

This section describes two 'more reliable subsets' within the AMI addressee annotations (with the UNKNOWN label removed as discussed in Section 3). The first is centered around the multimodal context of the utterance. The second uses the context determined by the type of dialog act for which the addressee was annotated. The aim of these contextual agreement analyses, as described in the introduction to this paper, is to be able to pinpoint a more reliable subset in the data without having all training and test data be annotated by multiple annotators.

5.1   Context: Focus of Attention

Visual Focus of Attention (FOA) of speakers and listeners is an important cue in multimodal addressing behavior. In this section it is investigated to what extent

Table 7. The three different contexts defined by different conditions on the FOA annotation that are used to find more reliable subsets of the addressee annotations

Context	Description
I	Only those utterances during which the speaker does not look at another participant at all (he may look at objects, though)
II	Only those utterances during which the speaker does look at one other participant, but not more than one (he may additionally look at objects)
III	Only those utterances during which the speaker does look at one or more other participants (he may additionally look at objects)

this cue impacts the task of annotators who observe the conversational scene and have to judge who was addressing whom. FOA annotations are a manifest type of content, do not need extensive discourse interpretation, and can be annotated with a very high level of inter-annotator agreement. This makes them especially useful when they can serve as multimodal context for finding a more reliable subset of the addressing data, because it is more likely that this context can be retrieved for new, unseen data, too[3].

Table 7 lists three different FOA contexts (I, II and III) that each define a different subset of all addressee annotations. The contexts are defined with respect to the Focus of Attention of the speaker during the utterance. Context I concerns utterances during which the speaker's gaze is directed only to objects (laptop, whiteboard, or some other artefact) or nowhere in particular. One might expect that in this context the annotation task is harder and the inter-annotator agreement lower. Contexts II and III concern the utterances during which the speaker's gaze is directed at least some of the time to other persons (only one person, for context II, or any number of persons for context III). The expectation was that utterances in contexts II and III respectively would also exhibit a difference in inter-annotator agreement. When a speaker looks at only one participant, agreement may be higher than when the speaker looks at several (different) persons during an utterance.

Table 8 presents α values for the pairwise inter-annotator agreement for the three subsets defined by the three FOA contexts from Table 7, compared to the α values for the whole data set that were presented in Section 3.1. Inter-annotator agreement for the addressee annotation is consistently lowest for context I whereas contexts II and III consistently score highest. When a speaker looks at one or more participants, the agreement between annotators on addressing consistently becomes higher. Contrary to expectations there is no marked difference, however, between the contexts where, during a segment, a speaker only looks at one participant or at several of them (context II versus III).

---

[3] Although it should be noted that state-of-the-art recognition rates are still too low for this, in the order of 60% frame recognition rate [Ba and Odobez, 2007; Voit and Stiefelhagen, 2008b].

Table 8. Pairwise α agreement for the subsets defined by the three contextual FOA conditions, compared to α agreement for the full data set (without the label UNKNOWN)

	All (excl. UNKNOWN)	I	II	III
MA vs VKAR	0.67	0.60	0.78	0.77
DHA vs S95	0.47	0.41	0.57	0.57
S95 vs VKAR	0.63	0.59	0.69	0.66
DHA vs VKAR	0.47	0.42	0.48	0.51
MA vs S95	0.59	0.57	0.63	0.62
DHA vs MA	0.43	0.32	0.53	0.56

In conclusion, it can be said that the subset of all utterances during which the speaker looks at some other participants at least some of the time, defined by context II or III, forms a more reliable subset of the addressee annotations as defined in the introduction to this paper. This subset contains two thirds of all utterances annotated with addressee.

5.2   Context: Elicit Dialog Acts

The second contextual agreement analysis presented here concerns a certain specific group of dialog acts. Op den Akker and Theune [2008] discussed that forward looking dialog acts, and more specifically, 'Elicit' types of dialog act (see Table 9), are more often I-addressed, and tend to be addressed more explicitly. If this were true, one would also expect elicit dialog acts to exhibit a higher inter-annotator agreement on addressing. This we can test on the data in the AMI corpus. Table 10 presents the pairwise α inter-annotator agreement values for all proper dialog acts, the 'elicit' dialog acts only, and the proper acts without the 'elicit' acts. Clearly, the agreement for only the 'elicit' acts is a lot higher. Apparently the intended addressee of elicits is relatively easy to determine for an outsider (annotator); this may support what Op den Akker and Theune [2008] say about the differences in how speakers express 'elicit' acts and other forward looking acts.

We tested this difference between Elicits and other dialog acts again using a second set of annotations, that were not yet introduced in this paper. The dialog acts of AMI meeting IS1003d, segmented and labelled by annotator

Table 9. Types of 'Elicit' dialog acts

Description	Dialog act label
Acts about information exchange:	ELICIT-INFORM
Acts about possible actions:	ELICIT-OFFER-OR-SUGGESTION
Acts that comment on the previous discussion:	ELICIT-COMMENT-ABOUT-UNDERSTANDING and ELICIT-ASSESSMENT

Table 10. Pairwise α agreement for all proper dialog acts and for the elicit dialog acts only

	All proper acts	Elicits only	No elicits
MA vs VKAR	0.67	0.87	0.64
DHA vs S95	0.47	0.84	0.38
S95 vs VKAR	0.63	0.80	0.61
DHA vs VKAR	0.47	0.58	0.41
MA vs S95	0.59	0.76	0.57
DHA vs MA	0.43	0.57	0.40

VKAR, were annotated for addressee by another 10 annotators. In this case the DA-segments as well as their labels were already given, so annotators only had to label the addressee (of the proper acts, i.e. excluding BACKCHANNELS, STALLS and FRAGMENTS). This implies that we can study inter-annotator agreement on the whole set of all proper DActs in this meetings which is 454 out of a total of 693 acts. In this case, annotators were not allowed to use the Unknown label, so they were asked to decide if a DA is addressed to the Group of to some individual, and in the latter case who is addressed.

For the addressee labeling task, we computed Krippendorff's pairwise α and Krippendorf's group α for the whole group both for the whole set of proper dialogue acts and for the subset of elicit acts.

The results are as follows. The pairwise α is significantly higher for Elicit-acts (50 units) than for all proper acts (454 units). A paired t-test was performed to determine if there is a real difference in the α values for pairs of annotators of addressees for all acts and α values for the same pair of annotators for only addressees labels of elicit acts. The mean difference (M=0.1718, SD =0.01412, N= 45) was significantly greater than zero, $t(44) = 12.16$, two-tail $p < 0.001$, providing evidence that their is a real difference. A 95% C.I. about the mean difference is (0.1433, 0.2001). The group wise α for elicit acts is 0.80 which is much higher than the group wise α for the whole set of proper acts, 0.65.

Since not all of these 44 pairs are independent we also performed the same test on 9 pairs of annotators that are independent (one fixed annotator paired with all other 9). The mean difference (M=0.1667, SD =0.00915, N= 9) was significantly greater than zero, $t(8) = 5.46$, two-tail $p < 0.001$, providing evidence that their is a real difference. A 95% C.I. about the mean difference is (0.09, 0.23).

These findings again support the claim that it is easier for annotators to tell if the group is addressed or some individual, when the act is an elicit act, than in general for dialogue acts, and that this subset of the data in the corpus has a high reliability.

6   Discussion and Summary of Addressing Agreement

Throughout this paper pairwise α agreement scores have been presented for different class mappings and subsets of the addressee annotations in the AMI corpus. The different effects noted about these scores were consistent. That is, although only a few combinations of scores are reported, all different combinations of mappings and subsets consistently show the same patterns. For example, all relative differences between the FOA contexts hold for the 'all agreed proper dialog acts' condition, the 'excluding UNKNOWN' condition, and for the $(A, B, C, D) => S$ class mapping.

The following conclusions can be summarized for the inter-annotator agreement of addressee annotations: (1) the label UNKNOWN does not give any information about the annotated content; (2) there is a large confusion between dialog acts being G-addressed or I-addressed, but if the annotators agree on an utterance being I-addressed they typically also agree on the particular individual being addressed; (3) utterances during which the speaker's focus of attention is directed to one or more other participants are consistently annotated with more agreement than those during which the speaker's FOA is not directed to any participant; and (4) 'elicit' dialog acts are easier to annotate with addressee than other types of dialog act.

The context defined by the different FOA conditions, and the context defined by the 'elicit' dialog acts, specify more reliable subsets of the annotated data. These subsets can be used in machine learning tasks in two ways. Firstly, classifiers can be trained on only the more reliable subset, in an effort to increase the relevance of the results. Secondly, classifiers can be built that restrict their judgements to those instances for which humans agree more easily (that is, the more reliable subset), yielding a 'no classification possible' judgement for instances that do not belong to the more reliable subset. This way, the consumer of the classifications can place more trust in the judgements returned by the classifier, even when the original annotations were produced with a low level of inter-annotator agreement. The approach set out in this paper might be used for other data sets as well, using in-depth analyses of the contextual agreement and disagreement patterns in annotations to gain more insight in the quality and usability of (subsets of) the data. It remains for future work to find out how much more this approach can make classifiers 'fit for purpose', but it is important to note that the FOA and the Elicit acts can be automatically detected with much better reliability than addressee.

References

AMI Consortium: Guidelines for dialogue act and addressee. Technical report (2005)

Ba, S.O., Odobez, J.-M.: A study on visual focus of attention recognition from head pose in a meeting room. In: Renals, S., Bengio, S., Fiscus, J.G. (eds.) MLMI 2006. LNCS, vol. 4299, pp. 75–87. Springer, Heidelberg (2006)

Ba, S.O., Odobez, J.M.: Head pose tracking and focus of attention recognition algorithms in meeting rooms. In: Stiefelhagen, R., Garofolo, J.S. (eds.) CLEAR 2006. LNCS, vol. 4122, pp. 345–357. Springer, Heidelberg (2007)

Beigman Klebanov, B., Beigman, E., Diermeier, D.: Analyzing disagreements. In: Artstein, R., Boleda, G., Keller, F., Schulte im Walde, S. (eds.) Coling 2008: Proceedings of the workshop on Human Judgements in Computational Linguistics, Manchester, UK, Coling 2008 Organizing Committee, August 2008, pp. 2–7 (2008) ISBN 978-3-540-69567-7

Beigman Klebanov, B., Shamir, E.: Reader-based exploration of lexical cohesion. Language Resources and Evaluation 40(2), 109–126 (2006)

Carletta, J.C.: Unleashing the killer corpus: experiences in creating the multi-everything AMI meeting corpus. Language Resources and Evaluation 41(2), 181–190 (2007)

Carletta, J.C., Ashby, S., Bourban, S., Flynn, M., Guillemot, M., Hain, T., Kadlec, J., Karaiskos, V., Kraaij, W., Kronenthal, M., Lathoud, G., Lincoln, M., Lisowska, A., McCowan, I., Post, W.M., Reidsma, D., Wellner, P.: The AMI meeting corpus: A pre-announcement. In: Renals, S., Bengio, S. (eds.) MLMI 2005. LNCS, vol. 3869, pp. 28–39. Springer, Heidelberg (2006)

Carletta, J.C., Evert, S., Heid, U., Kilgour, J., Robertson, J., Voormann, H.: The NITE XML toolkit: flexible annotation for multi-modal language data. Behavior Research Methods, Instruments and Computers 35(3), 353–363 (2003)

Carletta, J.C., McKelvie, D., Isard, A., Mengel, A., Klein, M., Møller, M.B.: A generic approach to software support for linguistic annotation using xml. In: Sampson, G., McCarthy, D. (eds.) Corpus Linguistics: Readings in a Widening Discipline. Continuum International, London (2005)

Goffman, E.: Footing. In: Forms of Talk, pp. 124–159. University of Pennsylvania Press, Philadelphia (1981)

Jovanović, N.: To Whom It May Concern - Addressee Identification in Face-to-Face Meetings. Phd thesis, University of Twente (2007)

Jovanović, N., op den Akker, H.J.A., Nijholt, A.: A corpus for studying addressing behaviour in multi-party dialogues. Language Resources and Evaluation 40(1), 5–23 (2006)

Krippendorff, K.: Content Analysis: An Introduction to its Methodology. The Sage CommText Series, vol. 5. Sage Publications, Beverly Hills (1980)

op den Akker, H.J.A., Theune, M.: How do I address you? modelling addressing behavior based on an analysis of multi-modal corpora of conversational discourse. In: Proceedings of the AISB symposium on Multi-modal Output Generation, MOG 2008, April 2008, pp. 10–17 (2008) ISBN 1-902956-69-9

Post, W.M., Cremers, A.H.M., Blanson Henkemans, O.A.: A research environment for meeting behavior. In: Proceedings of the 3rd Workshop on Social Intelligence Design, pp. 159–165 (2004)

Reidsma, D.: Annotations and Subjective Machines — of annotators, embodied agents, users, and other humans. PhD thesis, University of Twente (October 2008)

Reidsma, D., Carletta, J.C.: Reliability measurement without limits. Computational Linguistics 34(3), 319–326 (2008)

Reidsma, D., Hofs, D.H.W., Jovanović, N.: Designing focused and efficient annotation tools. In: Noldus, L.P.J.J., Grieco, F., Loijens, L.W.S., Zimmerman, P.H. (eds.) Measuring Behaviour, Wageningen, NL, September 2005a, pp. 149–152 (2005a)

Reidsma, D., Hofs, D.H.W., Jovanović, N.: A presentation of a set of new annotation tools based on the NXT API. Poster at Measuring Behaviour 2005 (2005b)

Voit, M., Stiefelhagen, R.: Deducing the visual focus of attention from head pose estimation in dynamic multi-view meeting scenarios. In: IMCI 2008: Proceedings of the 10th international conference on Multimodal interfaces, pp. 173–180. ACM, New York (2008a)

Voit, M., Stiefelhagen, R.: Visual focus of attention in dynamic meeting scenarios. In: Popescu-Belis, A., Stiefelhagen, R. (eds.) MLMI 2008. LNCS, vol. 5237, pp. 1–13. Springer, Heidelberg (2008)

Creating Standardized Video Recordings of Multimodal Interactions across Cultures

Matthias Rehm[1], Elisabeth André[1], Nikolaus Bee[1], Birgit Endrass[1],
Michael Wissner[1], Yukiko Nakano[2], Afia Akhter Lipi[2],
Toyoaki Nishida[3], and Hung-Hsuan Huang[3]

[1] Augsburg University, Institute of Computer Science, 86159 Augsburg, Germany
rehm@informatik.uni-augsburg.de
[2] Dept. of Computer and Information Science, Faculty of Science and Technology,
Seikei University, Japan
y.nakano@st.seikei.ac.jp
[3] Dept. of Intelligence Science and Technology, Graduate School of Informatics,
Kyoto University, Japan
nishida@i.kyoto-u.ac.jp

Abstract. Trying to adapt the behavior of an interactive system to the cultural background of the user requires information on how relevant behaviors differ as a function of the user's cultural background. To gain such insights in the interrelation of culture and behavior patterns, the information from the literature is often too anecdotal to serve as the basis for modeling a system's behavior, making it necessary to collect multimodal corpora in a standardized fashion in different cultures. In this chapter, the challenges of such an endeavor are introduced and solutions are presented by examples from a German-Japanese project that aims at modeling culture-specific behaviors for Embodied Conversational Agents.

1 Introduction

The acquisition of corpora as a basis for cross-cultural studies is a challenging endeavor. First of all, an enormous amount of data is required in order to shed light on culture-specific differences in behavior. Even when concentrating on one culture only, it is hard to assess how behavior is influenced by the context in which recordings are taken. Cross cultural studies introduce a further behavior determinant which needs to be separated out from other contextual variables, such as the situation in which the recordings are taken and the personality of the videotaped subjects. As a consequence, the acquisition of corpora needs to be carefully planned requiring cooperation between researchers across different countries. In the following, we discuss some general recommendations for the acquisition of cross cultural corpora, and detail this recommendation in later sections with examples from a large corpus study, which was conducted in Germany and Japan.

M. Kipp et al. (Eds.): Multimodal Corpora, LNAI 5509, pp. 138–159, 2009.

1.1 Application Scenario Match

The recorded scenario should match the envisioned application scenario as closely as possible. For example, when implementing an application for cultural training, it is advisable to record prototypical scenarios that constitute situations a tourist or any business canvasser is likely to encounter. Furthermore, we need to take into account how the user will interact with the application. If the user is just listening to an agent, the recording of monologues might suffice. In case the user is expected to engage in a dialogue with an agent, a sufficient amount of samples for dialogue and turn taking acts should be represented in the data as well. Culture is not only reflected by specific speaking behaviors. Listening behaviors may significantly differ from culture to culture as well. If a corpus is to feature typical interaction patterns, recordings of at least two people engaging in a conversation are required per culture. Further conversational phenomena arise in multi-party conversations. In a three-party conversation one person may not just listen to another person, but overhear the dialogue between two other people. Four-party conversations enable the participants to form sub groups and engage in multi-threaded conversations. Usually, a tourist or business canvasser encounters situations that include more than two conversational partners. Nevertheless, research has mostly concentrated on the recordings of two-party conversations so far.

1.2 Definition of a Common Protocol

Corpus studies have been conducted for a large variety of languages and cultures. However, since previous studies focused on different settings and phenomena, the results are difficult to compare. For example, it is hard to identify characteristic culture-specific interaction patterns if the recordings feature conversing friends in one culture and conversing foreigners in another. To conduct a comparative cross-cultural study, a common protocol needs to be defined which guides corpus collection across different cultures. On the one hand, we have to make sure that the protocol is explicit enough to enable the experimenters to replicate studies in different countries and get comparable results. On the other hand, the protocol should still allow for a sufficient amount of culture-specific variations. In particular, we have to make sure that culture-specific behaviors, such as greeting rituals, are not implicitly included in the protocol. As a minimum requirement, experimenters need to agree on the application scenarios (e.g. asking for directions or making a hotel reservation) and the conversational setting (monologue, dialogue or multi-threaded conversation). Another issue is to decide on which behavior determinants apart from culture to vary and which to keep constant. For instance, different gender constellations might be considered in order to investigate how gender affects the style of conversation in different cultures. Many factors might, however, have to be kept constant out of practical considerations in order to limit the amount of data to be recorded.

1.3   Phenomena Occurrences

We aim at recording multimodal communicative behaviors of naturally acting people, but at the same time a sufficient amount of data covering the phenomena we are interested in should occur. To ensure a high control over the recordings, the employment of actors who are not known to the subjects in advance might be a promising option. Actors may help keep the conversation going and provoke a sufficient amount and variety of behaviors from the subjects. Furthermore, we have to decide on which cultural dimensions to focus. For instance, to analyze the influence of the power distance index on communication, scenarios with people that represent a different status might yield more interesting results than scenarios with people of equal status. Again, actors may help ensure that differences in status are reflected in a controlled manner. Naturalness of the data would still be guaranteed by just considering the non-acted behaviors in the later analysis.

1.4   Separating Culture from Other Behavior Determinants

Contextual factors that might have an impact on behavior need to be controlled and to be separated out from cultural-specific behavior determinants. Such factors include the participants' gender, their personality, and their social status. For instance, it might be observed that the spatial extension of gestures in a corpus is unusually high. In Germany, this might easily be attributable to the recorded persons' extrovert personality trait. But what if the data were from a Southern European country like Italy? Then the observed expressive behavior might well just be the standard behavior pattern in this culture (e.g., Ting-Toomey 1999). In order to identify the potential influence of the subjects' personalities on their behaviors, it is highly recommended to record the personality traits of the participating subjects. In the ideal case, potential gender effects on dialogue may be taken into account by taking recordings of all possible gender combinations (female-female, female-male, and male-male) which is, however, not feasible when investigating multi-party conversations due to the many combinations to be considered.

1.5   Technical Requirements

The subjects need to be recorded from various viewing angles in order to ensure that their gestures and facial expressions are visible. When aiming at studying typical interaction patterns, not only the speakers, but also the addressees need to be videotaped. In order to allow for comparing cross-cultural studies, the recordings should be taken from similar angles in all participating countries. For example, a comparison might become difficult if gestures are better visible in one culture than in another or if a person appears more dominant in one culture due to the viewing angle chosen. For the same reason, the audio quality needs to be kept constant across cultures. Another question concerns the choice of an appropriate setting for the recordings. To ensure that the recordings match the application as closely as possible, they might be taken in a similar situation.

Here, we have to take into account, however, that the context introduces a new variable which might be difficult to separate out from culture-specific factors. A neutral room helps avoid any bias due to context, but people might behave differently than in the application situation.

2   Culture

Aiming at simulating culture-specific behavior in interactive systems, it is necessary to clarify first what is meant by culture and second which observable phenomena are influenced by culture. We will not discuss different cultural theories here, but present one theoretical school that defines culture as norms and values that guide the behavior of people from the given culture. Culture in this approach provides a set of heuristics that structure the behavior and its interpretation by the members of a culture. One representative of this line of thinking is Hofstede [15], who develops a dimensional model of culture. His theory is based on a broad empirical survey that gives detailed insights in differences of value orientations and norms. Hofstede defines five dimensions on which cultures vary, the best known is perhaps his identity dimension that distinguishes between collectivistic and individualistic cultures and defines to what degree individuals are integrated into a group. The other dimensions are hierarchy, gender, uncertainty, and orientation. Hierarchy denotes if a culture accepts unequal power distance between members of the culture or not. Identity defines to what degree individuals are integrated into a group. Gender describes the distribution of roles between the genders. In feminine cultures for instance roles differ less than in more masculine cultures. Uncertainty assesses the tolerance for uncertainty and ambiguity in a culture. Those with a low uncertainty tolerance are likely to have fixed rules to deal with unstructured situations. Orientation distinguishes long and short term orientation, where values associated with short term orientation are for instance respect for tradition, fulfilling social obligations, and saving one's face often resulting in elaborate systems of politeness. Following this approach, a given culture is defined as a point in a five-dimensional space.

According to Hofstede, nonverbal behavior is strongly affected by cultural affordances. The identity dimension for instance is tightly related to the expression of emotions and the acceptable emotional displays in a culture. Thus, it is more acceptable in individualistic cultures like the US to publicly display negative emotions like anger or fear than it is in collectivistic cultures like Japan. Based on Hofstede's dimensions, Hofstede, Pedersen, and Hofstede [16] define synthetic cultures as representations of the end points of the dimensions and show how specific behavior patterns differ in a principled way depending on where a culture is located. Table 1 presents a summary for the acoustic and spatial behavior of these synthetic cultures, which can serve as a starting point for modeling culture-specific behavior [27]. Using this information as a predictor for the acoustic and spatial behavior of the German and Japanese culture leads to some problems as is exemplified with the following example. High power distance

Table 1. Synthetic cultures and corresponding patterns of behavior for low and high values. For illustrative purposes, the positions of the German (G) and the Japanese (JP) culture are given. If they fall into the same category (e.g. high values on the gender dimension) the relative position is indicated.

Dimension	Synthetic Culture	Sound	Space	Example
Hierarchy	Low: Low Power	Loud	Close	German
	High: High Power	Soft	Far	Japanese
Identity	Low: Collectivistic	Soft	Close	Japanese
	High: Individualistic	Loud	Far	German
Gender	Low: Femininity	Soft	Close	
	High: Masculinity	Loud	Close	G < JP
Uncertainty	Low: Tolerance	Soft	Close	
	High: Avoidance	Loud	Far	G < JP
Orientation	Low: Short-Term	Soft	Close	German
	High: Long-Term	Soft	Far	Japanese

(hierarchy dimension) results standing further apart in face-to-face encounters whereas collectivism (identity dimension) generally means standing closer together in the same situation. Both attributions hold true for the Japanese culture. Thus, what will be the result of these correlations if they are combined? The most sensible solution would be to consider the semantics of the dimensional position. If a culture has a high power distance then there could be differences in proxemics behavior that are related to social status, for instance resulting in standing further away from high status individuals but closer together with peers. Another obvious problem with this information is that the actual behavior of an existing culture might be completely different from this stereotypical behavior. To realistically model culture-specific patterns of behavior for interactive systems, it becomes thus necessary to capture the necessary empirical data for a given culture.

3   Application Scenario Match

The verbal and non-verbal behavior of embodied conversational agents (ECAs) becomes more and more sophisticated. But this behavior is primarily based on a Western cultural background due to the available agent systems and their predefined animation sequences. But according to [31] the most profound misunderstandings in face-to-face communication arise due to misinterpretations of non-verbal cues. Thus, culture-adaptive behavior in embodied agents can further cross-cultural communication in two ways. (i) Employing an agent that adheres to culturally determined behavior programs will enhance the efficiency of information delivery. (ii) Agents capable of changing their "cultural programs" can serve as embarrassment-free coaching devices of culture-specific behaviors. Based on Hofstede's theory of cultural dimensions [15], the CUBE-G[1] project

---

[1] CUlture-adaptive BEhavior Generation for embodied conversational agents
http://mm-werkstatt.informatik.uni-augsburg.de/projects/cube-g/

investigates whether and how the non-verbal behavior of agents can be generated from a parameterized computational model, The project combines a top-down model-based approach with a bottom-up corpus-based approach which allows to empirically ground the model in the specific behavior of two cultures (Japanese and German).

One of the central goals of the project is to develop a role-playing scenario to increase cultural awareness following generally accepted learning steps. Bennett [2] as well as Hofstede [16] describe similar approaches that are widely used in real-world trainings and that will be adapted for the use in CUBE-G. The focus lies on scenarios that every tourist or ex-patriate is likely to encounter. A first meeting between strangers, a negotiation process, and an interaction of individuals with different social status have been identified to serve this purpose due to their prototypical nature, i.e. they can be found in every culture and they constitute situations a tourist or ex-patriate is likely to encounter. Thus, they present the three scenarios for collecting multimodal data on face-to-face interactions in the German and the Japanese culture.

3.1   Scenario 1: First Meeting

There are several specific reasons for including the first-meeting scenario. According to Kendon [18], it is not only found in all cultures but it also plays an important role for managing personal relations by signaling for instance social status, degree of familiarity, or degree of liking. There is also a practical reason for this scenario because it is the standard first chapter of every language textbook and thus known to everybody who ever learned a foreign language revealing a potential application of the results in a role-play for first meeting scenarios. For Argyle [1], a first meeting is a ritual that follows pre-defined scripts. Ting-Toomey [31] follows his analysis by denoting a first meeting as a ceremony with a specific chain of actions. Knapp and Vangelisti [19] emphasize a first meeting as a step into the life of someone else, which is critical for a number of reasons like face-keeping or developing a network of social relation. Thus, the ritualistic nature of a first meeting makes sense in order "to be on the safe side" by establishing such a new relationship in a satisfactorily, i.e. facekeeping, manner for both sides.

Previous studies established some differences in nonverbal behavior for the German and the Japanese cultures. According to [31], the actual greetings at the beginning of the first meeting scenarios can be supposed to take longer in Japan, which is a representative of a collectivistic culture. On the other hand, gesture usage should be more frequent in an individualistic country like Germany. It has been shown [11] that more body contact can be expected in Germany due to ritualistic handshakes during the greeting. The corpus analysis in CUBE-G could confirm these findings (only partially for the body contact claim, see [28]). Additional results include differences in posture and in gestural expressivity.

3.2 Scenario 2: Negotiation

Whereas the main focus in the first meeting scenario was on the nonverbal behavior of the interlocutors, which we expect to be qualitatively similar in both scenarios, the negotiation scenario adds an additional layer concerning differences in the styles and strategies for such a negotiation. Following [32] we categorize such strategies into three main classes:

- Avoidance: Using the avoidance strategy, a negotiation partner tries to avoid the negotiation which is undesirable for him in some manner. This might be performed by shifting the focus of the conversation to something different or trying to get completely out of the conversation.
- Integrative: Following the integrative strategy, the negotiation partner tries to find a solution for the given problem that is satisfying for all participants. This includes for example the aim to understand the other's perspective of the situation.
- Distributive: Being in a distributive strategy the conversation partner wants to carry out his point and to "win" the negotiation. This might either be conducted in an offensive way as in criticizing the negotiation partner or in a more defensive way such as referring to prior commitments.

This categorization originates from [26], who relate these categories to cultural differences in decision conferencing. They state that the higher a culture scores on Hofstede's hierarchy dimension, the higher the probability for choosing an avoidance strategy gets. The position on the uncertainty avoidance dimension also influences the style of a negotiation. The higher the value on this dimension gets the more emotion and aggression is to be expected in a negotiation as well as more interpersonal conflict. Thus, the urge to find a solution is very strong and with it the probability for an integrative strategy increases and the probability for an avoidance strategy decreases. But as in cultures that score low on this dimension everyone's opinion is taken into account, here too the integrative strategy is the most probable. The identity dimension suggests that people from individualistic cultures tend to stand behind their attitudes. As a consequence, for them the task itself, i.e. the negotiation, is always in the main focus of the conversation. For people from collectivistic cultures, harmony is more important and thus less interpersonal conflict arises in a negotiation. The same holds true for the gender dimension, where the probability for interpersonal conflict increases with increasing masculinity.

An alternative differentiation of negotiation styles is introduced by [36] focusing on how an argument is created:

- Authority: Referring to a well known person that holds the same view.
- Norms and laws: Claiming that one is stating a generally accepted norm.
- Facts: The argument is based on objective and provable facts.
- Experience: Claiming own experience to exemplify the point.
- Analogies: Putting things in perspective by comparisons.
- Logic: Drawing conclusions from a chain of logical arguments.

Still another categorization takes the communicative functions into account that can be observed during a negotiation [6]:

- Task: The conversation partners are busy with solving the task (negotiating with each other)
- Task-management: The conversation partners talk about the task (the negotiation or situation itself)
- Communication-management: The conversation partners aim at maintaining the conversation, focusing on contact, perception, and understanding.
- Other level: Here all other possible parts of a negotiation are summarized, such as small talk or jokes.

The frequency of these functions and their distribution in an actual negotiation depends on the cultural background of the interlocutors. For instance, acknowledging understanding (communication management) is more likely to occur in collectivistic cultures like the Japanese [31]. As Western cultures are on the individualistic and masculine sides of Hofstede's dimensions they are expected to take an aggressive approach to reach a solution exhibiting a structured and analytical approach in their negotiation [30]. This is supported by the fact that western cultures are short term cultures, which suggests that they tend to solve problems quickly and in a sequential manner focusing mainly on the task itself. Eastern cultures on the other hand are found on the collectivistic and long-term sides of the dimension resulting in a slower and more exhaustive way of problem solving where every opinion is taken into account and harmony is at stake resulting in an increased frequency of the communication management and other related contributions.

The negotiation scenario is a variant of the standard lost at sea scenario [37]. Subjects have to assume that they are shipwrecked in the Pacific Ocean. They have only time to take three items with them that could help them in surviving. On the boat there are fifteen items and thus they have to choose among those fifteen. Every subject has to choose his top three items from this list of fifteen and then they had to negotiate to come up with a single three item list ranked in order of importance for surviving. This is afterwards compared with the "official" list by the U.S. Coast Guard (see below). This scenario has the advantage of forcing the subjects to come to a consensus about the relevant items and as their monetary award depends on how close they come to the official list they have an intrinsic motivation to argue for their choices.

3.3 Scenario 3: Status Difference

The different positions of the German and the Japanese culture on Hofstede's hierarchy dimension lead to some obvious differences in behavior. The hierarchy dimension describes how cultures deal with differences in power among the members of the culture. Cultures with high power distance accept this difference as a natural phenomenon, accepting decisions by persons with higher power. In cultures with low power distance, power is often only given temporarily and does not constitute a merit in itself. Thus, decisions tend to be challenged regardless of the actual position of the interlocutors.

For the task of planning video recordings of such interactions, it becomes very relevant how status is created in the experimental condition. A literature review revealed that it is quite difficult to create a natural situation with status differences and that most studies rely on a task-oriented design, where the status of the interlocutors is ascribed by their roles in a role-play (e.g. one subject is teacher, the other is student). The difficulties start even earlier with defining what is meant by status. Berger and colleagues [3] distinguish between diffuse and (task-)specific status, where diffuse status denotes characteristics that are not relevant to the task at hand, e.g. gender, race, age, occupation or education, and (task-)specific status denotes characteristics and abilities that are relevant to solving the task at hand, for instance mechanical skills to solve a problem with a car. A similar suggestion is made by Trompenaars and Hampden-Turner [34], who distinguish between ascribed and achieved status. Ascribed status summarizes characteristics that describe what a person is, e.g. age, gender, social connections, education, or profession and thus correspond to the diffuse status by Berger and colleagues. Achieved status on the other hand is constituted by characteristics that describe what a person does, e.g. a person's track record and correspond to the specific status as one's track record can only establish a higher status if it is relevant to the task at hand.

The next challenge to be solved is how to assign status to the participants of the video recordings. Different suggestions have been made to deal with this problem. Hall and Friedman [14] choose subjects among members of the same company, thus ensuring that a natural status difference is in place. On the other hand, this didn't allow for controlling how status is created and thus it became difficult to pinpoint behavior differences to specific aspects of status. Others have deliberately created status differences in experimental situations. Leffler and colleagues [22] assigned different roles to their subjects like teacher and student and observed how interaction changed due to this role assignment. The problem here is that students had to act like teachers without being ones. This means that they acted the stereotypes they know about teachers and it cannot be claimed that the result resembles an actual teacher student interaction. Knoterus and Greenstein [20] create status difference by seemingly objective manners. For instance, two subjects had to take an IQ test before an intelligence-based experiment. Task-specific status was faked by telling each subject that they scored average while the other scored extremely high or extremely low. Ungar [35] suggests to concentrate on diffuse status by relying on superficial features like clothes. In his studies he observed how subjects interacted with confederates, whose status was faked by clothing, for instance suit, tie, topcoat vs. overall and construction helmet.

For the corpus study we were interested in how subjects interact with interlocutors of seemingly higher status. We focused on diffuse status to establish this difference by exploiting the cover story of the study. Subjects were recruited by flyers telling them that a large consulting company for the automobile industry is conducting a study on negotiation styles in different countries. Thus, there was a representative from this consulting company present as the main leader of the experiment and he was the one doing the debriefing session after subjects had finished their negotiation task. The representative was of course dressed accordingly, he was equipped with some articles bearing the logo of the consulting company, and he had the "official" list from the U.S. coast guard to match the subject's result against. Although such a list does exist, it is modified dynamically according to the result of the negotiation process in order to create the following specific situations:

1. Positive: The first answer of the subjects is rated as being among the top three items and indeed ranked as the number one item ensuring the subject 10 Euro.
2. Neutral: The second answer of the subject is rated as being among the top three items but not ranked as the second important item. Thus, the monetary reward only increased by 5 Euro.
3. Negative: The third answer of the subject is rated as completely wrong resulting in no additional monetary reward.

For the third scenario we expected different behaviors between the two cultures as well as between this scenario and the preceding two in the same culture. Leffler and colleagues [22] describe three different categories of status dependent nonverbal behavior:

- Proxemics: High status individuals take more space and are less invaded by others.
- Vocalic: High status individuals talk more, longer, and louder (see also [5]), interrupt more frequently and successfully, and laugh less frequently.
- Symbolically intrusive: High status individuals may point at others, direct them or shut them up with a gesture.

Ellyson and colleagues [8] add that high status individuals have a higher visual dominance ratio, i.e. they look at others more when speaking than listening. Johnson [17] observed that low status individuals use more verbal facilitators like "yeah" or "mhmm".

These findings suggest that our subjects will stand further away from the interlocutor in the third scenario than in the other two scenarios, that the subjects might talk in a softer voice, and that the subjects will interrupt the interlocutor less frequently in the third scenario. Moreover, we expect differences between the cultures based on their position on the hierarchy dimension. The Japanese subjects are expected to accept the statements of the high status interlocutor more readily than the German subjects that are expected to question the "official" answer or at least to demand an explanation for the "official" ranking.

4   Definition of a Common Protocol

To ensure the replication of conditions in all cultures, a common protocol has to be established on how to conduct the study with detailed instructions to be followed at every step. These instructions have to cover recruiting of subjects and actors, the timeline of each recording, scripts for the people conducting the experiment as well as detailed information about the necessary materials and the setup of the equipment. The CUBE-G protocol is detailed here as an example of such a protocol. Another necessary prerequisite is a common language for the researcher, which is English in the case of CUBE-G.

4.1   Recruiting

To recruit subjects, a believable cover story had to be manufactured that produces plausible answers for what is going on during the recordings. A flyer was produced stating that a large consulting company for the automobile industry is conducting a study simultaneously in different countries and that Augsburg (Kyoto) has been chosen as one of the locations in Germany (Japan). The objective of the study was to investigate negotiation styles in the participating countries. A monetary award was promised, the amount of this award depending on the outcome of the negotiation process. This was to ensure that subjects had an intrinsic motivation in the negotiation. The negotiation partner of each subject is played by an actor to ensure comparable conditions for each subject (see Section 5 for more details). The first meeting was introduced as a prerequisite to the negotiation process, ensuring a minimal acquaintance of the interlocutors, the high status scenario was introduced as the debriefing from the negotiation process with the representative of the consulting company, which was also played by an actor.

4.2   Timeline

To illustrate the timeline, the study was piloted several times in detail and an audiovisual protocol of this pilot was created. It turned out that this material is well suited to serve as a kind of "storyboard" illustrating the general timeline of the study. Figure 1 gives an impression of such a "storyboard". The subject is welcomed and asked to fill out the personality questionnaire as well as some additional information concerning data protection issues before it is let to the recording room. There the actor playing the second subject is already waiting. The subject is welcomed again this time by the representative of the consulting company and another lab person, who also introduces the goal of the study. Together with the actor playing the second student the subject is led to the recording area where they have time to get acquainted for the actual experiment. After five minutes, another lab person disrupts the conversation and leads the two subjects back to their tables where they have time to read the experimental instructions and prepare the negotiation task. After ten minutes, subjects are led back to the recording area, where they start negotiating. Discussions continue until they reach a consensus (10 to 15 minutes). Then the actor playing the role of the second subject is led out of the room to allow for separate debriefings. The representative of the consulting company enters the recording area with the "official" list and the subject has to report and defend their choices.

Fig. 1. "Storyboard" to illustrate the timeline of the study

Fig. 2. Snapshots from application with virtual characters

As can be seen in Figure 1, subjects and actors are recorded standing. Although sitting at a table would seem to be a more natural setting for the task, this would prevent us from eliciting most of the non-verbal behaviors we are interested in like proxemics, gestures and postures. Additionally, the envisioned application will take place in a virtual meeting place where groups of agents and users stand together and interact (see Figure 2). Thus, doing the recordings as shown in Figure 1 increases the application scenario match significantly.

4.3   Instructions

Along with the information about the timeline of the experiment, detailed instructions are necessary for each participant in the study. In the case of the CUBE-G project, these are two lab people welcoming the subject and introducing the task to the subjects, and two actors, one acting as another student and one acting as the principal investigator, i.e. the representative from the consulting company.

Lab people. To ensure the same conditions and especially the same amount of information for every subject, it is important to define in detail what is said and done by the people running the study. The welcoming people are only allowed to recite the cover story and to instruct subjects about the personality test and the data protection issues (formal protocol that has to be approved by the local data protection officer). The lab people in the recording room need a standardized text for a short introduction based on the cover story and detailed experimental instructions in written form for the subjects. They are entitled to answer questions that might arise concerning the mechanics of the study but otherwise have to stick to the cover story.

Actors. Instructions for the actors differ depending on their roles. The student actor is supposed to assume a passive role letting the subject lead the discussion and only take the initiative when this strategy fails. For the first meeting, the actor can rely on his own background story for everything that does not concern his university life. For this part of his biography he is supplied with a cover story that ensures that he does not study the same subject as the participant to prevent detailed discussion about specific courses or teachers, which might easily blow the cover. For the negotiation scenario, the actor has to ensure that at the beginning he agrees only on one item with the subject, ensuring that they have to discuss at least four items. For the discussion, actors have been supplied with pro and contra arguments for each item to ensure that they (i) have enough arguments and (ii) that every subject has to face the same arguments for a given object on the list.

The high status actor acts as the representative of the consulting company from the back story. He follows a more constrained script to induce certain affective states in the subjects in order to analyze the potential differences in reacting to these situations. The first item from the subject's list has to be the top item of the "official" list ensuring a high monetary award and thus inducing a positive state in the subject. The second item had to be the third on the list, thus being just not right and ensuring less money. The third item had to be completely wrong, resulting in no money for this item and thus inducing a negative state in the subject. The hypothesis is that German subjects start to question the "official" list more often than the Japanese subjects.

4.4   Material and Technical Setup

Apart from the above mentioned instructions, material for the study includes personality questionnaires in German and Japanese and additional instructions for filling out the questionnaires in German and Japanese (see Section 5). Instructions for the subjects include detailed information for the negotiation task, i.e. the variation of the lost at sea scenario, and an informed consent concerning the data protection issues. How this issue is dealt with depends on local regulations in the countries that participate in the study. For the technical setup, materials include schematic figures on the configuration of the cameras, microphones, and other equipment, which is accompanied by audio-visual material from the piloting sessions from which the "storyboards" described above have been extracted. Most of the material has to be translated into the target language of the study (here German and Japanese).

Apart from the material presented, the recording sessions for the CUBE-G project were followed in each country by a representative from the organizing team to ensure that conditions match each other as close as possible.

5   Phenomena Occurrences

This challenge is not specific for capturing cultural-specific behavior but is of a more general kind. It concerns the decision which phenomena will be analyzed and how it can be ensured that enough occurrences of these phenomena are elicited during the recordings. In CUBE-G, we decided to make use of actors as interaction partners for our subjects based on two considerations. First, we wanted to make sure that all subjects are confronted with the same conditions. By using actors, we were able to create scripts for each scenario that defined (sometimes strictly, sometimes loosely) how the interaction should take place. The second reason was to ensure that enough material is elicited. Our fear was that subjects would agree very soon on three items during the negotiation to get done with it. Using actors we could ensure that subjects really had to argue to make their point.

The next challenge concerns the question how the material is processed for the analysis. Multimodal corpora have been in the center of research in computer science for over a decade now. Thus, a large amount of annotation schemes have been proposed to cover the analysis of such data on which one can draw. Additionally, standards have been introduced for evaluating the validity of a scheme (e.g. [21]). The CUBE-G corpus allows for analyzing verbal as well as nonverbal behavior. Currently, the analysis is focusing on nonverbal behavior employing the following annotation schemes:

- Verbal channel: Currently, the dialogue is transcribed in the language of the interlocutors and an English translation of this transcript is provided.
- Gesture channel: Gestures are analyzed on two different levels of granularity. Following a well-established coding scheme by McNeill [24], the type of gestures is analyzed focusing on conversational gestures and distinguishing between emblematic, deictic, iconic, and metaphoric gestures. Additionally, it is analyzed how a gesture is performed relying on features of expressivity that have been described by Efron [7] (for examining cultural differences) as well as Gallaher [10] (for examining differences in personal style) and taking aspects like the spatial extent of a gesture and its speed into account.
- Posture channel: Postures are annotated based on Bull's suggestions [4], who defined coding schemes for head, trunk, arm, and leg movements.
- Proxemics channel: This channel describes the overall spatial behavior of the interlocutors. Coding of this channel follows Hall's [13] definition of spatial areas that trigger different behavioral routines, distinguishing between intimate, personal, social, and public spaces.
- Speech volume: As is evident from Table 1, volume depends on a culture's position on Hofstede's dimensions and is coded here in terms of three values (low, med, high). Preliminary observations showed that volume of speech seem to be gender related as well.

An in-depth description of the annotation schemes for gestures and postures as well as some results from the corpus study can be found in [28]. As we expect culture-specific differences in the observed behavior, we also have to assume culture-specific differences in the analysis of this behavior. For instance, if it is typical in a given culture to use a lot of space to perform gestures, then this might be regarded as the baseline against which the observed behavior is matched. Thus, what is interpreted as a large gesture in Germany might just be medium in Italy. This is one of the main reasons why for instance Northern Europeans are perceived as cold and distant by Southern Europeans. Consequently, standardized instructions for the analysis of the data are necessary, defining in detail what constitutes for instance high, medium, and low spatial extent in general to avoid culture-specific interpretations.

6 Separating Culture from Other Behavior Determinants

Although definitions of culture state that norms and values lie at the bottom of heuristics of behavior and interpretation of behavior (see Section 2), it is not obvious if a specific behavior that is observed in an interaction is determined or at least influenced by the interlocutor's cultural background or has quite different origins, for instance rooting in the interlocutor's personality. Other influencing factors can be the interlocutor's gender, his age or even his current emotional and motivational state. For instance, it might be the case that mixed-gender pairs show different interaction patterns than same-gender pairs, and that male pairs again show differences compared to female pairs. In the CUBE-G corpus, we observed for instance that female Japanese subjects spoke in a quieter voice when interacting with males compared to their interactions with females.

Preparing for the video recordings in the CUBE-G project, we decided to control for gender and personality effects and to keep other factors like age and educational background as constant as possible by recruiting students of a specific age group at the universities in Augsburg and Kyoto.

6.1 Controlling for Gender

To control for gender, we took all possible pairings into account for the video recordings. For combinations of more than two interlocutors, this control mechanism soon becomes unfeasible due to the number of combinations that have to be considered. One of the interaction partners in each scenario was an actor (see previous section) following a script for the specific situation. After having met the actor for the first time, subjects negotiate with the same actor. Afterwards they interact with a person of seemingly higher status who is played by a different actor. Table 2 summarizes the design of the recordings. To control for gender effects, a male and a female actor were employed in each scenario interacting with the same number of male and female subjects. Actors in scenarios (i) and (ii) played the other students, whereas the actors in scenario (iii) played

Table 2. Design of the corpus study to control for gender effects

First Meeting		Negotiation		Status Difference	
Actor	Subjects	Actor	Subjects	Actor	Subjects
M_{A1}	M_{S1}–M_{S5}	M_{A1}	M_{S1}–M_{S5}	M_{A2}	M_{S1}–M_{S5}
	F_{S1}–F_{S5}		F_{S1}–F_{S5}		F_{S1}–F_{S5}
F_{A1}	M_{S6}–M_{S10}	F_{A1}	M_{S6}–M_{S10}	F_{A2}	M_{S6}–M_{S10}
	F_{S6}–F_{S10}		F_{S6}–F_{S10}		F_{S6}–F_{S10}

the roles of representatives of the consulting company that conducted the study. Thus, apart from the two male (M_{A1}, M_{A2}) and two female actors (F_{A1}, F_{A2}), ten male (M_{S1}-M_{S10}) and ten female subjects (F_{S1}-F_{S10}) were needed for this corpus study.

Due to some over recruiting we recorded 21 pairs in Germany and 26 pairs in Japan. The recordings took place over four days in each country, where the first day was used for rehearsals with the actors.

6.2   Controlling for Personality

The main focus in CUBE-G is on culture-specific differences in nonverbal behavior. In Section 3 it was detailed what kind of differences can be expected deriving from different cultural backgrounds. For instance, gestural expressivity is often linked to cultural variables. For instance, Southern Europeans tend to use gestures more frequently than Northern Europeans [31], and Italian immigrants to the US show more expansive gestures than Jewish immigrants [7]. Others have shown that similar effects can be seen when the focus is laid on personality instead of culture. Gallaher describes gestural expressivity as a function of personal style and links it to different personality traits. Thus, the extensive gesture use of an interlocutor is not necessarily attributable to his Southern European origin; instead it could just be a trait of his extrovert personality. As a consequence, it seems inevitable to control for personality when investigating cultural differences in nonverbal behavior.

The best strategy would be to test subjects beforehand and design the experiment in order to capture all combinations of personality traits x gender. This is just not possible due to the large amount of material that would be produced and that would just not be possible to analyze. Thus, we opted for an a posteriori solution. All subjects had to take part in a personality assessment, which allows us to take the subjects' personality into account for the later analysis and perhaps even get indications on correlations between personality profiles and cultural dimensions. It is a question of some dispute if such correlations exist. Triandis and Suh [33] for instance review work on cultural influences on personality and culture and give an excellent overview of their interrelations. Thus, in the long run, an integrated model is needed that combines cultural variables and other influence factors. Nazir and colleagues [25] e.g. propose a first model that relates culture and personality in a cognitive architecture. A number of standardized tests exist for which it has been shown that they are applicable in different cultures. We chose the NEO-FFI assessment, which defines personality as a five dimensional space. It has been shown to work well in different cultures [23].

7   Technical Requirements

To produce comparable data sets it is indispensable to define technical requirements for the video recording sessions. This includes the specifications for the recording equipment as well as the layout of the recording area to be able to reproduce the recording conditions. Both aspects are determined by the phenomena that are captured. For instance, if the focus is on the automatic analysis of facial expressions, it becomes necessary to capture the subject's face with the camera face-to-face with the subject. As the camera itself can have an influence on the subject's behavior, such a setting might prove too obtrusive to capture the relevant phenomena. Thus, the dilemma has to be solved to provide a situation that is as natural as possible while still allowing capturing the relevant phenomena. Another decision concerns the recording area itself. In CUBE-G, we opted for a neutral room that does not provide any distractions from the task. To be able to establish similar conditions in both countries, the specification for the recording area as well as for the technical equipment has to provide a high level of detail.

7.1 Specifying the Recording Area

The room was designed in order to focus subjects on the task at hand, i.e. interacting with the interlocutor, providing as little contextual cues as possible that could attract the attention of the participants. Additionally, the actual recording equipment was integrated in such a way that it remained as far in the background as possible. Figures 3 gives an impression of the recording rooms in Germany and Japan. The most obvious piece of equipment in each case is the microphone that had to be placed in a prominent place to capture the audio information. An alternative would have been to use headsets but it was decided that the use of headsets would have been even more obtrusive than placing the microphone in the recording area. The area itself was around 3 x 5m with a single entrance that allowed for controlling the location of the subject relative to the actor by leading the subject into the room first, which resulted naturally in the subject choosing the position opposite of the entrance. Additionally, in the third scenario, it was a natural move to lead the actor subject out of the recording area because his location was near the entrance, allowing us starting the debriefing session with the actual subject.

7.2 Specifying the Technical Equipment

Figure 3 gives an impression of the technical equipment that was used. Two video cameras capture the actions by the actor and the subject, one focusing on the actor, the second one focusing on the subject. A webcam was installed on the floor outside the recording area that captured the feet of the interlocutors allowing for analyzing the proxemics behavior. Audio was captured by an external microphone that was connected to the camera capturing the subject. Because our focus was primarily on the subject's behavior, we refrained from synchronizing the cameras. Although layout and equipment had been tightly specified, it turned out that some uncontrollable effects made it necessary to adjust this setting on the fly. Some of the Japanese subjects sat down on the floor for the interaction. In hindsight this is not a surprising effect but neither

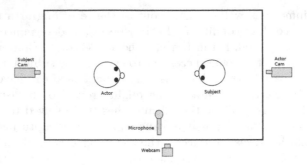

Fig. 3. Layout of the recording area

the Western nor the Japanese researchers took this as an option into account. Thus, the camera positions had to be adjusted during the recordings in two cases. Additionally, the placing of the microphone was also tailored to standing interactions, resulting in bad audio quality for these pairs.

8   Conclusion

The work presented in this article is part of a larger research endeavor that aims at enculturating interactive systems acknowledging the fact that the user's cultural profile provides heuristics of behavior and interpretation that influence his interactions. Non-verbal behavior, which was the focus in this article, is only one aspect of this endeavor. Other aspects include verbal behaviors like small talk, emotional facial displays, cognitive abilities like the appraisal of incoming data, or the appearance of the agent. Research in this area is in its infancy and one of the current challenges is to determine the importance of the different factors on the interaction. Complexity arises from the ill-defined nature of the domain which makes it difficult to reliably specify the links between cultural profiles and behavior traits. In this article, we gave an introduction into the specific challenges that arise by recording multimodal corpora in different cultures in order to capture behavior patterns that are attributable to the cultural background of the interlocutors with the aim of explicating some of these links. These challenges include the decision for appropriate scenarios, the establishment of common protocols for the recordings, the elicitation of relevant behavior, the identification of influencing variables, and the technical requirements for the actual recordings. Solutions to these challenges have been proposed by examples from the CUBE-G project, which aims at modeling culture-specific behaviors for Embodied Conversational Agents.

Following the suggestions given in this chapter produces a large amount of data that has to be analyzed. So far, purely statistical analyses have been conducted on the annotations of posture and gestural expressivity data. The results reveal significant differences between German and Japanese samples in preferred hand and arm postures, in most of the dimensions for gestural expressivity as well as in communication management and small talk behavior. Details of the analyses can be found in [28] and [9]. As has been noted earlier, it can be expected that such a purely statistical analysis does only reveal some general trends and that the semantics of the dimensions and the interaction context have to be taken into account. For this purpose, it is indespensable to take the semantics of Hofstede's dimensions into account. To this end, we controlled for gender effects and status differences in order to be able to compare differences in behavior and link these differences to Hofstede's dimension like gender or hierarchy.

The question has been raised if the use of students is a valid approach for capturing relevant data of culture-specific interactions as they represent at best a subgroup of the culture. Relying on Hofstede's theory of culture, we define culture as national culture and from this perspective the German students can be expected to adhere in general to the cultural heuristics for the German national culture and the Japanese students to the heuristics for the Japanese national culture. Thus, the question is more fundamental in asking if the cultural theory of Hofstede is a good choice. The undeniable advantage of Hofstede's approach (and similar ones like Hall [12] or Schwartz and Sagiv [29]) is the very clear level of abstraction, i.e. national cultures. A popular counter argument runs like this: National cultures are all very well but our systems do not deal with THE German user but with a bank accountant from Berlin or a farmer from the heart of Bavaria. We would like to draw an analogy here to the treatment of different languages in HCI. Although there is without question a difference in how the Bavarian farmer and the bank accountant from Berlin speak, localizing a system for the German market nevertheless assumes something like a standard German language, which is as fictional as the standard German culture. Nevertheless, this abstraction works very well for the time being. Thus, it remains to be shown if a system that equally idealizes cultural heuristics on a national level does not have its merits in serving as a starting point for enculturating interactive systems.

The CUBE-G corpus presents a rich resource of cross cultural data. By and by, starting with the end of 2009, chunks of the corpus will be made available to the research community. For up-to-date information and condition please check the project website[2].

Acknowledgements

The work described in this article is funded by the German Research Foundation (DFG) under research grant RE 2619/2-1 (CUBE-G) and the Japan Society for the Promotion of Science (JSPS) under a Grant-in-Aid for Scientific Research (C) (19500104).

References

1. Argyle, M.: Bodily Communication. Methuen & Co. Ltd., London (1975)
2. Bennett, M.J.: A developmental approach to training for intercultural sensitivity. International Journal for Intercultural Relations 10(2), 179–195 (1986)

---

[2] http://mm-werkstatt.informatik.uni-augsburg.de/projects/cube-g/

3. Berger, J., Fisek, M.H., Norman, R.Z., Zelditch Jr., M.: Status Characteristics and Social Interaction: An Expectation-States Approach. Elsevier, Amsterdam (1977)
4. Bull, P.E.: Posture and Gesture. Pergamon Press, Oxford (1987)
5. Burgoon, J.K., Buller, D.B., Woodall, W.G.: Nonverbal Communication: The Unspoken Dialogue. Harper and Row, New York (1989)
6. Core, M., Allen, J.: Coding Dialogs with the DAMSL Annotation Scheme. In: Proceedings of the AAAI Fall Symposium on Communicative Action in Humans and Machines, Boston, MA (1997)
7. Efron, D.: Gesture, Race and Culture. Mouton and Co., Netherlands (1972)
8. Ellyson, S.L., Dovidio, J.F., Fehr, B.J.: Visual behavior and dominance in women and men. In: Mayo, C., Henely, N.M. (eds.) Gender and nonverbal behavior. Springer, Heidelberg (1981)
9. Endrass, B., Rehm, M., André, E.: Culture-specific communication management for virtual agents. In: Proceedings of AAMAS (2009)
10. Gallaher, P.E.: Individual Differences in Nonverbal Behavior: Dimensions of Style. Journal of Personality and Social Psychology 63(1), 133–145 (1992)
11. Greenbaum, P.E., Rosenfeld, H.M.: Varieties of touching in greeting: Sequential structure and sex-related differences. Journal of Nonverbal Behavior 5, 13–25 (1980)
12. Hall, E.T.: The Silent Language. Doubleday (1959)
13. Hall, E.T.: The Hidden Dimension. Doubleday (1966)
14. Hall, J.A., Friedman, G.B.: Status, gender, and nonverbal behavior: A study of structured interactions between employees of a company. Personality and Social Psychology Bulletin 25(9), 1082–1091 (1999)
15. Hofstede, G.: Cultures Consequences: Comparing Values, Behaviors, Institutions, and Organizations Across Nations. Sage Publications, Thousand Oaks (2001)
16. Hofstede, G.J., Pedersen, P.B., Hofstede, G.: Exploring Culture: Exercises, Stories, and Synthetic Cultures. Intercultural Press, Yarmouth (2002)
17. Johnson, C.: Gender, legitimate authority, and leader-subordinate conversations. American Sociological Review 59, 122–135 (1994)
18. Kendon, A.: Conducting Interaction: Patterns of Behavior in Focused Encounters. Cambridge Univ. Press, Cambridge (1991)
19. Knapp, M.L., Vangelisti, A.L.: Interpersonal Communication and Human Relationships. Pearson Education, Inc., Boston (1984)
20. Knoterus, J.D., Greenstein, T.N.: Status and performance characteristics in social interaction: A theory of status validation. Social Psychology Quarterly 44(4), 338–349 (1981)
21. Knudsen, M.W., Martin, J.-C., Dybkjær, L., Ayuso, M.J.M., Bernsen, N.O., Carletta, J., Heid, U., Kita, S., Llisterri, J., Pelachaud, C., Poggi, I., Reithinger, N., van Elswijk, G., Wittenburg, P.: ISLE Natural Interactivity and Multimodality Working Group Deliverable D9.1: Survey of Multimodal Coding Schemes and Best Practice (2002), http://isle.nis.sdu.dk/reports/wp9/D9.1-7.3.2002-F.pdf (07.02.07)
22. Leffler, A., Gillespie, D.L., Conaty, J.C.: The effects of status differentiation on nonverbal behavior. Social Psychology Quarterly 45(3), 153–161 (1982)
23. McCrae, R.R., Allik, J. (eds.): The Five-Factor Model of Personality Across Cultures. Kluwer Academics, Dordrecht (2002)
24. McNeill, D.: Hand and Mind — What Gestures Reveal about Thought. The University of Chicago Press, Chicago (1992)

25. Nazir, A., Lim, M.Y., Kriegel, M., Aylett, R., Cawsey, A., Enz, S., Zoll, C.: Culture-personality based affective model. In: Proceedings of the IUI workshop on Enculturating Conversational Interfaces, Gran Canaria (2008)
26. Quaddus, M.A., Tung, L.L.: Explaining cultural differences in decision conferencing. Communications of the ACM 45, 93–98 (2002)
27. Rehm, M., Nakano, Y., André, E., Nishida, T.: Culture-specific first meeting encounters between virtual agents. In: Prendinger, H., Lester, J.C., Ishizuka, M., et al. (eds.) IVA 2008. LNCS (LNAI), vol. 5208, pp. 223–236. Springer, Heidelberg (2008)
28. Rehm, M., Nakano, Y., André, E., Nishida, T., Bee, N., Endrass, B., Huang, H.-H., Lipi, A.A., Wissner, M.: From Observation to Simulation — Generating Culture Specific Behavior for Interactive Systems. In: AI & Society (in press)
29. Schwartz, S.H., Sagiv, L.: Identifying culture-specifics in the content and structure of values. Journal of Cross-Cultural Psychology 26(1), 92–116 (1995)
30. Teng, J.T.C., Calhoun, K.J., Cheon, M.J., Raeburn, S., Wong, W.: Is the east really different from the west: a cross-cultural study on information technology and decision making. In: Proceedings of the 20th international conference on Information Systems, pp. 40–46 (1999)
31. Ting-Toomey, S.: Communicating Across Cultures. The Guilford Press, New York (1999)
32. Traum, D., Swartout, W., Marsella, S., Gratch, J.: Fight, Flight, or Negotiate: Believable Strategies for Conversing Under Crisis. In: Panayiotopoulos, T., Gratch, J., Aylett, R.S., Ballin, D., Olivier, P., Rist, T. (eds.) IVA 2005. LNCS (LNAI), vol. 3661, pp. 52–64. Springer, Heidelberg (2005)
33. Triandis, H.C., Suh, E.M.: Cultural influences on personality. Annual Review of Psychology 53, 133–160 (2002)
34. Trompenaars, F., Hampden-Turner, C.: Riding the Waves of Culture. McGraw-Hill, New York (1998)
35. Ungar, S.: The effects of status and excuse on interpersonal reactions to deviant behavior. Social Psychology Quarterly 44(3), 260–263 (1981)
36. http://www.jobware.de/ra/fue/vhs/41.html (last visited: November 25, 2008)
37. Warwick, T.: Function analysis for team problem solving. In: SAVE Annual Proceedings (1994)

Multimodal Intercultural Information and Communication Technology – A Framework for Designing and Evaluating Multimodal Intercultural Communicators

Jens Allwood and Elisabeth Ahlsén

SSKKII Interdisciplinary Center, University of Gothenburg

Abstract. The paper presents a framework, combined with a checklist for designing and evaluating multimodal, intercultural ICT, especially when embodied artificial communicators are used as front ends for data bases, as digital assistants, as tutors in pedagogical programs or players in games etc. Such a framework is of increasing interest, since the use of ICT across cultural boundaries in combination with the use of ICT by persons with low literacy skills is rapidly increasing. This development presents new challenges for intercultural ICT. A desideratum for interculturally sensitive artificial communicators is a generic, exportable system for interactive communication with a number of parameters that can be set to capture intercultural variation in communication. This means a system for a Generic, Multimodal, Intercultural Communicator (a GMIC).

Keywords: multimodal ICT, intercultural ICT, virtual communicator, ECA (embodied communicative agent).

1 Purpose

This paper presents a framework, combined with a checklist, for designing and evaluating multimodal intercultural ICT (MMIICT). After motivating the study of MMIICT and defining the concept, the paper focuses on how a GMIC can be designed and/or evaluated with respect to adaptation to variation in activity and culture, using the checklist. Finally, an illustrating example of an evaluation of a web based embodied communicative agent (ECA) used in many countries is given.

2 Why Multimodal Intercultural ICT is an Area of Increasing Importance

The use of ICT to support communication and information transfer across national, ethnic, cultural boundaries is becoming more and more common. Intercultural ICT, in this sense, can be present in intercultural use of e-mail, chat, digital news broadcasts,

M. Kipp et al. (Eds.): Multimodal Corpora, LNAI 5509, pp. 160–175, 2009.

blogs, games, intercultural education and multimodal websites. Especially interesting here is the use of multimodal agents, avatars and robots to communicate and give information across cultural boundaries. The use of such devices as front ends of data bases, in games and chat fora (Life World etc) is quickly increasing.

It is likely that this use will increase even more as people with low literacy skills become users of ICT, since this will be the most natural way for them to communicate. In this situation, it will become more and more interesting to have avatars and other ECA:s who possess natural (human like) communication skills. This development points to an increased need for ECA:s that can be adapted for use in different cultures and different activities of these cultures.

3 Definition of Multimodal Intercultural ICT

By "Multimodal Intercultural ICT", we mean ICT which employs a multimodal GUI. Such a GUI uses two or more of the visual, auditory, tactile, olfactory and gustatory sensory modalities. It also uses two or more of the Peircean modes of representation (index, icon and symbol) [1]. Our focus will be on dynamic, interactive ICT employing avatars or other artificial communicators, across national, ethnic, cultural boundaries. We characterize an "avatar" as a VR representation of a user and an "artificial communicator" as any communicative agent with a multimodal or multirepresentational front end (cf. above). An avatar will in this way be a special case of an "artificial communicator" or "embodied communicative agent" (ECA).

4 Activity Dependence of ICT

Both in design and evaluation, it is important to relate ICT to the social activity it is supposed to be a part of. Thus, there are different activity requirements if we compare an "artificial communicator" that has been constructed as a front end to a data base (e.g. for a multinational company to present its products), as a personal digital assistant, as a friendly tutor teaching small children to read and write or as an avatar which is to represent a player in a game like War Craft.

Everywhere the social activity, with its purpose, its typical roles, its typical instruments, aids, procedures and environment, determines what are useful characteristics of the "artificial communicator". Both in designing a specification and in designing an evaluation schema, it is therefore important to build in systematic ways of taking activity dependence into account [2].

5 Generic Applicability and Multimodal Robustness

A second desideratum for interculturally sensitive artificial communicators is to base them on a generic system for interactive communication with a number of parameters that can be set to capture intercultural variation in communication. For interesting suggestions in this direction, see [3], [4]. Kenny et al. [3] focus on Virtual Humans used for training leadership, negotiation, cultural awareness and interviewing skills. Their goal is to create engaging characters that convey the three main characteristics of being *believable* (giving the illusion of human-like behavior), *responsive* (to the human user and the surrounding events, by having a rich inner dynamic) and *interpretable* (using the same "verbal and nonverbal cues that people use to understand one another"). They also distinguish three layers in a Virtual Human Agent: *the cognitive layer*, which "makes decisions, based on input, goals and desired behavior", *the virtual human layer*, or body, including input processing (e.g. vision, speech, smell) and output processing (verbal speech, body gestures and actions) and *the simulation layer* (environment). Further, Kenny et al. point to the role of emotions in recognition and expression. This is also stressed by Kopp et al. [5].

A model presented by Jan et al. [4] provides parameters for different cultures (North American English, Mexican Spanish and Arabic) for a chosen subset of conversational behavior: *proxemics*, *gaze* and *overlap in turn taking*. Their scenario is also Virtual Humans in environments used mainly for training intercultural communication. They advocate a modular design where functional elements can be mapped to culture-specific surface behaviors. This has been done, for example, in the ECA GRETA [6].

There are not very many studies of the effects of cultural variation in avatars. Koda studied Japanese designed avatars in different Asian countries in and, in a follow-up study, western designed avatars also in North and South America. He found that there are cultural differences in how facial expressions are interpreted and that gestures could interfere with the interpretation of facial expressions [7], [8]. Koda and coworkers found a wide variation in the interpretation of positive expressions, whereas negative expressions were recognized more accurately [9]. Based on claims about cultural differences in the perception of avatars, Johansen [10] compared avatar perception by American and German users. The hypotheses were that American users, coming from an image dominated culture [11], would be more sensitive to attractiveness in an avatar, while German users would place more importance on credibility [12]. The study was also based on claims by Barber and Barde [13] and Chau et al. [14] about cultural differences in reactions to stimuli, for example, that a global interface has to be localized or designed according the cultural nuances of the target audience in order to be effective. Johnson's results did show that Germans reacted more positively to a credible avatar than Americans, but in general similarities between the two groups were greater than expected. A generic multimodal intercultural communicator (GMIC), thus, has to be flexible and easily adapted to similarities as well as differences between different cultures and different activities.

Constructing a GMIC would mean constructing a generic system that in principle would allow similar contents or functions to be localized in a culturally sensitive manner which often might mean slightly different ways. It is important here to say "similar", since the contents (e.g. news casts) or functions (e.g. giving advice) could themselves be affected by cultural variation [15]. Below, we will provide a suggestion (in the form of a kind of check list) for some of the parameters that could characterize such a system.

A third desideratum for the system is "multimodal robustness" in the sense that the system should be able to handle difficulties in text understanding, difficulties in speech recognition and difficulties in picture/gesture recognition in a sensible way. The system should not halt or respond by "unknown input" or "syntax error" each time routines for recognition or understanding break down. The GMIC should provide routines for how, given a particular activity, such problems can be handled, e.g. by being able to record user contributions, even if they are not recognized or understood and then playing them back to the user as a repetition with question intonation, or by giving minimal feedback through head movements or minimal vocal contributions (which have the function of encouraging the user to continue).

6 Some Intercultural Parameters of a GMIC

Below, we will present a number of features of communication, which exhibit cultural variation. The features are based on earlier work [20],[15], [3], [4].

6.1 Cultural Variation in Expressive Behavior

Some expressive communicative behavior exhibits large scale cultural variation [16]. Besides verbal parameters, a GMIC needs to have parameters for

- head movements (nods, shakes, backward jerks, left turn, right turn, forward movement, backward movement)
- facial gestures (smiles, frowns, wrinkle, mouth movements other than speech)
- eye movements and gaze
- eye brow movements
- posture shifts
- arm and hand movements
- shoulder movements
- intonation in speech
- intensity, pitch and duration in speech

In all of these parameters [17] several fairly well attested (stereotypical) cultural differences exist, e.g. head movements for "yes" vary between typical European-style nodding and the Indian sideways wagging. Similarly, head movements for "no" vary between headshakes and the backward jerk with an eye-brow raise (sometimes called "head toss"), which is common from the Balkans through the Middle East to India [18], [19].

6.2 Cultural Variation in Content and Function

Expressive behavior does not exist for its own sake, but in order to convey content. National, ethnic cultures vary in what expressions, content and functions are seen as allowable and appropriate in different contexts [20]. Should we always smile to strangers? Should women smile to men? Should voices always be subdued and modulated or only when talking to people with higher status? How permissible are white lies? What is worse, a lying system or an insulting system?

Below are some content areas, where studies have shown cultural variation [16].

- Emotions. What emotions are acceptable and appropriate in different activities? E.g. is it permissible for two colleagues at work to quarrel and show aggression or is this something that should be avoided at all costs?
- Attitudes. What attitudes, e.g. regarding politeness and respect, are appropriate? Should titles and formal pronouns, rather than first names and informal pronouns be used?
- Everyday topics. What topics are regarded as neutral and possible to address, even for strangers, e.g. politics, the weather, job, income etc.?
- Common speech acts, e.g. greetings and farewells. Are greetings and farewells always in place or should they be reserved only for some occasions?

6.3 Intercultural Variation in Perception, Understanding and Interpretation

Besides cultural variation in the production of communicative behavior, there is also cultural variation in the perception, understanding and interpretation of such behavior. If a male person A does not know that males of group B think that in a normal conversation it is appropriate to stand 10 cm apart (rather than, say, 30 cm), and sometimes touch, their male interlocutors, he might misinterpret what a member of group B does when he steps closer and now and then touches him (A). For an interesting computational model of proximity in conversation, see [4]. In general, all cultural differences in occurring expressive behavior are sensitive to expectations concerning appropriate contents and functions and can therefore be misinterpreted. Since many of the expectations are emotional habits on a low level of awareness and control, they might in many cases, more or less automatically, affect perception and understanding [21]. Thus, a GMIC also needs to have a set of parameters for expectations (e.g. values) and other factors that influence perception, understanding and interpretation.

6.4 Interactive Features

Besides parameters for expressive behavior, content, function, and interpretation, other parameters need to be set up to cover variation in interactive features between people with differing cultural backgrounds. Such parameters concern

- Turntaking: How do we signal that speaker change is about to occur? Is it ok to overlap with other speakers? Is it OK to interrupt other speakers? When should interruptions occur? How long should the transition time be from one speaker to the next speaker? Is it OK to do nothing or to be silent for a while in a conversation? What should we do to keep a turn? How do we signal that we don't want the turn, but rather want the other speaker to continue? [22], [15].

- Feedback: How do speakers indicate, display and signal to each other that they can/cannot perceive, understand or accept what their interlocutor is communicating [19]. Is this done primarily by auditory means (small words like *mhm, m, yeah* and *no*) or by visual means (head nods, head shakes, posture shifts etc.) [23], [24]? What emotions and attitudes are primarily used? Is very positive feedback preferred or is there a preference for more cautious feedback? [5].
- Sequencing: What opening, continuing and closing communication sequences are preferred in the culture, e.g. What is the preferred way of answering telephone calls in different activities (opening sequence)? What is the preferred way of ending telephone calls (closing sequence)? When and how should you greet friends and unknown persons when you meet them (opening sequence) [17]?
- Spatial configuration: This includes variation in the size of the distance between the speakers and differences in how speakers orient to each other in different settings (e.g. side by side, face-to-face, 90 degrees etc.)

6.5 Social Activity and Other Kinds of Context Dependence

Besides the social activity that the communication is part of, there are other contextual features, that can influence communication, e.g. such features may be connected with the deictic features of a language (in English, e.g. words like *I, you, here, now* or tense endings), which in many languages (but not all) are dependent on features of the immediate speech situation. Other factors that might be influential are beliefs, expectations and values that are relevant for several social activities, e.g. ways of showing or not showing respect for persons of another gender, older people or powerful people.

6.6 Impression Created in an External Observer

Over and above the features of communication introduced above, the behavior of an artificial communicator may also be described according to features introduced by an external evaluator, concerned with establishing whether the behavior of the artificial communicator is believable, responsive and/or interpretable. An evaluation might also be concerned with the quality of what is being simulated, e.g. aspects of cognition, the human body, the environment, emotions, mirroring behavior etc.

6.7 A Set of Parameters for Evaluation and Suggested Functions in an Embodied Communicative Agent

The overview presented above provides us with a number of desirable features in an ECA. They are summarized in table 1 below.

Table 1. Summarizing checklist of communicative features in an ECA

Features	Specification
Activity dependence	goals, roles, artifacts, environment
Generic applicability – parameters for cultural adaptation:	
Expression:	Eye brow movements
	Eye movements
	Arm and hand movements
	Shoulder movements
	Intonation in speech
	Intensity, pitch, duration in speech
Content + function	Emotions
	Attitudes (e.g. politeness)
	Common speech acts
	Everyday topics
Interactive functions	Turn taking
	Feedback
	Sequences
	Spatial configuration
Other types of context dependence	e.g. deixis, beliefs, expectations, values

7   An Example - An Evaluation of an Artificial Communicator Used in Many Cultures – The Case of IKEA's Anna

7.1   Anna in Different Countries

In order to make our discussion more concrete, we will exemplify it by taking a closer look at an artificial communicator used by a multinational company, IKEA, based in Sweden. We are using IKEA's Anna as an example of the variation that currently exists in commercial artificial communicators between different countries/cultures. We will also use it to exemplify how the framework introduced above can be used to discuss what could be modified with respect to audiences with different cultural backgrounds.

Anna is an interface to a database of a furniture company. Her main task is, thus, to present web pages with pictures and prices of different types of furniture, but she also provides information about some other aspects of the company. Anna is a fairly simple application, with a neutral-friendly facial expression, some head and posture movements, eye blinks and a very limited set of facial expressions which can be matched to written messages produced by the user or by Anna herself.

The Swedish and "generic" Anna figure is shown in figure 1.

Fig. 1. Anna (Sweden + "generic")

Whereas Anna's clothes display the nationality of the company (yellow and blue clothes – colors of the Swedish flag) and indicate selling activity through the outfit of an IKEA sales clerk and with a headset, her skin (fair), hair (red) and eye color (blue) seem to be chosen to show a woman who could come from any European country or North America.

An IKEA web page with an artificial communicator exists in the following parts of the world: *Europe:* Belgium, the Czeck Republic, Denmark, Germany, France, Iceland, Italy, Hungary, Netherlands, Norway, Austria, Russia, Poland, Portugal, Switzerland, Slovakia, Finland, Sweden, United Kingdom, *North America:* Canada, United States, *Middle East*: United Arab Emirates/Dubai, *Asia Pacific*: Australia, China, Japan.

The following countries have an IKEA web page without an artificial communicator: Europe: Spain, Greece, Cyprus, Romania, Turkey, *Middle East:* Kuwait, Israel, Saudi Arabia, *Asia Pacific:* Hong Kong, Malaysia, Singapore, Taiwan. (Data from: IKEA web pages Nov. 2008 and Apr. 2009)

A first question might now be whether IKEA in a particular country chooses to have an artificial communicator like Anna or not. Not all countries have an artificial communicator on their web page. Most European countries, Australia and Japan have an Anna agent and Dubai has a similar agent with darker hair.

The choice of *having or not having an artificial communicator* could clearly be culturally influenced, both with respect to whether it is culturally acceptable or good to have an ECA at all, or specifically a female ECA and with respect to her appearance. We can note that most European countries and Australia have the generic Anna figure and it is IKEA's official policy to have the same figure. The generic Anna has an appearance, which is typical many women in most of the countries where she appears (Europe and North America). The question of whether to use *a generic or a culturally adapted ECA*, in terms of appearance, is present for all multinational companies.

A next question might be *what an artificial communicator should look like in different cultural contexts*. Here, we can note that three different female agents can be found on the web pages. The Swedish/generic red haired Anna which is most frequent, a blonde "stereotypically Swedish-looking" Anna, which appears on the German and British web pages (see Figure 2), and a dark haired ECA which appears on the web pages of IKEA in Dubai (see Figure 3).

Fig. 2. Anna in Germany, UK

Fig. 3. ECA in Dubai

The blonde Anna emphasizes that IKEA is a Swedish company and links this to the typical image of a Swedish girl, as a sales promoting strategy. The agent in Dubai is perhaps rather an adaptation to the way a modern business-woman might look in Dubai.

If we turn to *the parameters* mentioned above for the behavior or an artificial communicator, we note that Anna moves her head, blinks, uses facial expressions and moves her lips a little when conveying a message. (We will return to this more in detail below.) Her message, however, appears as written text.

Concerning *activity dependence* and roles, the Swedish/generic and the German/British Anna both have the dress of a salesperson and a headset indicating a phone service. She is, thus, adapted to her activity role. The Dubai Anna, on the other hand has a more neutral or formal look, but this might of course be the way an IKEA employee looks in Dubai. She also does not carry a headset. Her picture is accompanied by the question: "Please ask me where our locations are.", so her activity role is clearly a bit different and more restricted than the role Anna has in other places.

Concerning *generic applicability and parameters that can be varied*, there probably are restrictions on what Anna can look like or if an ECA of this type at all is acceptable or even allowed, due to cultural conventions.

If we turn to her conversation, features of feedback, head movements and facial expressions can potentially be very important. Interestingly, for example, the Swedish and Australian Anna do not give equivalent text answers or facial expressions when they are given corresponding input. See Tables 2 and 3.

Why we find these particular differences is an open question. The facial expressions are chosen among a small number of available alternatives. We can speculate about cultural differences concerning different features of the interaction. Directness would be one variable, where the Swedish Anna goes directly from a short greeting to giving directions about typing in codes etc. The Australian Anna instead gives a longer greeting, possibly indicating a difference in politeness. Both of them

Table 2. Example of interaction with Swedish Anna

Input	Answer	Facial expression
Swedish:		
Hej	Hej hej. Ställ en fråga till mig	Big smile
(*Hi*)	så ska jag hjälpa dig. Om du	
	söker en produkt går det bra att	
	skriva det åttasiffriga	
	artikelnumret så visar jag mer	
	information om produkten.	
	(*Hi, hi. Pose a question to me*	
	and I will help you. If you are	
	looking for a product you can	
	type the eight digit number and	
	I will show more information	
	about the product.)	
Swedish:		
Jag vill köpa en säng	Här hittar du enkelsängar	Brows lowered,
(*I want to buy a bed*)	(*Here you find single beds*)	mouth to side, looks
		doubtful or maybe
		joking
Swedish;		
Nej	Det var tråkigt	Makes face with her
(*No*)	(*That was sad*)	mouth, pulling
		corners of lips down

Table 3. Example of interaction with Australian Anna

Input	Answer	Facial expression
English (Australia):		
Hi	Hello there, nice to meet you!	Big smile
English (Australia):		
I want to buy a bed	Please have a look at the beds	Big smile with raised
		eyebrows (happy
		look)
English (Australia):		
No	Don't hesitate to speak to me	Big smile
	again if you have another	
	IKEA question	

smile. To the request for beds, the Swedish Anna gives a surprisingly doubtful facial expression with the direct information about single beds, whereas the Australian Anna provides a big smile. To the somewhat rude answer from the customer, who says "no", the Swedish Anna says "That was sad" and makes a quite expressive face with her mouth. The Australian Anna, on the other hand, more or less ignores the "no" and invites a new question with a smile. Do Australians typically display more happiness, more politeness and are they less direct than Swedes? We don't really know the answer to these questions. The more interesting question is perhaps why there is a difference in interface design. Is the difference based on intuition or on empirical research available to interface designers?

7.2   A Checklist of Possible and Existing Features in an ECA Like Anna

Table 4. Features of Anna: existing features and suggested improvements, additions

Features	Specification	IKEA's Anna	Possible improvement
Activity dependence	goals, roles, artifacts, environment	Very activity specific/ limited	Could be extended within activity. Some everyday topics could be added.
Generic applicability - parameters:			
Expression	Head movements	small move- ments, no nods, head shakes etc.	Feedback in terms of nods and head shakes could be added. Cultural adaptations could be made of these.
	Facial gestures	3	Should be extended.
	Eye brow movements	In set expressions	Could be made more varied.
	Eye movements	-	Could be used more with some recognition of face or gaze, also for directions.
	Arm and hand movements	-	Could be added and used for feedback, typical gestures of culture, directions etc.
	Shoulder movements	-	Could be added. Maybe not needed for activity or for politeness.
	Intonation in speech	NA(?) text output	
	Intensity, pitch, duration in speech	NA(?) text output	
Content + function	Emotions	Has 3 emotions	Should be improved, extended repertoire needed.
	Attitudes (e.g. politeness)	Has 3 emotions	Should be improved, extended repertoire needed.
	Common speech acts	Has some	Could be extended with respect to some everyday needs.
	Everyday topics	-	Some could be added.
Interactive functions	Turn taking	Reacts after written message is sent.	Some incremental processing would increase human-like feature and make quicker responses possible.
	Feedback	Varied in text + 3 facial express- ions	Should be improved considerably, e.g. by added head movements.
	Sequences	Only responses to previous request (?)	
Other context dependence	e.g. deixis, beliefs, expectations, values	-?	

7.3 Evaluation of Anna and Suggested Improvements

Table 4 is an example of how one can go through the checklist given in Table 1, in order to evaluate the features of an artificial communicator and suggest improvements. The checklist can also be used for comparing repertoires of behavior and functions in different artificial communicators.

More advanced agents, like Max, GRETA and others [5], [6], [25], [26] have many of the features mentioned as absent or insufficient (and possible to add or improve) in Anna, in table 4 and that would make her appearance more believable, responsive and interpretable. These agents have a much advanced underlying architecture than most web based agents. Since Anna today is a fairly simple web front-end to IKEA's database, she perhaps does not need as many and advanced functions as the artificial communicators mentioned above have. There are, however, a number of improvements and/or additions that could be made with less advanced methods and that would make her a more pleasant and believable agent. Some feasible and worthwhile changes would be the ones listed below.

I.   Features that would be possible to add without too much added technology making cultural adaptation possible:

The main suggested additions are 1) head movements for feedback (e.g. for *yes* and *no*, positive and negative information and attitudes), 2) some arm and hand movements, which could enhance interpretability by adding redundancy and also could provide deictic information and added expressiveness, 3) an improved and extended repertoire of facial expressions, which can be linked to text output in a more advanced way, and 4) some extended content in terms of frequent everyday topics, which would make her more believable and user friendly.

Motivation for 1-4 above:

1) The addition of head movements, i.e. head nods to go with *yes* and positive information and attitudes and head shakes to go with *no* and negative information and attitudes would make Anna a more pleasant and believable agent.

2) Arm and hand movements are a resource that has not yet been exploited in Anna. They could add to expressiveness and redundancy in information, information structuring. (Shoulder movement is a more debatable feature in an agent with this particular role, since it might be interpreted as impolite, even if it adds expressiveness.)

3) Anna's has three facial expressions, which are holistic composites representing approximately (i) happiness/big smile, (ii) hesitation?, scepticism?, joking attitude?, and (iii) "I'm sorry", "I can't help you", "something is wrong" etc.? They are expressed in the following ways:

(i) Happy: eye brows raised, mouth open with big smile
(ii) Hesitant: eye brows lowered with inner ends lowered, eyes narrowed, mouth closed and drawn to one side
(iii) Sad: Eye brows drawn together with inner ends raised, mouth with lower lip, especially the corners of the mouth lowered, showing teeth ("Making face")

In general, these three facial expressions are too few and too hard to map to the text output to be really helpful, rather than confusing. Facial expressions 2 and 3 are especially hard to interpret. This might be one reason for the choice of the blonde Anna in Germany and the UK, since she does not have expression 2, which seems to be replaced by expression 1 in many cases, making her seem more friendly and polite (this might also be a result of the specific mapping to text). We can also see that the mapping between the facial expression (even of the generic Anna) and the corresponding text messages is not the same in the Anna's of different cultures (see the Swedish and Australian examples above). This could be an attempt at cultural adaptation and it can give this impression, especially in connection with the differences in text responses. The facial expressions would be possible to a) improve and make clearer/less ambiguous, b) extend, making more expressions possible, c) link in better ways to emotions, attitudes and factual information.

In combination with head movements for feedback and possibly some arm and hand movements, improved and added facial expressions would improve Anna's communicative repertoire and "believability". For facial expressions, the studies discussed above can provide information for improvements, e.g. emotions and attitudes could be expressed more efficiently by adding facial expressions, head movements for feedback functions and some arm-hand movements. These features would also add redundancy and thus possibly interpretability to common speech acts.

Concerning content, additions could be made, adding some very common everyday topics and some more topics relevant for an IKEA customer. There are studies with artificial communicators as front ends to databases in public places, which show typical and frequent questions, requests and attempts at small talk that users initiate and which could be used for identifying a set of topics and typical contributions [26]. The ability to handle at least some of these topics would make Anna more human like and user friendly.

II.   Additional suggested features

It would also be fairly simple to add more alternative looks to Anna that might make her look more believable for customers from different cultures. However, this is probably against IKEA's present policy.

III.   Features that require more technology and development

Some features that have not been suggested here, since they are more complex and require more research and development than the features mentioned under I and II above are: 1) detection of the user's face, eye gaze or hand movements, which would create a more naturalistic eye gaze and perhaps even make possible some mirroring of behavior, such as nodding or waving, 2) speech output, which would have to be prosodically adapted to the content of written messages and the emotional output of facial expressions.

1) If the user's face, eyes or hands could be detected and followed in space, Anna could be made to direct her eye gaze and provides some response to movements, such as saying *hallo* and *good bye* at the right moment while waving or pointing. This would add to her naturalness and impression of interactive reliability. The ability to

use eye gaze and pointing by Anna would also make improved deictic functions possible. However, both these features are demanding with respect to technology research and development.

2) Anna does not have speech output. Speech output would certainly be possible using recordings or a TTS system, whereas speech recognition would be far more demanding and require much more technological development and error management. The prosodic features of the spoken output would probably have to be linked to the written messages and to attitudes and emotions expressed in them in a similar way to what should be done for facial expressions. This would require extra design and resources. The female agent of IKEA in Dubai speaks a pre-recorded text with good intonation, but her speech is not really interactive and her facial expression does not vary.

7.4 Cultural Specification of Parameters

Given the improvements suggested in I and II above, cultural adaptation could be done with respect to: 1) The text output (adapted to the specific activity in the specific culture), e.g typical sequences and speech acts, choice of word, politeness etc., 2) Type of feedback words and phrases, showing Contact, Perception, Understanding and Attitudinal reactions (CPUA), 3) What type of response/information to give, where some variables might be the following: formal – informal, long – short, general – specific, direct – indirect, neutral – polite, neutral – expressive, 4) Head movements for feedback, showing CPUA, 5) Facial expressions, CPUA, emotions and attitudes, and 6) Possibly the looks/appearance of the ECA in different cultures.

8   Concluding Remarks

In this paper, we have given a first outline of a framework, which attempts to highlight some of the parameters to be taken into account in designing and evaluating a system for multimodal intercultural ICT. We have then exemplified the use of this framework in describing the features of an embodied communicative agent used by an international company in different cultures and suggesting features which could be improved or added.

References

1. Peirce, C.S.: Collected Papers of Charles Sanders Peirce, 1931-1958. In: Hartshorne, C., Weiss, P., Burks, A. (eds.) vol. 8, Harvard University Press, Cambridge (1931)
2. Allwood, J.: Capturing Differences between Social Activities in Spoken Language. In: Kenesei, I., Harnish, R.M. (eds.) Perspectives in Semantics, Pragmatics and Discourse, pp. 301–319. John Benjamins, Amsterdam (2001)
3. Kenny, P., Harholt, A., Gratsch, J., Swartout, W., Traum, D., Marsella, S., Piepol, D.: Building Interactive Virtual Humans for Training Environments. In: Proceedings of I/ITSEC (2007)

4. Jan, D., Herrera, D., Martinovski, B., Novick, D., Traum, D.: A computational Model of Culture-specific Conversational Behavior. In: Pelachaud, C., Martin, J.-C., André, E., Chollet, G., Karpouzis, K., Pelé, D. (eds.) IVA 2007. LNCS (LNAI), vol. 4722, pp. 45–56. Springer, Heidelberg (2007)
5. Kopp, S., Allwood, J., Ahlsén, E., Stocksmeier, T.: Modeling Embodied Feedback with Virtual Humans. In: Wachsmuth, I., Knoblich, G. (eds.) ZiF Research Group International Workshop. LNCS (LNAI), vol. 4930, pp. 18–37. Springer, Heidelberg (2008)
6. Poggi, I., Pelachaud, C., de Rosis, F., Carofiglio, V., De Carolis, N.: GRETA. A Believable Embodied Conversational Agent. In: Stock, O., Zancarano, M. (eds.) Multimodal Intelligent Information Presentation. Kluwer, Dordrecht (2005)
7. Koda, T.: Cross-cultural study of avatars' facial expressions and design considerations within Asian countries. In: Ishida, T., Fussell, S.R., Vossen, P.T.J.M. (eds.) IWIC 2007. LNCS, vol. 4568, pp. 207–220. Springer, Heidelberg (2007)
8. Koda, T., Rehm, M., André, E.: Cross-cultural Evaluations of avatar facial expressions designed by Western and Japanese Designers. In: Prendinger, H., Lester, J.C., Ishizuka, M. (eds.) IVA 2008. LNCS (LNAI), vol. 5208, pp. 245–252. Springer, Heidelberg (2008)
9. Koda, T., Ishida, T.: Cross-Cultural Study of Avatar Expression Interpretations. In: SAINT 2006, pp. 130–136 (2006)
10. Johansen, S.: Avatars in Global E-Commerce: A Cross-Cultural Analysis of the Effects of Avatars on Online Consumer Behavior in Germany and the U.S. Journal of Undergraduate Research 6(8), 32611 (352) 846–2032 (2006)
11. Kilbourne, J.: Deadly Persuasion. Free Press, New York (1999)
12. Hofstede, G.: Cultural Constraints in Personnel Management. Journal of International Business, Special Issue 2/98, Management International Review, 8–9 (1998)
13. Barber, W., Badre, A.: Culturability: the merging of culture and usability. Human Factors and the Web (1998),
    http://www.research.att.com/conf/hfweb/proceedings/barder/index.htm
14. Chau, P., Cole, M., Massey, A., Montoya-Weiss, M., O'Keefe, R.: Cultural differences in the online behavior of consumers. Journal of the Association for Computing Machinery 45(10) (2002)
15. Allwood, J.: Are There Swedish Patterns of Communication? In: Tamura, H. (ed.) Cultural Acceptance of CSCW in Japan & Nordic Countries, pp. 90–120. Kyoto Institute of Technology, Kyoto (1999)
16. Lustig, M., Koester, J.: Intercultural Competence: Interpersonal Communication across Cultures. Longman, New York (2006)
17. Allwood, J., Cerrato, L., Jokinen, K., Paggio, P., Navaretta, C.: The MUMIN Annotation Scheme for Feedback, Turn Management and Sequencing. In: Proceedings from the Second Nordic conference on Multimodal Communication. Gothenburg Papers in Theoretical
18. Morris, D.: Manwatching. Jonathan Cape, London (1977)
19. Allwood, J.: Bodily Communication – Dimensions of Expression and Content. In: Granström, B., House, D., Karlsson, I. (eds.) Multimodality in Language and Speech Systems, pp. 7–26. Kluwer Academic Publishers, Dordrecht (2002); Linguistics, 92. University of Gothenburg, Department of Linguistics (2006)
20. Allwood, J.: Intercultural Communication. In: Allwood, J. (ed.) Papers in Anthropological Linguistics 12. University of Gothenburg, Department of Linguistics, Göteborg (1985)
21. Hofstede, G.: Cultures and Organizations: Software of the Mind. McGraw-Hill, New York (1997)

22. Sacks, H., Schegloff, E.A., Jefferson, G.: A simplest systematics for the organization of turn-taking for conversation. Language 50, 696–735 (1974)

23. Allwood, J., Nivre, J., Ahlsén, E.: On the semantics and pragmatics of linguistic feedback. Journal of Semantics 9(1), 1–26 (1992)

24. Cassell, J., Thórisson, K.: The power of a nod and a glance. Envelope vs. emotional feedback in animated conversational agents. Applied Artificial Intelligence 13, 519–538 (1999)

25. Kopp, S., Wachsmuth, I.: Synthesizing Multimodal Utterances for Conversational Agents. The Journal Computer Animation and Virtual Words 15(1), 39–52 (2004)

26. Kopp, S.: How Humans Talk to Virtual Humans - Conversations From a Real-World Application. In: Fischer, K. (ed.) How People Talk to Computers, Robots, and Other Artificial Interaction Partners, SFB/TR 8 Report No. 010-09/2006, pp. 101–113 (2006)

Tools and Resources for Visualising Conversational-Speech Interaction

Nick Campbell

The University of Dublin, Trinity College
nick@tcd.ie
http://people.tcd.ie/nick

Abstract. This chapter describes both a video corpus (collected at ATR in Japan) and web-based tools to view, browse, search and export corpora of multi-party video-recorded conversions. One of the challenges presented by multimodal corpora, because of their enormous size, is making them available to other interested parties in a way that they can directly assess, to see if the corpus incorporates relevant data for their research, and then only access the relevant parts that they are interested in. The chapter presents a number of innovative ideas of how to browse a large corpus and some insight into what conversational phenomena this corpus features. The transcriptions and recordings are made available as part of SSPNet under a Creative Commons 'share-alike' license.

1   Introduction

With ever-growing increases in the amount of data available for speech technology research, it is now becoming increasingly difficult for any one individual to be personally familiar with *all* of the data in any given corpus. Yet without the insights provided by first-hand inspection of the types and variety of speech material being collected, it is difficult to ensure that appropriate models and features will be used in any subsequent processing of the speech data.

For data-handling institutions such as ELDA (the European Evaluations and Language-resources Distribution Agency [1]) and LDC (the US Linguistic Data Consortium [2]) whose main role is the collection and distribution of large volumes of speech data, there is little need for any single staff member to become familiar with the stylistic contents of any individual corpus, so long as teams of people have worked on the data to verify its quality and validate it as a reliable corpus. However, for researchers using those data as a resource to help build speech processing systems and interfaces, there is a good case to be made for the individual researchers to become personally familiar with the contents and characteristics of the speech data in the corpora that they use.

It is perhaps not necessary (and often physically very difficult) to listen to all of the speech in a given corpus but it is essential to be able to select in a non-random manner specific sections of the corpus for closer inspection and analysis. If the data is transcribed, the transcriptions will provide the first key into the speech data but there are many aspects of a spoken message that are

M. Kipp et al. (Eds.): Multimodal Corpora, LNAI 5509, pp. 176–188, 2009.

not well described by a plain text rendering of the linguistic content. Matters relating to prosody, interpretation, speaking-style, speaker affect, personality and interpersonal stance are very difficult to infer from text alone [3], and almost impossible to search for without specific and expensive further annotation of the transcription.

Multimodal corpora compound this problem by both proliferation of data and proliferation of interaction modalities. Perhaps the best-known example of a large multimedia corpus is that of the European-funded AMI project (FP6-506811 [8]) whose Meeting Corpus is created by a 15-member multi-disciplinary consortium dedicated to the research and development of technology that will help groups interact better [9]. A primary AMI focus is on developing meeting browsers that improve work-group effectiveness by giving better access to the group's history. Another is considering how related technologies can help group members joining a meeting late or having to 'attend' from a different location.

"In both cases, a key part our approach is to index meetings for the properties that users find salient. This might mean, for instance, spotting topic boundaries, decisions, intense discussions, or places where a specific person or subject was mentioned. To help with developing this indexing the consortium has collected the AMI Meeting Corpus, a set of recorded meetings that is now available as a public resource" [8].

The AMI data set was designed specifically for the project and consists of 100 hours of meeting recordings, using a range of signals, synchronised to a common timeline, and include close-talking and far-field microphones, individual and room-view video cameras, and output from a slide projector and an electronic whiteboard. The meetings were recorded in English using three different rooms with different acoustic properties, and include mostly non-native speakers. All the data is available from a public website and includes the following infomrmation (though not all for all recordings): Observation (meeting id), abstract summary, decision point, dialogue acts, extractive summary, focus of attention, hand movement, head movement, leg movement, named entities, topic seg.mentationm and manual transcript. The materials are distributed under a Creative Commons Share-Alike license [10]. However, the amount of data is enormous and although Metadata annotations are extensively prepared [11], in practice, download times prohibit easy access to the full corpus, which is presently being distributed on several DVDs to interested researchers.

At ATR [4], we have now collected several thousand hours of conversational speech data and have prepared a comparable web-based interface with cgi-scripts programmed in Perl that incorporate Java and JavaScript to facilitate first-hand browsing of the corpora. More recently, but on a smaller level than AMI, we have also started collecting multimodal recordings of multi-party conversational interactions. References to related work and more detailed descriptions of the corpora can be found in [5,6,7]. Some of the features of the software we produced will be described in the sections below. In the following text, Section 2 illustrates the top-level interface to the data, Section 3 gives an example of an interface that offers fast browsing based on dialogue structure, and Section 4 illustrates facilities for display and retrieval of multi-modal data using Flash movies.

2 Browser Technologies

With the growing recent interest in processing rich multimodal interaction, beginning with projects such as AMI [9], NIST Rich Transcription [12], and CHIL [13], there has been considerable research into collecting and annotating very large corpora of audio and visual information related to human spoken interactions [6], and subsequently huge efforts into mining information from the resulting data [14] and making the information available to researchers in various related disciplines [15]. Consequently, much research has also been devoted to interface and access technologies, particularly using web browsers [17].

Our own corpora, produced at ATR with funding assistance from the JST [16], illustrate different forms of spoken dialogue and are related by contextual features such as participant identity, nature of the interlocutor, mode of conversation, formality of the discourse, etc. They are stored as speech wave files with time-aligned transcriptions and annotations in the form of equivalently-named text files. Since they come from various sources, there is no constraint on file naming conventions so long as there is no duplication of identifiers. The files are physically related by directory structure and can be accessed through a web-page which hides the physical locations and provides access information in human-readable form.

Examples are given in Figures 1 & 2 which show the top-level pages for two sections of the corpus. The pages provide access to all the conversations from each participant, grouped in one case (Fig. 1) according to serial order of the dialogue sequence, and another (Fig. 2) by interlocutor, showing topic of the conversations as determined by manual labelling of the speech.

These summary pages allow the browsing researcher to visualise the style and content of each corpus with only minimal effort. In each case, the LIST option offers a quick route to the full transcriptions, although these themselves may be long and difficult to visualise.

Because of the very large number of conversations in the ESP_C subset, clicking on any link (shown in Figure 2) will bring up a text-free page, such as the one illustrated in Figure 3, which facilitates direct browsing access to the data as well as allowing immediate visualisation of its structure. We have found that this graphical way of illustrating a conversation speeds up access by allowing the researcher to see the dynamics of the discourse before having to access its transcription as text. The display makes use of the time-alignment information inherent in each transcription.

3 Browsing Based on Dialogue Structure

Whereas complete manual transcriptions are available for most conversations in the corpus, the difficulty of time-aligning such texts for graphic display is

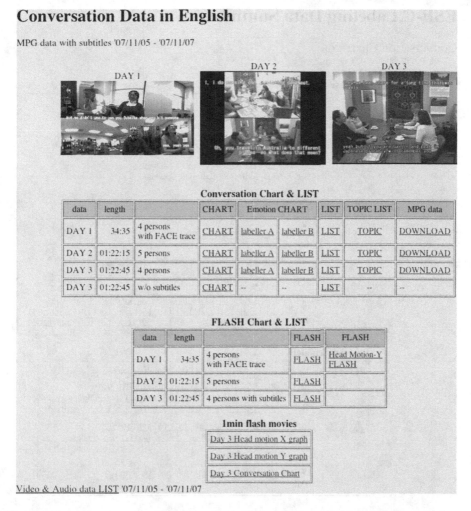

Fig. 1. The top page for accessing ATR dialogue data at http://feast.atr.jp/non-verbal/project/html_files/taba/nov07/ showing some of the annotated files for a series of video conversations (password & userid are available from *nick@tcd.ie*)

well known to conversation analysts, who have devised orthographic layout conventions that allow visualisation (to some extent) of the timing and sequential information of the dialogues [18,19]. Since overlapping speech is common in conversational interactions, the nature of the discourse can often be estimated from the structure of these overlaps.

Figure 3 demonstrates our solution to the problem of displaying and time-aligning such speech data. We take advantage of the two-dimensional interface of an interactive web page to plot utterance sequences graphically aligned for maximal visual impact. This screenshot shows two speakers' time-aligned utterance activity. On screen, each speaker's data are shown using a different

ESP-C Labeling Data Summary

Conversation Chart (CGI)
T-a : TOPIC labelled by Y-san (rule)
T-b : TOPIC labelled by N-san (rule)

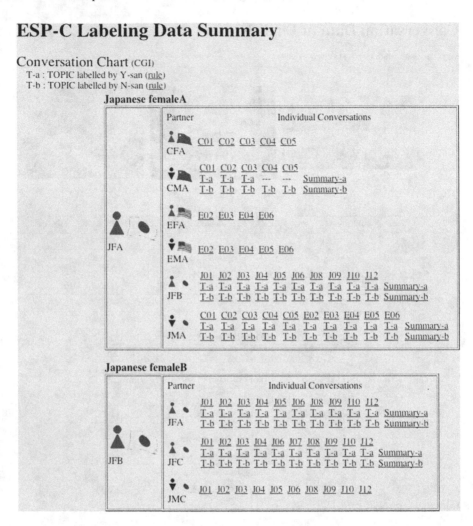

Fig. 2. The top page for accessing Japanese telephone conversations at http://feast.atr.jp/non-verbal/project/html_files/taba/top_esp-c/ showing interlocutor (by nationality and sex) and topic number, with access to summary data and topic annotations as well as to the actual sequential conversations

colour-coding to aid identification and each utterance is accessible by mouse-based interaction. Moving the mouse over a bar reveals its text (see e.g., the last row in the figure) and clicking on the bar will play the speech-wave associated with the utterance. This graphical form of layout makes it particularly easy to search utterance sequences based on dialogue structure and speech overlaps. A more conventional view of the transcriptions can be accessed by clicking the LIST option in the upper right-hand corner of this page. This reveals text in the form shown in Figure 4, with utterance timing, speaker, and transcription displayed vertically. Two modes of audio output are offered for dialogue speech, since it

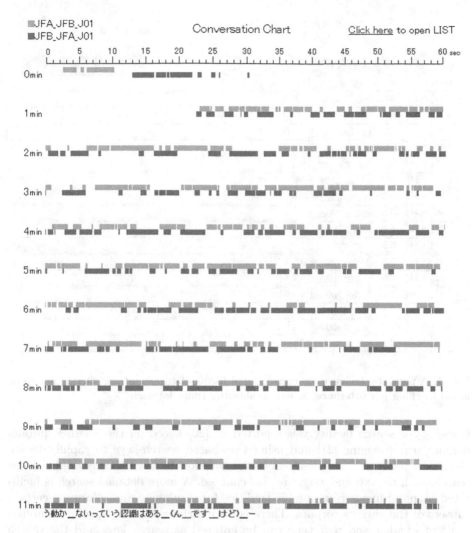

Fig. 3. A page showing speech interaction in a Japanese telephone conversation accessed from Figure 2, where the speech activity (on/off) for each speaker is displayed as a series of bars, allowing immediate visualisation of the overlaps and the dynamic structure of the interaction. Mousing over a bar displays its text (shown here in Japanese) and clicking on it brings up the speech data in a separate window for browsing. The width of each row shows one minute of speech activity.

is sometimes preferable to hear a stereo recording, which provides simultaneous natural access to both speaker's overlapping segments, and sometimes better to hear a monaural recording, where overlapping speech does not intrude on the ease of listening. Separate speech files are employed in each case.

Rapid search is an essential facility for any corpus, and several ways are offered for thus constraining the displayed data to specific subsets. A fast

■JFA_JFB_J03
■JFB_JFA_J03   Conversation List

start	end	speaker	PLAY	
0:19	0:21	JFA	stereo mono	十二月二__十日木曜日
0:21	0:22	JFA	stereo mono	三__時四__十__五__分
0:22	0:25	JFA	stereo mono	被験者__ツカモト__収録__を__開始__し__ます
0:25	0:26	JFB	stereo mono	十二月二__十日
0:27	0:28	JFB	stereo mono	三__時四__十
0:29	0:29	JFB	stereo mono	五__分
0:30	0:31	JFB	stereo mono	被験者アオヤマユカコ
0:31	0:33	JFB	stereo mono	収録__を__開始__し__ます
0:46	0:46	JFA	stereo mono	つ
0:56	0:56	JFA	stereo mono	ないすせ
1:12	1:14	JFB	stereo mono	ズー
1:31	1:32	JFB	stereo mono	もしもし
1:32	1:33	JFA	stereo mono	もしも(し__ー)
1:32	1:34	JFB	stereo mono	あっはい__アオヤマ__です__ー
1:34	1:35	JFA	stereo mono	ツカモトです__ー
1:35	1:36	JFB	stereo mono	こんにち(は__ー)ー
1:35	1:37	JFA	stereo mono	こんにち(は__ー)

Fig. 4. A page displaying more conventional forms of transcription, offering stereo or mono listening per utterance, as well as showing times for each

Google-type search facility was reported in [20] based on the Swish-E public-domain search-engine [21] and using text-based search-keys to rapidly locate given text sequences and their associated waveforms. Logical constraints on the search, such as AND and NOT, are also enabled. A more detailed search is facilitated by providing corpus specific facilities for displaying and reforming certain subsets of the various corpora. There is an interface whereby specific combinations of speaker and text type can be entered as search keys and the search constrained by e.g., interlocutor type, gesture dynamics, or discourse mode, by making use of the higher-level annotations on the data.

A Join-Play interactive-editing feature allows the user to simply append the latest utterance segment (video and audio, or audio alone) to a list of related segments to build up a novel data sequence with the speech files and associated text files zipped in a form ready to burn to DVD for wider distribution. This facility has proved useful in the rapid provision of materials for perceptual experiments as well as providing topic-specific subsets of the corpus for analysis at a separate site.

Figure 5 shows the join-play 'download' facility being used with the output of one of the recordings illustrated in Figure 1. The small squares around each head have been automatically generated by video signal processing and are used

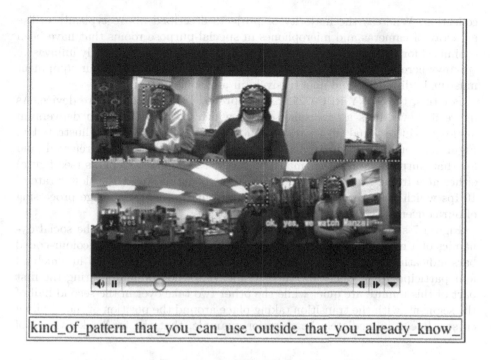

kind_of_pattern_that_you_can_use_outside_that_you_already_know_

download
[0:02:29.5799-0:02:34.1000]

Fig. 5. Selected portions of a conversation can be downloaded for concatenation into fresh dialogues. A time window can be selected interactively to include portions before and after the transcribed segment. A karaoke style subtitle provides visual display of the speech.

for movement tracking and analysis of the head and body interactions for each participant.

4   Display of Multi-modal Metadata

An increasing amount of our data is multi-modal. We now use 360-degree cameras as well as regular video when recording fresh dialogue data, and use computer programmes to produce derived data from the aligned video and audio.

Perhaps the greatest difference between the corpus material we present here and that which is currently available worldwide lies in our approach to the data collection. Whereas the majority of projects described above typically utilise an array of cameras and microphones in special-purpose rooms that have been optimised for data collection, we prefer a more portable and certainly uninvasive 'go-anywhere' approach to recording conversational speech data. Our equipment must fit in discreetly and unobtrusively in any social setting.

For this, the SONY RPU-C251 has an proved ideal video capture device. As figure 6 shows, it is a very small device which in its native form delivers an analogue video signal in a variety of formats, such as the one illustrated in Figure 5. For image signal-processing though, a digital signal is preferred, and for that purpose we use the small Pointgrey 'Flea2' video cameras (see figure) either at a frame-rate of 60 fps for raw data collection, or at the slower rate of 10 fps which has proved optimal for the automatic real-time image processing of our conversational data [6].

Figure 7 shows the output of this camera and illustrates how the social dynamics of a multi-party interaction can be readily visualised using colour-coded bars indicating speech activity [7]. We see that after a brief period in which all four participants are speaking, the two speakers who dominate during the first part of this minute are quiet while the other two take over in the second half of the segment, with the transition taking place around the position of the scrolling cursor. It can immediately be seen, for example, that the feedback pattern of

Fig. 6. The lens taken from a SONY RPU-C251 attached to a Pointgrey 'Flea2' digital video camera (right), and in the original analogue video housing (left) fitted with a soft cover for protection, and a similar 'Palnon' 360-degree lens mounted on a Pointgrey 'Firefly' digital capture device (bottom)

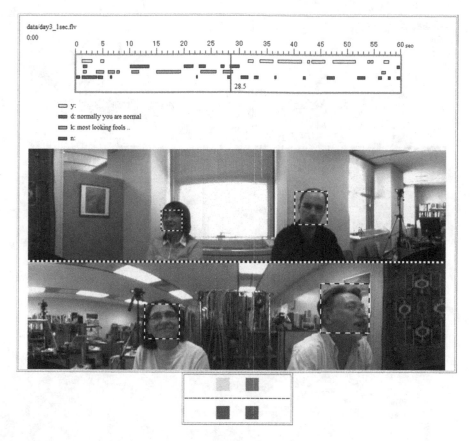

Fig. 7. Another method of interacting with multimodal data. Colour-coded bars (with key below showing speaker position) reveal the dynamics of the interaction, and a moving cursor marks the point in the discourse as the movie is played, with the transcriptions of each talker provided in animated form between the bar-plot and the video.

the former two speakers utterances is very different in style from that of the two speakers in the latter part of the segment. The areas around 'transition points' (such as the one marked by the cursor in the top part of the figure at time 28.5) can also be of great interest [22]. These types of states are immediately recognisable when scrolling through such graphical displays of speech interaction.

Similar interaction plots, automatically derived, can be related to the video sequence using Flash software for dynamic effect. Figure 8 shows how similar colour-coding can help to identify the movements of each speaker when numerical data are plotted. Here, face-detection software is employed to find the faces in each image, and then image-flow technology tracks the movements around and below each face to provide a measure of body and head movements for the different speakers. The derived metadata are displayed in the same clickable form as the text, allowing simple search and control of the video replay.

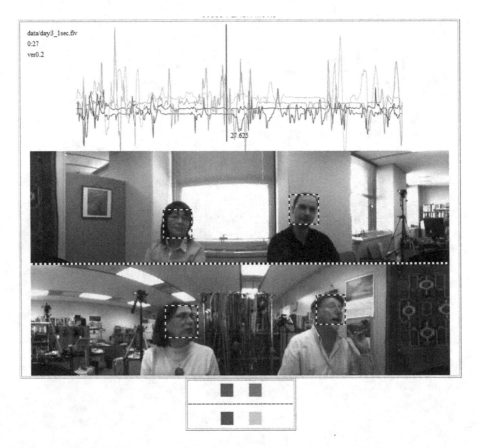

Fig. 8. Using Flash software to animate the automatically-derived movement data. Here the vertical head movement estimates are displayed time-aligned with the video. The cursor can be scrolled through each page of display to control the video and audio output. Again, the dynamics of the interaction become apparent and rapidly guide the researcher.

5   Conclusion

This chapter has described our approach to data collection and management, and introduced some of the hardware and software used for the recording and display of large-corpus data. The web-based tools and interface are now being used by a small community of international researchers working with the dialogue data. However, because of the large amount of personal information included in these highly natural conversations it is not feasible to make the entire corpus publicly available at this time. Representative samples can be seen at the FEAST web pages (Feature Extraction & Analysis for Speech Technology [23]), and interested researchers should apply to the author for access to specific subsets for research purposes. The software, however, can be made freely available to interested researchers with similar data in the hope that standards might then emerge for the interfacing of different types of discourse materials for future technology research and development.

Samples of the above data are also being made more generally available for research purposes under the new 'Social Signal Processing' EU Network [24].

References

1. ELDA - Evaluations and Language Resources Distribution Agency,
   http://www.elda.org
2. LDC - The Linguistic Data Consortium, http://www.ldc.upenn.edu/
3. Campbell, N.: On the Use of Nonverbal Speech Sounds in Human Communication. In: Esposito, A., Faundez-Zanuy, M., Keller, E., Marinaro, M. (eds.) COST Action 2102. LNCS (LNAI), vol. 4775, pp. 117–128. Springer, Heidelberg (2007)
4. ATR: The Advanced Telecommunications Research Institute, Keihanna Science City, Kyoto, Japan
5. Campbell, N.: Databases of Expressive Speech. Journal of Chinese Language and Computing 14(4), 295–304 (2004)
6. Douxchamps, D., Campbell, N.: Robust real-time tracking for the analysis of human behaviour. In: Popescu-Belis, A., Renals, S., Bourlard, H. (eds.) MLMI 2007. LNCS, vol. 4892, pp. 1–10. Springer, Heidelberg (2008)
7. Campbell, N.: Individual traits of speaking style and speech rhythm in a spoken discourse. In: Esposito, A., Bourbakis, N.G., Avouris, N., Hatzilygeroudis, I. (eds.) HH and HM Interaction. LNCS (LNAI), vol. 5042, pp. 107–120. Springer, Heidelberg (2008)
8. AMI Project: http://corpus.amiproject.org/documentations/overview
9. Carlette, J., et al.: The AMI Meeetings Corpus. In: Proc. Symposium on Annotating and Measuring Meeting Behaviour (2005)
10. Share-Alike License:
    http://en.wikipedia.org/wiki/Creative_Commons_licenses
11. Popescu-Belis, A., Estrella, P.: Generating Usable Formats for Metadata and Annotations in a Large Meeting Corpus. In: Proc. ACL, Prague, pp. 93–95 (2007)
12. The NIST Rich Transcription Evaluation Project, Meeting Recognition Evaluation, Documentation, http://www.nist.gov/speech/tests/rt/rt2002/
13. Waibel, A., Steusloff, H., Stiefelhagen, R.: CHIL - Computers in the human interaction loop. In: 5th international workshop on image analysis for multimedia interactive services, Lisbon (April 2004)
14. Tucker, S., Whittaker, S.: Accessing Multimodal Meeting Data: Systems, Problems and Possibilities. In: Proc. Multimodal Interaction and Related Machine Learning Algorithms, Martigny, Switzerland (2004)
15. Cremers, A.H.M., Groenewegen, P., Kuiper, I., Post, W.: The Project Browser: Supporting Information Access for a Project team. In: Jacko, J.A. (ed.) HCI 2007. LNCS, vol. 4553, pp. 571–580. Springer, Heidelberg (2007)
16. JST – The Japan Science & Technology Agency: http://www.jst.go.jp/EN/
17. Rienks, R., Nijholt, A., Reidsma, D.: Meetings and Meeting Support in Ambient Intelligence, ch.17. Mobile Communication series, Artech House, pp. 359–378 (2006) ISBN 1-58053-963-7
18. Sacks, H., Schegloff, E.A., Jefferson, G.: A simplest systematics for the organization of turntaking for conversation. Language 50, 696–735 (1974)

19. Local, J.: Phonetic Detail and the Organisation of Talk-in-Interaction. In: Proceedings of the XVIth International Congress of Phonetic Sciences, Saarbruecken, Germany: 16th ICPhS (2007)
20. Campbell, N.: Synthesis Units for Conversational Speech. In: Proc. Acoustic Society of Japan Autumn Meeting (2005)
21. SWISH-E – Simple Web Indexing System for Humans, Enhanced Version: http://swish-e.org/
22. Campbell, N.: How Speech Encodes Affect and Discourse Information - Conversational Gestures. NATO Security thr' Science, vol. 18, pp. 103–114. IOS Press, Amsterdam (2007)
23. ATR's FEAST, http://feast.atr.jp/non-verbal/project/html_files/taba/top.html
24. SSPNet – EU-funded 'Social Signal Processing' Network: http://www.sspnet.eu/

Accessing a Large Multimodal Corpus Using an Automatic Content Linking Device

Andrei Popescu-Belis[1], Jean Carletta[2], Jonathan Kilgour[2], and Peter Poller[3]

[1] Idiap Research Institute
Rue Marconi 19, P.O. Box 592, 1920 Martigny, Switzerland
andrei.popescu-belis@idiap.ch
[2] Human Communication Research Centre, University of Edinburgh
10 Crichton Street, Edinburgh EH8 9AB, Scotland, UK
J.Carletta@ed.ac.uk, jonathan@inf.ed.ac.uk
[3] DFKI GmbH, Stuhlsatzenhausweg 3
D-66123 Saarbruecken, Germany
peter.poller@dfki.de

Abstract. As multimodal data becomes easier to record and store, the question arises as to what practical use can be made of archived corpora, and in particular what tools allowing efficient access to it can be built. We use the AMI Meeting Corpus as a case study to build an automatic content linking device, i.e. a system for real-time data retrieval. The corpus provides not only the data repository, but is used also to simulate ongoing meetings for development and testing of the device. The main features of the corpus are briefly described, followed by an outline of data preparation steps prior to indexing, and of the methods for building queries from ongoing meeting discussions, retrieving elements from the corpus and accessing the results. A series of user studies based on prototypes of the content linking device have confirmed the relevance of the concept, and methods for task-based evaluation are under development.

Keywords: multimodal corpora, meeting corpora, speech-based retrieval, meeting assistants, meeting browsers.

1 Introduction

Researchers often think of multimodal corpora as simply a research tool – something which yields samples of information about human behaviour that will allow component technologies, such as gesture recognizers, to be built. However, technology makes it currently affordable to record data from relatively complex sensors, such as cameras or microphone arrays, in a variety of settings. Rich historical archives related to organizations, events, projects or people can thus easily be set up and continuously extended, in the form of multimodal corpora. This opportunity is currently being explored in many different ways, from attempts to capture all of the events in an individual's life to analyses of activities in public spaces. In such uses, the multimodal corpus is both a research tool – for

M. Kipp et al. (Eds.): Multimodal Corpora, LNAI 5509, pp. 189–206, 2009.

developing the automatic analyses that underpin the ability to make use of large amounts of recorded material – and a platform for developing, demonstrating and refining the new application concepts that these automatic analyses enable.

One commercially important application of this general approach is on meeting archives. The AMIDA Automatic Content Linking Device (ACLD) performs real-time searches over a multimodal meeting archive using automatic speech recognition, thus providing assistance with past information during an ongoing meeting, at a minimal attentional cost for the participants. Throughout the process of developing the ACLD from the initial concept to a standalone demonstration, we have been completely reliant on the AMI Meeting Corpus. Taking this process as a case study, we explain how we leveraged this multimodal recorded data set in order to create an application for online use, without the need for staging frequent live meetings to test the application.

We begin with an explanation of the content linking concept (Section 2), followed by a description of the AMI Meeting Corpus (Section 3) and a discussion of the uses to which it has been put during the development of our technology demonstration (Section 4). The four main stages of the content linking approach – corpus preparation and indexing, query preparation, retrieval, and access to multimodal data – are described respectively in Sections 5.1 through 5.4. Initial results from user studies, based on reactions from focus groups (Section 6.1) and on feedback from commercial partners on pilot versions of the ACLD (Section 6.2), are encouraging but do not preclude more systematic evaluation in the future (Section 6.3). The plans for future development of the ACLD are finally outlined in Section 7.

2   The Content Linking Concept

2.1   Scenario of Use and Inferred User Needs

Imagine for a moment that your company is moving into a new office building. The meeting rooms in the building are instrumented with cameras, microphones, and other devices to record what happens in them. On the day that you move in, the rooms are turned on, recording everything that happens in them, unless someone presses a privacy switch to disable the system temporarily. Over the course of a year, a large meeting archive is built up. As well as allowing meeting playback, it contains information about when meetings happened, who attended them, what slides were shown at what times, and what documents were presented or consulted during a meeting, or were produced as a result of a meeting. What use would the company wish to make of such an archive, and what tools would employees need for that use?

Although this scenario may sound far-fetched, many companies already make recordings of their most important meetings for their archives, and can see a use for recording all meetings, as long as the benefits to the company's employees are high enough for them to leave the system on. The problem comes with sifting through the archive to find the right bits. Although there are many times at which one might wish to search the archive, this problem is especially severe during meetings themselves. Meetings take a great deal of staff time, which is expensive. Often people have a feeling during meetings that they need some piece of information, but they can't lay their hands on it, at least not during the meeting itself. And yet, producing the right piece of information at the right time can change the course of a meeting, and sometimes, even determine the future of a company. This is the problem that motivates our design of a *content linking* application.

2.2   Outline of the Proposed Solution

Our solution to this problem is to have the room not just record the meetings that happen in it, but also "listen" to them and search quietly in the background for the most relevant documents and meeting segments from the archive, ready to be consulted whenever someone in the meeting feels the need. A system providing tailored access to potentially relevant fragments of recorded meetings or documents could be very valuable in improving group communication and individual awareness. Participants in a meeting often mention previous discussions, or documents related to them, containing facts that are relevant to their current discussion, but accessing them requires more time than participants can afford to spend during the discussion. If provided with an efficient device for searching past meetings and documents, participants only need to decide if they want to explore any further, and possibly introduce in the current discussion, the meeting fragments or documents retrieved automatically for them. The system could be used privately by every participant, or its results could be shown to the entire group on a separate projection screen.

2.3   Previous Work

The real-time content linking application put forward here borrows from several other applications described in the literature, with the main notable differences being the access to multimodal processed data, in real-time, through a speech-based, autonomously functioning system. Our system is also – to our knowledge – the first one that is fully implemented in a multimodal interaction context, giving access to indexed multimedia recordings as well as websites, based on automatic speech recognition and keyword spotting.

The initial versions of the content linking concept were introduced either as *query-free search*, which was implemented in the Fixit system [1], or as *just-in-time retrieval*, implemented in the Remembrance Agent [2,3]. Fixit is an assistant to an expert diagnostic system for the products of a specific company, such as fax machines and copiers. Fixit monitors the state of the user's interaction with the diagnostic system, in terms of positions in a belief network, and runs searches on a database of maintenance manuals to provide additional support information related to the position in the network. The results of the searches are in fact precomputed for each node of the belief network, in order to speed up the process at run time.

The Remembrance Agent is much closer, in its design, to the AMIDA content linking approach. The agent, which is integrated to the Emacs text editor, runs searches at regular intervals (every few seconds) using a query that is based on the last typed words (the size of the set of words is configurable, e.g. from 20 to 500). Results from a repository of emails or text notes are displayed in a separate frame, and can be opened within Emacs as well.

Both terms that refer to these two systems – query-free search and just-in-time (information) retrieval – capture important aspects of the general approach: there is no need for the user to formulate explicit queries, and results are updated regularly so that the users receive them, in theory, exactly when they need them. Several other systems have pursued and extended the approach. Watson [4] monitors the user's operations in a text editor, but proposes a more complex mechanism than the Remembrance Agent for selecting terms for queries, which are directed to the Altavista web search engine. Besides automatic queries, Watson also allows users to formulate queries and disambiguates them using the terms that were selected automatically.

Another query-free search system was designed for enriching television news with articles from the Web [5]. The system annotates TV broadcast news, using queries derived from closed captioning text, with links to potentially relevant news wire from the Web. A related type of work, though from a different perspective not inspired by information retrieval, are systems for document/speech alignment [6,7] specifically applied to meeting browsers. These systems typically perform the alignment offline, though online techniques can also draw inspiration from them [8].

Turning to speech-based systems, the creators of the Remembrance Agent have also designed Jimminy, a wearable assistant that helps users to take notes and to access information when they cannot use a standard computer keyboard [9]. Jimminy uses a number of contextual capture devices, in particular a positioning device that detects the room where the user is situated, and a device for identifying the user's interlocutors based on their badges. However, the use of speech was not implemented, and the detection of the subject of conversation was simulated by entering this topic as real-time notes. The testing of the system concerned in fact mostly the note-taking function. More recently, several speech-based search engines have been proposed, for instance a spoken interface to Google [10], or a spoken interface for a mobile device [11]. Such systems are comparatively less common than systems for searching spoken document archives [12] or for multimedia information retrieval [13].

3   The AMI Meeting Corpus

The AMI Meeting Corpus [14,15,16] consists of 100 hours of recordings from rooms like the one described in our opening scenario. The recordings use a range of signals synchronized to a common timeline. These include close-talking and far-field microphones, individual and room-view video cameras, and output from a slide projector and an electronic whiteboard. During the meetings, the participants also have unsynchronized pens available to them, which record what they write. The meetings were recorded in English, in three different rooms [17, p. 6–12], and include mostly non-native English speakers.

It was important for us to be able to understand what was happening during the meetings in the corpus. Real groups are messy – they have a shared understanding built up over their shared history, they sometimes are not sure what they are meant to achieve, and their participants are sometimes motivated by things that bear no relationship to the actual task. Although the AMI Corpus contains some real meetings of real groups to ensure that we do not diverge from reality too far, most of the material in the corpus is elicited experimentally to be as similar to real meetings as possible, but to ensure that we can capture everything there is to know about the groups involved.

In our elicitation technique, a group of four people come together in a one-day role-playing exercise in which they act as a team that needs to design a new kind of remote control for a TV set. At the beginning of the day, they are given separate crash courses in the specialty roles that such a team might contain, learning how to be a project manager, industrial designer, user interface designer, or marketing expert. They then engage in a series of four meetings which take them from an introduction to the problem that they need to solve, all the way through to their final design of the remote control. In between meetings, the participants do individual work towards the remote control design, receive emails from other people in "the company" that supply new information, and fill out some questionnaires that can be used *a posteriori* to assess things like how efficient the group is being or whether a leader is emerging.

During both the individual work and the team meetings, everything the team members produce is collected – emails, presentations, hand-written notes – so that it is available to the research team. The AMI Meeting Corpus is a publicly available [14] interdisciplinary resource, and the work that has been done on it contributes to organizational psychology and corpus linguistics as well as serving as material for the development of a range of multimodal processing and language recognition technologies.

4   The Many Uses of a Corpus

One way of viewing the AMI Meeting Corpus is as a collection of features, with training and test data, that allow us to develop component technologies. Since most corpus users, especially those involved in international evaluations, are concerned with improving the performance of some component or other, this is the dominant view. However, we have relied on the corpus not just during component development, but during all stages of the software lifecycle.

Our first use for the corpus was simply as inspiration for the kinds of applications we might build. With hindsight, it may seem obvious that we could build a content linking device using our technologies, and that the end users would be enthusiastic about it. However, it was not something we considered doing until we considered precisely how people actually behave in the recorded meetings. There is no substitute for this kind of observation. In particular, potential users can usually identify things they do not need, but are less good at introspecting about what they do need. This is why advanced user studies make use of recorded data among other observation and elicitation techniques [18].

Our second use was for the capture of user requirements. Potential users are able, given a concrete enough concept, to make suggestions about what would make for useful software features, and a way of making a concept concrete for them is by showing them how the concept would work. In the very early stages, before any programming is done, two techniques are helpful. One is describing specific meeting problems, either taken from or inspired by the corpus, and having users talk around them. The other is to use materials from the corpus to create mock-ups – still images that show a series of screenshots for an interface that could potentially be built. We used both techniques to inform our development.

Our final use was during application development itself. Part of this is continuing work on user requirements by taking prototypes to focus groups in the same way as the initial mock-ups, and of course, giving demonstrations to potential vendors and future funders, using the AMI Corpus in the following way. Working on an application that applies to live meetings creates particular challenges for development and demonstration. One cannot know what will happen in a live meeting ahead of time. This makes demonstrating on a live meeting fraught with danger, especially for early system versions. For this reason, we usually demonstrate using a recorded meeting, by playing it back in a separate frame or window and feeding its signals into the system as if they were live. For this purpose, the AMI Corpus design of meetings in series helps us considerably. We use a group's last meeting (a meeting labeled with 'd', e.g. 'ES2008d') to simulate a live meeting, treating segments from the three previous meetings (labeled 'a', 'b' and 'c') and associated documents as the group's history to be linked. This method makes it possible to demonstrate our technology when no meeting is happening, and, essentially, to replicate the same behaviour over and over again, a crucial property during software development and debugging.

There is one final point worth making about development of this kind of application. Making the componentry work online, fast enough for live use, is something that the research community often considers to be an uninteresting engineering task. Online processing usually involves trading off speed against accuracy, which is unattractive when one is judged by one's results without reference to processing time. Partly, it is the possibility of end user applications like our content linking device that motivates having this engineering work done. Because we demonstrate on a recorded meeting, at least at first, none of our componentry need work online. We can simply pre-process the recorded meeting and store the results for use during the demonstration, feeding them into the system as if they were live just as we do with the signals. To find out how the technology would actually work given the constraints of on-line processing, we gradually replace our simulated components with real online ones as the researchers make them available.

5   The AMIDA Automatic Content Linking Device

In a nutshell, the Automatic Content Linking Device performs searches at regular intervals over a database of documents and meeting recordings – derived from the AMI Meeting Corpus at this stage – with a search criterion that is constructed based on the words that are recognized automatically from an ongoing discussion. This requires the following processing stages. The corresponding modules and data exchanges between them are represented in Figure 1, and are further described in Sections 5.1 through 5.4 below.

1. *Document Bank Creator and Indexer*: Prepares, and updates before each meeting, a database of documents and of snippets of previous meetings in which media and annotations are aligned.
2. *Query Aggregator*: At regular and frequent intervals during a meeting (e.g. every 30 seconds or on the user's demand by clicking a button), prepares a query to this database, derived from the ongoing conversation through automatic speech recognition (ASR) or keyword spotting (KWS), possibly emphasizing certain keywords. The module then executes the query, retrieves the results, and integrates them with previous ones, so that their variation is smoothed in time.
3. *User Interface*: Displays the current search results, as clickable document links, and provides through them access to past documents and meeting recordings, but also to web pages through a web search API.

These functionalities are supported by a modular architecture called *The Hub* – represented as an area connecting several modules in Figure 1 – which allows communication through a subscription-based client/server protocol [19].

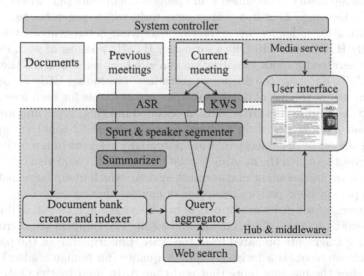

Fig. 1. Main components of the AMIDA ACLD. The two areas labeled as "Hub & middleware" and "Media server" represent the connection between all modules covering the respective areas. The Hub ensures real-time annotation exchange, while the Media server enables playback of audio and video from files or capture devices. ASR stands for automatic speech recognition, and KWS for keyword spotting.

The Hub allows the connection of heterogeneous software modules, which may operate locally or remotely, and ensures that data exchange is extremely fast – a requirement for real-time processing. Data circulating through the Hub is formatted as timed triples – i.e. tuples of (time, object, attribute, value) – and is stored in a relational database, which is able to deal with large-scale, real-time annotations of audio and video recordings. 'Producers' of annotations send triples to the Hub, which are received automatically by the 'consumers' that subscribed to the respective types, defined by pattern matching over object names. Consumers can also query directly the Hub's database for past annotations and metadata about meetings.

An annotation-playback function that resubmits existing annotations to the Hub, without duplication, is required by the ACLD for simulating online processing and is currently under implementation. Until this becomes available, real time is simulated using data streamers that produce data from the files containing AMI Corpus annotations in the NITE XML Toolkit (NXT) format [20].

Complementing the Hub, the HMI Media Server broadcasts audio and video that was captured in an instrumented meeting room to various media consumers, mainly the ASR, KWS, and User Interfaces. The media sources are the various files stored on the Multimodal Media File server [14].

5.1 Data Preparation: Pre-processing of Past Meetings

The *Document Bank Creator* (DBC) is run offline before a meeting, to create or update the repository of documents and pseudo-documents that will be searched during the meeting. This is a preparation task, which generates text versions of documents for indexing, by extracting text from heterogeneous file formats (essentially HTML and MS Office formats). HTML versions of each document are also generated for quick visualization in a web browser. The DBC then inserts into the Hub's database the document metadata – including URIs of source files – which identifies the list of documents that are available for each meeting, and lists their main properties: title, date, associated meeting, type, and authorship information when available. In a future scenario, the DBC could automatically construct the set of documents that are potentially relevant to a meeting, based on the project to which the meeting is related. The DBC could also be connected to an organizational content management system, which many large institutions set up as part of their policies regarding document sharing.

The document set includes snippets of previous meetings, as well as documents such as reports, memos, slides, emails, and so on. The snippets are currently one minute long fragments prepared from the ASR transcript [21] of the past meetings, which can be obtained with acceptable quality (for human readers) a couple of hours after the meeting (note that real-time ASR, used by the Query Aggregator, has a significantly lower accuracy). The trade-off in choosing the length of these snippets is between the need to have enough content words in each snippet, and the need for precision when snippets are opened in a meeting browser: if they are too large, then the user cannot easily find the region of interest. The segmentation into snippets currently avoids cutting through a speech segment.

The use of topic segments as snippets is under study, the main limitation being the large granularity of thematic episodes.

The text version of the files is indexed using the Apache Lucene open-source software, creating indexes for each meeting of the AMI Meeting Corpus (in the present demonstration version). Indexing optimizes word-based search over large document sets. Here, all words are used as keywords, and the index is optimized using word stemmers and the TF*IDF weighing scheme.

5.2 Sensing the User's Information Needs

The retrieval of relevant fragments from past meetings, or of related documents, requires input about the current topic of conversation of meeting participants, in an ongoing or replayed meeting. Although many capture devices could be used to provide such input, we believe that the most informative cues lie in the words that are spoken by the participants. Therefore, our main goal at this level is to use Automatic Speech Recognition and/or Keyword Spotting modules to construct queries over the meeting/document database.

Real-time large vocabulary speech recognition is still a challenging objective for the ASR community, but within the AMIDA project such a system has recently become available [22]. One of its main features is the trade-off between speed and accuracy, which allows it to run in real-time (with a slight but constant delay only) even on standard workstations. The AMI Corpus is also accompanied, for internal use, by sample results from the offline ASR system developed within the AMIDA project [21]. Three ways of running the ACLD are thus mainly distinguished here by the origin of the ASR output:

1. Real-time ASR from signals captured in a smart meeting room (here, the audio setting has a strong influence on the recognition accuracy).
2. Real-time ASR over recorded signals (for demonstration purposes).
3. Simulating real-time ASR by producing and sending to the Hub the results of higher-quality offline ASR (for development and demonstration purposes).

The words from the ASR are filtered for stopwords, so that only content words are used for search. Our list of stopwords has about 80 words, including the most common function words, interjections and discourse markers. Furthermore, we believe that existing knowledge about the important terminology of a project can be used to increase the impact of specific words on search. A list of pre-specified keywords can thus be defined, and if any of them are detected in the ASR from the meeting, then they can be specifically marked in the query so that their importance is increased when doing the search (see next section). A specific list was defined by the user-study group for the AMI Meeting Corpus, and at present it contains words or expressions such as 'cost', 'energy', 'component', 'case', 'chip', 'interface', 'button', 'L_C_D', 'material', 'latex', 'wood', 'titanium', and so on, for a total of about 30 words. This list can be modified online by the users of the ACLD, by adding or removing words. If no list of keywords is available, then all words from the query (except for the stopwords) simply receive equal weight.

The list of keywords can also be used directly by a real-time keyword spotting system, which identifies their occurrence in speech without performing ASR on the entire signal. We experimented with a system available within AMIDA [23], which allows to update the list of keywords during execution, i.e. during a meeting. The results are encouraging, especially for long keywords (short ones tend to be over-recognized), and current work is aimed at combining the KWS results with those from the real-time ASR, in order to increase the precision and the coverage (e.g. for out-of-vocabulary words) of speech recognition.

The functions described in this sub-section are performed by the *Query Aggregator* (QA) module. The QA periodically obtains from the Hub the words or keywords that were recognized, and processes them in batches corresponding to time frames of fixed size, e.g every 20-30 seconds – this can be modified when running the application. This typical duration is a compromise between the need to gather enough words for search, and the need to refresh the search results reasonably often. Instead of the fixed time frame, information about audio segmentation into spurts or utterances could be used for a more natural segmentation of the ASR input. Additionally, the QA can also launch a query when a user demands it by pressing a button in the interface.

5.3   Retrieval of Documents and Snippets

The QA uses the query words obtained from the ASR and/or the KWS to formulate a query which is addressed to an information retrieval engine (Apache Lucene), over the index of documents created by the DBC's indexer. If any of the pre-specified keywords are detected in the speech, then they are specifically marked in the query, and their importance is increased when doing the search. Using this keyword boosting mechanism (specific to the Lucene engine), the weight of keywords is currently set at five times the weight of the other, non-boosted, words. The results returned by the Lucene engine are the meeting fragments and documents that most closely match the query – in information retrieval terms – in the respective time frame.

The QA then returns to the Hub the results, specifically, as a list of structured records such as: (meeting, time, keyword, relevance, document type, URL). To improve the informativeness of the result displayed in the user interface, it is useful to include in this record the keywords that were matched, i.e. the ones that helped to retrieve the specific document, as well as a relevance score produced by the search engine. This retrieval task has thus a similar goal as speech/document alignment [7,6], except that alignment is viewed here as the construction of sets of relevant documents for each meeting segment, and not only as finding the document that the segment "is about". The retrieval techniques that are employed here are therefore quite different too, as speech/document alignment relies on precise matching between a referring expression and one of the elements of a document.

To avoid inconsistent results from one time frame to another, due to the fact that word choice varies considerably in such small samples, and therefore search results vary as well, a persistence (smoothing) mechanism was defined, partly inspired by the notion of perceptual salience of entities: the relevance of the meeting fragments and documents amounts to a form of conceptual salience that evolves in time.

The persistence mechanism adjusts the current relevance scores for each document returned by the search engine, considering also the documents from the previous time frame and their own adjusted relevance scores. If t_n denotes the current time frame and t_{n-1} the previous one, and if $r(t_n, d_k)$ is the raw relevance of document d_k computed by the search engine after a query at time t_n, then the *adjusted relevance* $r'(t_n, d_k)$ computed using the persistence (smoothing) mechanism, is defined as follows (we note $r(t_n, d_k)$ as r_n for clarity reasons): $r'_n = \alpha * r_n + (1 - \alpha) * r'_{n-1}$ – with a typical value of $\alpha = 0.8$ being used. The larger the α factor, the more persistent the documents tend to be in the display interface, where they are sorted by relevance. Additionally, a filtering mechanism deletes the least relevant of the documents which are sent to the Hub and to the interface, using absolute and relative thresholding, as described in [24, p. 280].

Some user groups encouraged an extension of the Query Aggregator to provide web search as a complement to the existing document search. This was implemented using the Google API, which, like other web search engines but unlike Lucene, does not allow keyword boosting in queries and limits query size (32 words for Google). Therefore, the web query is built in a slightly different way: if any keywords from the pre-specified list are detected during the latest time interval, only these keywords are appended to build the query; if no keywords are detected, then all detected words are used. The web domain which is searched can be specified and changed during the meeting by the users (for the moment, it is set to http://en.wikipedia.org).

5.4   Accessing the Meeting Corpus and Documents

A number of concepts for the *User Interfaces* (UI) are currently being developed and tested: user-friendliness is one of the main criteria orienting our design. Two examples are shown here: a full-screen UI (Figure 2) that displays simultaneously, in several frames, all the information related to content linking, and a widget UI (Figure 3), which minimizes the use of the screen's real estate through the use of tabs, and the opening of documents and meeting snippets in separate viewers.

Figure 2 shows a snapshot of the full-screen UI over meeting ES2008d. On the top left, the list of recognized keywords, referring to important concepts for the group's activity, reassures the user about the search terms being used, as they were recognized from the audio. Every 30 seconds or on demand (by pressing the "update" button), a newly recognized keyword set is added in the top left frame; this also triggers and immediate query in the QA, and the update of results (documents/snippets, and websites). The bottom left frame, which scrolls in the same way as the keywords, shows the five most relevant document names for that time in the meeting, as well the five most relevant web pages, ordered by relevance. The frame can also display all past results as well, appended to the current one, if the user wishes so ("show all" checkbox at the bottom left).

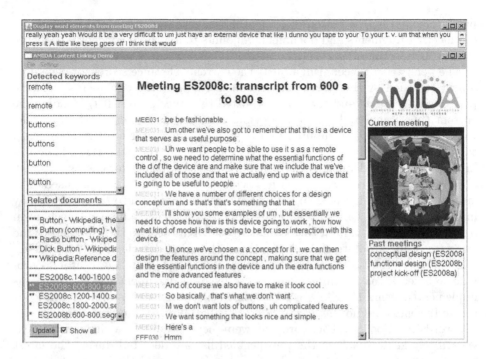

Fig. 2. Snapshot of the ACLD's full-screen UI, showing a fragment of a past meeting being retrieved among the list of relevant documents at the bottom left corner, and being opened in the central frame. The window above the ACLD displays the words as they are recognized by the ASR, or are streamed into the Hub from offline ASR.

At the bottom right of the full-screen UI is a static display showing the three meetings in the history, giving access to their contents, metadata and summaries. Above that, the interface displays a room-view video of the ongoing meeting, with the audio in the case of past meetings. The UI displays in the centre frame a text or HTML version of the selected document, or opens the selected web page.

Figure 3 shows a snapshot of the widget UI, taken at some time during replay of meeting ES2008d. This version of the UI is a deliberately simplified window frame reduced to show exclusively content that is actually delivered by the ACLD at runtime, split into three tabs, which contain respectively:

1. Labels of the relevant documents and past meeting snippets found in the meeting index, preceded by an appropriate icon corresponding to the document type, to support faster identification by the user.
2. Relevant web links found within the pre-specified web domain.
3. Keywords recognized in the respective system turn, or alternatively all recognized words with highlighted keywords.

The rank of a label in the document result list, as well as its font size, indicate its relevance within the query result; for web search results, the only indicator

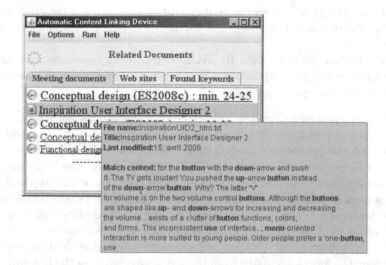

Fig. 3. Snapshot of AMIDA ACLD's widget UI, showing the tab with the list of relevant documents at a given moment, with explicit document and snippet labels. Hovering over a label displays the metadata associated with the document, as well as excerpts where the keywords were found. Tabs displaying detected keywords and retrieved websites are also available.

of relevance is the rank. Hovering over a result link (document, meeting snippet, web link) provides metadata about it in a pop-up window, including most importantly the *match context* shown in Figure 3. The match contexts which shows excerpts of the document that match keywords and words detected from speech, with surrounding words. Clicking on a link opens the respective document using an appropriate viewing program – respectively, a native editor, a meeting browser (JFerret, a successor to Ferret [25]), or a web browser.

6   Evaluation

Several approaches were considered for the evaluation of the ACLD application, but all of them require a significance investment of resources, in terms of human subjects or of ground truth data, which amounts to human annotators as well. If reference-based and task-based evaluation methods are distinguished, then the first two of the following approaches are reference-based, and the last two are task-based:

1. Construct ground truth data by asking human annotators to associate to each meeting segment the documents they believe are relevant, from a pool of limited size; then, check whether the ACLD actually finds those documents.
2. Ask human judges to assess the relevance of each document returned by the ACLD for a given meeting recording.

3. Test the ACLD *in use* on the participants to an ongoing meeting, by measuring for instance how often and for how long they consult the proposed documents.
4. Assess user-satisfaction with the ACLD (e.g. using questionnaires or interviews) after using the application in a meeting, or after seeing a demonstration of the concept.

The first two approaches provide "objective" measures of performance, in terms of precision and recall, but they evaluate the performance of the retrieval engine (Lucene and the persistence model) rather than the entire application, which includes a larger set of components. Therefore, the task-based or user-centric evaluation appears to be more suitable for evaluating the entire application, by assessing its utility for a specific use. Of course, many factors beyond the concept and the technology contribute to overall utility of an application, such as the user-friendliness of the UI, the IT literacy of the users, and so on.

In the two following sub-sections, we summarize initial evaluation results obtained using the fourth approach from the list above, while in the last sub-section we outline the setting that will be used for the third approach, evaluation in use.

6.1   Feedback from Focus Groups

The ACLD concept was shown to two focus groups of about eight persons each, one concerned with the military domain, and the other with meetings in large organizations [26].

The groups found the general concept of content linking useful for groups that have a large information-base from which to draw material, but suggested that content be linked only on demand, not continually. The content linking concept was seen as adding value also, or sometimes mostly, for the individual meeting participant, by helping them retrieve information that has been forgotten and even catch up with parts of a meeting missed through inattention or non-attendance. Access to personally held information was seen as useful, but so was sharing personal linked content with the group, as long as it would be possible to separate private and common spaces. The capacity to add one's own keywords to the system was seen as crucial, although it appeared clearly that keywords alone could not be used exclusively to find the right information. Other search aids that could enrich the ACLD should focus on information about the people involved in meetings, and other meeting metadata such as location and attendance. One group thought that it would be useful to look back at the documents or presentations used during previous meetings; documents should be identified by author, version number, date, and time. To avoid distracting the user, the ACLD needs to work as much as possible autonomously in the background.

6.2   User Feedback to Prototype Demonstrations

We have demonstrated the ACLD to potential industrial partners, namely, about forty representatives of companies that are active in the field of meeting technology. Typically, a series of sessions, lasting 30 minutes each, started with a presentation of the ACLD and continued with a discussion, during which notes were taken. The participants found that both online and offline application scenarios seemed promising, as well as both individual and group uses. The ACLD received very positive verbal evaluation, as well as useful feedback and suggestions for future work [27, p. 18-21]. Several companies are negotiating with us to demonstrate the technology on their own meetings.

6.3   Evaluation in Use: The TBE Setup

We have selected the same Task-Based Evaluation (TBE) method that we have previously used to evaluate meeting browsers [28,29, p. 8-18 and 31-35] for the ACLD meeting assistant as well. The protocol makes use of the AMI Meeting Corpus, and requires a group of four subjects to carry out a remote control design task that was started by a previous group recorded in the corpus, from which three recorded meetings ('a', 'b' and 'c' from a series) and the related documents are available. In the original TBE campaign, we tested various groups that either only had access to the documents that came out of the previous meetings, or could use one of three types of meeting browser. The evaluation measures were the efficiency of the groups in solving the task, their satisfaction with the tools, but also the analysis of tool usage in itself. These experiments provide a "baseline" to which groups carrying out a similar task, but using now the ACLD to access previous recordings and documents, can be compared, so that the benefits of the ACLD can be assessed. We are currently at the stage of pilot testing this form of evaluation, and adapting the ACLD software to the testing conditions.

7   Conclusion and Future Work

The ACLD is currently a research prototype that demonstrates how access to a very large corpus can be made easier in a context where automatic, query-free retrieval can be used to facilitate access to past meetings and documents from ongoing meetings. The complexity of the demonstrator, and the challenges of real-time processing, were gradually solved by using offline annotations from the AMI Meeting Corpus. Therefore, at present, the ACLD offers a sound platform for experimenting with access techniques to multimodal corpora, to which new data processing modules can be added, followed by tests of their effectiveness in improving retrieval or visualisation of corpus data.

The first implementation of the ACLD allowed us to demonstrate the concept and to collect feedback that tells us what is most important for turning it into a real-world application. For instance, potential users have made clear that the graphical layout of the interface is important, leading us to experiment with the full-screen and widget UIs. A general goal is to reduce the number of mouse clicks required to access the content of documents. Color-coding the document types and displaying their relations to the (key)words recognized from the audio might also improve user experience, according to the feedback obtained.

Potential users suggested some additional functionalities that we are considering. For instance, keeping a record of the documents that were consulted during a meeting might help users who want to go back to them after the meeting, and is of course essential for evaluation. Retrieval could be improved by including a relevance feedback mechanism for the returned documents, by representing keywords in a structured manner, e.g. using tag clouds, and by using word sense disambiguation to improve the precision of the retrieval.

The ACLD could also be useful, in the future, in a series of meetings to understand what topics re-occur, when a discussion is being repeated, and also which topics never get discussed because they are forgotten. Tag clouds for topics can help to support this understanding. This kind of functionality would take the concept from information presentation towards intervention in the current group discussion, and could make the ACLD part of a broader-scope meeting assistant.

Modern recording techniques open out many possibilities for new technologies that exploit archived multimodal data. Our Automatic Content Linking Device is just one possible example, but one that has excited the interest of companies that work in the area of meeting support or are potential consumers of such technology. We relied on a recorded corpus throughout the process of creating it – as inspiration, to capture user requirements, and as a platform for development, demonstration, and evaluation. The same process could be applied for a wide range of novel applications that exploit the same kind of underlying resource.

Acknowledgments

This work was supported by the European Union's IST Programme, through the AMIDA Integrated Project FP6-0033812, Augmented Multiparty Interaction with Distance Access, and by the Swiss National Science Foundation, through the IM2 National Center of Competence in Research. The authors would like to thank here their colleagues from the ACLD and Hub development teams: Erik Boertjes, Sandro Castronovo, Michal Fapso, Mike Flynn, Alexandre Nanchen, Theresa Wilson, Joost de Wit, and Majid Yazdani, as well as Danil Korchagin and Mike Lincoln for help with real-time ASR.

References

1. Hart, P.E., Graham, J.: Query-free information retrieval. IEEE Expert: Intelligent Systems and Their Applications 12(5), 32–37 (1997)
2. Rhodes, B.J., Starner, T.: The Remembrance Agent: A continuously running information retrieval system. In: PAAM 1996 (1st International Conference on Practical Applications of Intelligent Agents and Multi-Agent Technology), London, pp. 486–495 (1996)
3. Rhodes, B.J., Maes, P.: Just-in-time information retrieval agents. IBM Systems Journal 39(3-4), 685–704 (2000)

4. Budzik, J., Hammond, K.J.: User interactions with everyday applications as context for just-in-time information access. In: IUI 2000 (5th International Conference on Intelligent User Interfaces), New Orleans, LA (2000)
5. Henziker, M., Chang, B.W., Milch, B., Brin, S.: Query-free news search. World Wide Web: Internet and Web Information Systems 8, 101–126 (2005)
6. Popescu-Belis, A., Lalanne, D.: Reference resolution over a restricted domain: References to documents. In: ACL 2004 Workshop on Reference Resolution and its Applications, Barcelona, pp. 71–78 (2004)
7. Mekhaldi, D., Lalanne, D., Ingold, R.: From searching to browsing through multimodal documents linking. In: ICDAR 2005 (8th International Conference on Document Analysis and Recognition), Seoul, pp. 924–928 (2005)
8. Nijholt, A., Rienks, R., Zwiers, J., Reidsma, D.: Online and off-line visualization of meeting information and meeting support. The Visual Computer 22(12), 965–976 (2006)
9. Rhodes, B.J.: The wearable Remembrance Agent: A system for augmented memory. Personal Technologies: Special Issue on Wearable Computing 1, 218–224 (1997)
10. Franz, A., Milch, B.: Searching the Web by voice. In: Coling 2002 (19th International Conference on Computational Linguistics), Taipei, pp. 11–15 (2002)
11. Chang, E., Seide, F., Meng, H.M., Chen, Z., Shi, Y., Li, Y.C.: A system for spoken query information retrieval on mobile devices. IEEE Transactions on Speech and Audio Processing 10(8), 531–541 (2002)
12. Garofolo, J.S., Auzanne, C.G.P., Voorhees, E.M.: The TREC spoken document retrieval track: A success story. In: RIAO 2000 (6th International Conference on Computer-Assisted Information Retrieval), Paris, pp. 1–20 (2000)
13. Lew, M., Sebe, N., Djeraba, C., Jain, R.: Content-based multimedia information retrieval: State of the art and challenges. ACM Transactions on Multimedia Computing, Communications, and Applications (TOMCCAP) 2(1), 1–19 (2006)
14. AMI Consortium: The AMI Meeting Corpus, http://corpus.amiproject.org (accessed November 18, 2008)
15. Carletta, J.: Unleashing the killer corpus: experiences in creating the multi-everything AMI Meeting Corpus. Language Resources and Evaluation Journal 41(2), 181–190 (2007)
16. Carletta, J., Ashby, S., Bourban, S., Flynn, M., Guillemot, M., Hain, T., Kadlec, J., Karaiskos, V., Kraaij, W., Kronenthal, M., Lathoud, G., Lincoln, M., Lisowska, A., McCowan, I., Post, W., Reidsma, D., Wellner, P.: The AMI Meeting Corpus: A pre-announcement. In: Renals, S., Bengio, S. (eds.) MLMI 2005. LNCS, vol. 3869, pp. 28–39. Springer, Heidelberg (2006)
17. AMI Consortium: The AMI multimodal meeting database – infrastructure, data and management. Deliverable 2.2, AMI (Augmented Multi-party Interaction) Integrated Project FP 6506811 (August 2005)
18. Whittaker, S., Tucker, S., Swampillai, K., Laban, R.: Design and evaluation of systems to support interaction capture and retrieval. Personal and Ubiquitous Computing 12(3), 197–221 (2008)
19. AMI Consortium: Commercial component definition. Deliverable 7.2, AMIDA (Augmented Multi-party Interaction with Distance Access) Integrated Project IST 033812 (November 2007)
20. Carletta, J., Evert, S., Heid, U., Kilgour, J.: The NITE XML Toolkit: Data model and query language. Language Resources and Evaluation 39(4), 313–334 (2005)

21. Hain, T., Burget, L., Dines, J., Garau, G., Karafiat, M., Lincoln, M., Vepa, J., Wan, V.: The AMI system for the transcription of speech in meetings. In: ICASSP 2007 (32nd International Conference on Acoustics, Speech, and Signal Processing), Honolulu, pp. 357–360 (2007)
22. Garner, P.N., Dines, J., Hain, T., El Hannani, A., Karafiat, M., Korchagin, D., Lincoln, M., Wan, V., Zhang, L.: Real-time ASR from meetings. Technical report (2009)
23. Szoke, I., Schwarz, P., Matejka, P., Burget, L., Karafiat, M., Fapso, M., Cernocky, J.: Comparison of keyword spotting approaches for informal continuous speech. In: Eurospeech 2005 (9th European Conference on Speech Communication and Technology), Lisbon, pp. 633–636 (2005)
24. Popescu-Belis, A., Boertjes, E., Kilgour, J., Poller, P., Castronovo, S., Wilson, T., Jaimes, A., Carletta, J.: The AMIDA automatic content linking device: Just-in-time document retrieval in meetings. In: Popescu-Belis, A., Stiefelhagen, R. (eds.) MLMI 2008. LNCS, vol. 5237, pp. 272–283. Springer, Heidelberg (2008)
25. Wellner, P., Flynn, M., Guillemot, M.: Browsing recorded meetings with Ferret. In: Bengio, S., Bourlard, H. (eds.) MLMI 2004. LNCS, vol. 3361, pp. 12–21. Springer, Heidelberg (2005)
26. AMI Consortium: HCI evaluation of prototype applications. Deliverable 6.3, AMIDA (Augmented Multi-party Interaction with Distance Access) Integrated Project IST-033812 (October 2008)
27. AMI Consortium: AMIDA proof-of-concept system architecture. Deliverable 6.7, AMIDA (Augmented Multi-party Interaction with Distance Access) Integrated Project IST 033812 (March 2008)
28. Post, W.M., Elling, E., Cremers, A.H.M., Kraaij, W.: Experimental comparison of multimodal meeting browsers. In: Smith, M.J., Salvendy, G. (eds.) HCII 2007. LNCS, vol. 4558, pp. 118–127. Springer, Heidelberg (2007)
29. AMI Consortium: Meeting browser evaluation. Deliverable 6.4, AMI (Augmented Multi-party Interaction) Integrated Project FP 6506811 (December 2006)

An Exchange Format for Multimodal Annotations

Thomas Schmidt[1], Susan Duncan[2], Oliver Ehmer[3], Jeffrey Hoyt[4],
Michael Kipp[5], Dan Loehr[4], Magnus Magnusson[6], Travis Rose[7],
and Han Sloetjes[8]

[1] University of Hamburg
[2] University of Chicago
[3] University of Freiburg
[4] MITRE Corporation
[5] DFKI Saarbrücken
[6] Human Behavior Laboratory Reykjavik
[7] Virginia Tech
[8] MPI for Psycholinguistics Nijmegen

Abstract. This paper presents the results of a joint effort of a group of multi-modality researchers and tool developers to improve the interoperability between several tools used for the annotation and analysis of multimodality. Each of the tools has specific strengths so that a variety of different tools, working on the same data, can be desirable for project work. However this usually requires tedious conversion between formats. We propose a common exchange format for multimodal annotation, based on the annotation graph (AG) formalism, which is supported by import and export routines in the respective tools. In the current version of this format the common denominator information can be reliably exchanged between the tools, and additional information can be stored in a standardized way.

1 Introduction

This paper presents the results of a joint effort of a group of multimodality researchers and tool developers (see [16, 17]) to improve the interoperability between several tools used for the annotation and analysis of multimodality. We propose a common exchange format for multimodal annotation, based on the annotation graph formalism, which is supported by import and export routines in the respective tools.

The paper is structured as follows: section 2 gives an overview of the multimodal annotation tools involved. Section 3 discusses the main commonalities and differences in these tools' data models and formats. Section 4 describes the main characteristics of the exchange format. Section 5 is concerned with the implementation of conversion routines from the tools' formats to the exchange format and vice versa. Section 6, finally, discusses some possible future improvements or extensions of the exchange format. The appendix contains an exemplary, commented annotation file in the multimodal annotation exchange format.

M. Kipp et al. (Eds.): Multimodal Corpora, LNAI 5509, pp. 207–221, 2009.

2 Tools

The following tools were considered in this effort:

- ANVIL, a video annotation tool, developed by Michael Kipp at the DFKI in Saarbrücken (see [1, 11, 12] and figure 1). ANVIL's main application area is the study of multimodality. Other application fields include human-computer interaction, psychology, ethnology, conversation analysis and dance studies.

Fig. 1. User interface of ANVIL

- C-BAS, a tool for coding events on video or audio tracks, developed by Kevin Moffit at the University of Arizona (see [7]).
- ELAN, a tool for multi-level annotation of video and audio, developed by the Max-Planck-Institute for Psycholinguistics in Nijmegen(see [6, 9, 27]). ELAN's main application areas include studies of multimodality, studies of sign language and field linguistics (documentation of endangered languages).
- EXMARaLDA Partitur-Editor, a tool for transcription of audio or video recordings of spoken language, developed by Thomas Schmidt at the University of Hamburg (see [10, 23, 24] and figure 3). EXMARaLDA is mostly used in conversation and discourse analysis, language acquisition studies and dialectology (multimodality being an issue in all fields except dialectology).
- MacVisSTA, a tool for annotation and visualization of multiple time-synchronized videos, developed by Travis Rose, Francis Queck and Chreston Miller at Virginia Tech (see [21, 22]).

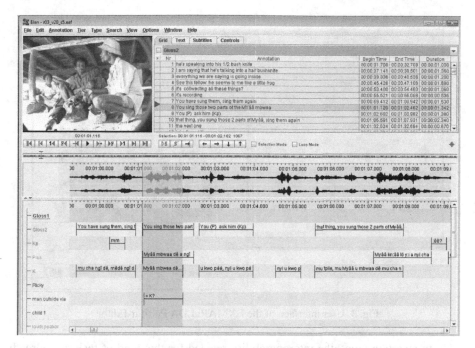

Fig. 2. User interface of ELAN

- Theme, a commercial software tool for finding patterns in temporally annotated data, developed by Magnus Magnusson for Noldus (see [25]).
- Transformer, a tool for exchanging annotation data between different annotation tools and for creating customizable printable transcripts, developed by Oliver Ehmer at the University of Freiburg (see [26]).

These tools differ greatly in their technical details, in their intended target audiences, in the design of their user interfaces and in the specific tasks they help to solve. They have in common, however, that they all allow the creation of or the work with analytic textual data which is time-aligned to a video recording. They are therefore all used to carry out multi-modal annotation and analysis.

It is not uncommon, though, that a researcher wants to exchange data between two or more of them, because no single tool offers all the functionality required for a given task. This is all the more true of large distributed projects where different operations on the data are carried out at different locations and by different people. For instance, a typical processing pipeline could look like this:

1) EXMARaLDA is used to transcribe the verbal behavior in an interaction,
2) ELAN's advanced video support is needed to add detailed annotation of multi-modal behavior,
3) Theme is used to carry out an analysis of the annotated data,
4) Transformer is used to generate a visualization of the annotated data.

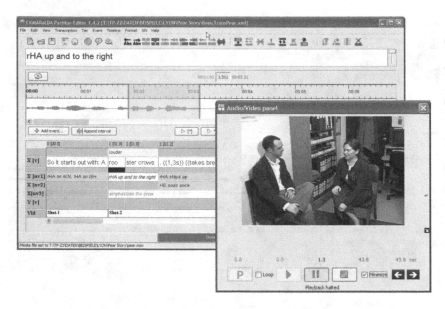

Fig. 3. User interface of the EXMARaLDA Partitur-Editor

Up to a certain point, the interoperability needed for this kind of task was already provided before our effort by some of the tools in the form of import and export routines converting between the tools' own data format and that of another. However, this was an inefficient and unreliable solution because it meant that each tool developer had to keep track of and react to changes in all other tools. The obvious solution therefore was to agree on a common exchange format which can accommodate all the information contained in the individual tools' formats.

3   Comparison of Data Formats

As a first step towards this goal, a thorough analysis and comparison of the different tool formats was carried out. All formats have in common that their basic building blocks are annotation tuples consisting of a start and an end point (with, typically, a temporal interpretation) and one or more text labels (with no fixed interpretation). Since this is precisely the principle on which the annotation graph formalism (AG, see [4]) is based, it was natural to choose AGs as a general framework for our task. As a further advantage, several software packages facilitating the work with AGs already exist [2].

However, there are differences between the formats (1) with respect to the way the basic building blocks are organised into larger structures, (2) with respect to semantic specifications of and structural constraints on the basic and larger structural entities, and (3) with respect to organization on the storage level, for storing the underlying scheme and projects containing multiple data files. The following section discusses the differences in the formats which were identified to be relevant in terms of interoperability.

3.1 General Organisation of the Data Structure

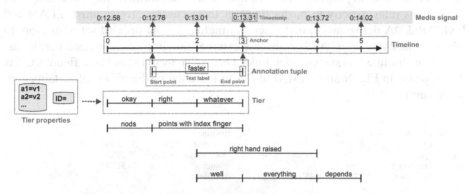

Fig. 4. Schematic diagram of basic elements of the data models

3.1.1 Tier-Based Data Formats vs. Non-Tier-Based Formats

In ANVIL, ELAN, EXMARaLDA and Transformer, all annotations are partitioned into a number of tiers such that each annotation is part of exactly one tier, and no two annotations within a tier overlap. These tiers are usually used to group annotations which belong to one level of analysis (e.g. verbal vs. non-verbal behaviour, hand movements vs. facial expression) or to one participant (in multi-party interaction). By contrast, C-BAS, MacVisSTA and Theme do not have the concept of a tier; they keep all annotations in a single list. When converting from a non-tier-based format to a tier-based format, a partition of this list into tiers must be found. In the other direction, the grouping can be ignored or, if the target format provides this possibility, the category underlying the grouping can be represented as a property of an individual annotation.

3.1.2 Single vs. Multiple Labels

Annotations consist of a single label in ELAN, EXMARaLDA, MacVisSTA and Transformer, while ANVIL, C-BAS and Theme can have multiple (typed) labels for one and the same annotation. In ANVIL, these are organized by tier. Each tier T can have a set A_1-A_n of typed attributes. Every added annotation can then fill these attributes. When converting from multi-label formats to a single-label format, each multi-label annotation has to be split into a corresponding number of single-label annotations on different tiers. For instance, as figure 5 illustrates, an ANVIL track T with attributes A_1-A_n (left) would be translated to n separate tiers in ELAN (right).

```
<track name="speaker_1">                          <tier name="speaker_1_words">
  <el start="0.12" end="0.27">                      <annotation start="0.12" end="0.27">you</annotation>
    <attribute name="words">you</attribute>         <annotation start="0.27" end="0.36">lie</annotation>
    <attribute name="POS">PRO</attribute>         </tier>
  </el>                                            <tier name="speaker_1_POS">
  <el start="0.27" end="0.36">                      <annotation start="0.12" end="0.27">PRO</annotation>
    <attribute name="words">lie</attribute>         <annotation start="0.27" end="0.36">V</annotation>
    <attribute name="POS">V</attribute>           </tier>
  </el>
</track>
```

Fig. 5. Correspondences between multi-label (left) and single-label (right) annotation

3.1.3 Implicit vs. Explicit Timeline

In ANVIL, C-BAS MacVisSTA, Theme and Transformer, the timestamps of annotations refer directly to media times in the recording. By contrast, ELAN and EXMARaLDA define an explicit external timeline, i.e. an ordered set of anchors to which annotations refer. Anchors in this external timeline can, but need not, be assigned an absolute timestamp which links them to the media signal (see figure 6). It is thus possible in ELAN and EXMARaLDA to leave the media offsets of certain annotations unspecified.[1]

```
<tier name="speaker_1_words">
   <annotation start="0.12" end="0.27">
      you
   </annotation>
   <annotation start="0.27" end="0.36">
      lie
   </annotation>
</tier>
<tier name="speaker_1_POS">
   <annotation start="0.12" end="0.27">
      PRO
   </annotation>
   <annotation start="0.27" end="0.36">
      V
   </annotation>
</tier>
```

```
<timeline>
   <anchor id="T0" time="0.12"/>
   <anchor id="T1" time="0.27"/>
   <anchor id="T2" time="0.36"/>
</timeline>

<tier name="speaker_1_words">
   <annotation start="T0" end="T1">you</annotation>
   <annotation start="T1" end="T2">lie</annotation>
</tier>
<tier name="speaker_1_POS">
   <annotation start="T0" end="T1">PRO</annotation>
   <annotation start="T1" end="T2">V</annotation>
</tier>
```

Fig. 6. Implicit (left) and explicit (right) timeline

In terms of interoperability, the difference between implicit and explicit timelines poses two problems: First, the former do not permit unspecified media offsets. When going from a format with an explicit to a format with an implicit timeline, missing offsets therefore have to be calculated. The simplest way to achieve this is through (linear) interpolation. Second, in going from an implicit to an explicit timeline, the question arises of how to treat points with identical offsets. If two such points are mapped to different anchors (the EXMARaLDA and ELAN formats allow this[2]), there is no straightforward way of ordering them and contradictory data structures (i.e. annotations whose endpoint precedes their startpoint in the timeline) may result. This has to be taken care of in the conversion routines.

---

[1] In other words: the annotator can freely determine the degree of precision of the alignment between annotations and recordings. By the same logic, it becomes possible to have a completely non-temporal interpretation of start and end points – for instance, when the annotated object is not a recording, but a written text.

[2] In contrast to EXMARaLDA, however, ELAN places certain restrictions on the sharing of anchors. It does not allow single anchors per time value to be shared by different annotations on tiers that are independent of each other. Sharing of anchors is only used to consistently link the begin point and end point of chains of annotations on parent and child tiers and for the construction of annotation chains on time-aligned dependent tiers that do not allow gaps. This is a kind of object-oriented approach to managing time anchors.

3.2 Semantic Specifications and Constraints

The properties of the multimodal annotation formats discussed so far, just like the AG framework in general, are on a relatively high level of abstraction. That is, they concern very general *structural* characteristics of annotation data, and they do not say very much about their *semantics*.[3] While a high level of abstraction is beneficial to interoperability in many ways, actual applications profit from more concrete semantic specifications. All of the tools considered in our effort introduce such specifications as a part of their data models and formats, thereby often imposing further structural constraints on annotations which may have to be taken into account in data conversion.

3.2.1 Speaker Assignment of Tiers

In EXMARaLDA and ELAN, a tier can be assigned to one member of an externally defined set of speakers. In all other tools, speaker assignment can only be expressed on the surface, e.g. by using appropriate tier names, but speakers and speaker assignment are not an integral part of the semantics of the respective data model.

3.2.2 Parent/Child Relations between Tiers

In Anvil, ELAN and Transformer, tiers can be explicitly assigned to a parent tier. Tied to this assignment is the constraint that annotations in child tiers must have an annotation, or a chain of annotations, in the parent tier with identical start and end points. This relationship can be used, for example, to ensure that annotating elements (e.g. POS tags) always have an annotated element (e.g. a word) they refer to. In fact, in ANVIL and ELAN, certain annotations in child tiers do not even get an immediate reference to the timeline. Instead, they inherit their start and end points from the corresponding annotation in the parent tier.[4] This increases robustness since a misalignment of such logically related elements can never occur. Apart from such structural constraint on the tiers' content, ANVIL also allows to organize tiers themselves hierarchically into groups and subgroups for visual organization (like directory folders) and inheritance of coding scheme properties (group attributes are inherited by all contained tracks).

3.2.3 Tier Types

All tier-based tools define some kind of tier typology, i.e. ways of classifying individual tiers with respect to their semantic or structural properties. Thus, tiers in ANVIL can be of type 'primary' 'singleton' or 'span', reflecting structural properties related to the parent/child distinction described above. Similarly, ELAN distinguishes between the 'symbolic' types 'time subdivision', 'included in', 'symbolic subdivision' and 'symbolic association' (Transformer uses the same distinctions), and EXMARaLDA has the tier types 'transcription', 'description' and 'annotation' .

All these type distinctions address a similar issue - they tell 'their' application about meaningful operations that can be carried out on the annotation data. However,

---

[3] It is in this sense that Bird/Liberman (2001:55) call their AG framework "ontologically parsimonious (if not positively miserly!)".

[4] In ELAN, this is done through an explicit reference from an annotation in the child tier to a parent annotation on the parent tier. In certain cases, this is combined with a reference to the preceding annotation on the same (child) tier. In that way, a chain of (ordered) child annotations with the same parent is formed.

the very fact that the typologies serve an application-specific purpose makes it difficult to map between them when it comes to data conversion.

However, some similarities exist, for instance, between ELAN-ANVIL types. Thus, the ANVIL 'singleton' type is equivalent to ELAN's 'symbolic association' (both types impose a one-to-one relationship between pairs of annotations on the two given tiers), and the ANVIL 'span' type is equivalent to ELAN's 'included in' (both types imply that an annotation on tier A (temporally) contains a series of annotations on tier B[5], possibly with gaps).

3.2.4 Restrictions on Label Content

Besides classifying annotations according to their structural properties, some tools also provide a way of prescribing permissible values for annotation labels. Anvil has the most far-reaching functionality in this respect – it allows the definition of possible annotation values in a separate 'specification file'. This file stores the complete syntactic 'blueprint' of the annotation (sometimes called the coding scheme), i.e. names and types of all tiers, including their corresponding typed attributes. A similar purpose is fulfilled by a so-called 'controlled vocabulary' in ELAN.

There was some discussion in our group as to whether these specifications are to be considered part of the tools' formats at all. In any case, the fact that not every tool format provides a place for specifying such restrictions on label content makes this kind of data problematic for data exchange. Moreover, the AG formalism and format do not (at least not in any straightforward way) support the definition of such sets.

4 Exchange Format

Given that AG had been chosen as the general framework, we decided to develop the exchange format on the basis of AG's XML-based file format, which is identical to level 0 of the Atlas Interchange Format (AIF, see [2, 13, 19]).[6]

We agreed to use the following strategy: First, we would define the greatest common denominator of all tool formats and make sure that we achieve lossless exchange of this information. Second, we would devise a way of uniformly encoding all information

---

[5] Similarly, EXMARaLDA requires that for every annotation A on a tier of type 'A', there must be a temporally contiguous set of annotations $B_1...B_n$ on a tier of type 'T', assigned to the same speaker, such that A and $B_1...B_n$ cover the same time interval. A is then interpreted as a (dependent) annotation of $B_1...B_n$ (e.g. a translation of a transcribed utterance). The EXMARaLDA editor, however, does not enforce these constraints during input (because EXMARaLDA was partly designed for post-editing large sets of legacy data in which such constraints had been inconsistently dealt with), but rather provides the user with a possibility to check the well-formedness of data structures in a separate step.

[6] It should be noted that, in one place, we did *not* adhere to the AG format specification: [19] prescribes the use of so-called 'fully qualified' identifiers for nodes, arcs, etc. in which the identifier attribute can be used to infer the place of an element in the document tree (e.g.: "an anchor 'Timit:AG1:Anchor2' belongs to the annotation graph 'Timit:AG1', which in turn belongs to the AGSet 'Timit'." [19]). Since, however, the XML specification explicitly disallows the use of colons in ID attributes (leading to various problems with XML parsers), we decided not to follow this convention in the exchange format.

which goes beyond the common denominator. In that way, the exchange format will at least capture all the available information, and each tool's import routine can decide whether and how it can make use of that information. While this manner of proceeding does not guarantee lossless round-tripping between different tools, it should at least make it possible for the user to work with a chain of tools with increasingly complex data formats without losing any information in the conversion process(es).

Essentially, the greatest common denominator consists in the basic building blocks (i.e. labels with start and end times) plus the additional structural entities (tiers and timeline) discussed in section 3.1. The concepts discussed in section 3.2., on the other hand, go beyond the common denominator information. Consequently, the main characteristics of the exchange format are as follows:

4.1 Annotations and Timeline

As prescribed by AIF, annotations are represented in <Annotation> elements which refer to external <Anchor> elements via 'start' and 'end' attributes. We decided to use the 'type' feature to specify the tier. Note that in AIF there is originally no concept of 'tier'. However, it makes sense to think of different tiers as different 'types' of information (see next section). The annotation content is represented in one or more[7] <Feature> elements underneath the <Annotation> element, e.g.:

```
<Anchor id="T6" offset="10" unit="milliseconds"/>
<Anchor id="T7" offset="30" unit="milliseconds"/> [...]
<Annotation type="TIE1" start="T6" end="T7">
        <Feature name="description">And so hee</Feature>
</Annotation>
```

As mentioned above, for tools without an explicit timeline, the <Anchor> elements have to be generated from timestamps within annotations. Conversely, when a tool with an explicit timeline defines an anchor without a timestamp, the timestamp is added in the exchange format by interpolating between the nearest preceding and following timestamps that *do* have a timestamp.[8]

4.2 Tier Assignment

AIF's <MetadataElement> element is used to record the existence of and information about tiers. We prescribe a fixed name 'Tier' for this kind of information and a nested <MetadataElement> element with the fixed name 'TierIdentifier' to provide each tier

---

[7] More than one <Feature> element is used whenever an annotation consists of more than one label (cf. section 3.1.2.). For instance, ANVIL allows a single annotation to contain a set of attributes A1..An. These can be represented in multiple <Feature name="A1">, ..., <Feature name="An"> tags.

[8] Actually AG/AIF allows anchors without timestamps, so the interpolation might just as well be deferred to the moment a tool without an explicit timeline imports the AG file. This would have the benefit that, in a conversion between tools with explicit timelines, no additional (and only approximately correct) timestamps would have to be generated. The decision not to proceed in this way is owing to pragmatic reasons (i.e. keeping conversion routines simple), but should possibly be revised in future versions of the exchange format.

with a unique identifier. This identifier is then referred to from the type attribute in the <Annotation> element. Tools with non-tier-based data formats can ignore this information when importing from the exchange format, but need to generate it from appropriate other elements of the data structure (i.e. from other categorizations of annotations) when exporting to the exchange format.

```
<MetadataElement name="Tier">
   <MetadataElement name="TierIdentifier">TIE1</MetadataElement>
</MetadataElement>
 [...]
<Annotation type="TIE1" start=" T6" end=" T7">
```

4.3 Additional Information

Further information about tiers is stored in nested <MetadataElement> elements with the fixed name 'TierAttribute'. Each tier attribute is represented by the fixed triple Source-Name-Value, where 'Source' describes the defining instance (i.e. the tool), 'Name' the name given by the tool for that attribute and 'Value' its value.

```
<MetadataElement name="Tier">
   [...]
   <MetadataElement name="TierAttribute">
       <MetadataElement name="Source">EXMARaLDA</MetadataElement>
       <MetadataElement name="Name">speaker</MetadataElement>
       <MetadataElement name="Value">SPK0</MetadataElement>
    </MetadataElement>
</MetadataElement>
[...]
```

5 Conversion Routines

All participating tool developers were asked to write routines which would convert between their tools' formats and the exchange format. The technology for implementing these routines could be freely chosen. Thus, the ANVIL and ELAN conversions are done using the (Java) AG programming library, the EXMARaLDA conversion is based on XSL stylesheets, the Theme converter is written in Perl, the Transformer converter is written in VisualBasic, and MacVisSTA uses Python scripts for the task. At this point in time, we see no disadvantage in this diversity. Rather, we think that the fact that all these technologies have led to working conversion routines can be seen as a proof of the flexibility of our solution.

Partly, the new conversion routines have been integrated into the respective tools. Partly, they can be used as standalone converters.

6 Conclusion and Outlook

Our effort so far has resulted in a format via which the common denominator information can be reliably exchanged between the tools and which stores additional information in a standardized way. The interoperability can be extended to other tools like Praat [5], Transcriber [3], the NXT toolkit [20] or the TASX Annotator [15] by making use of existing import and export routines which some of the tools offer. The new data exchange options and the fact that we have a systematic analysis of the tool formats' differences and commonalities are a major step forward towards the interoperability that many multimodality researchers expect from their tools.

Further developments should concern the information which goes beyond the common denominator. There are two areas in which we plan to extend the current specification of the exchange format within our approach:

- Simple partial correspondences: Some bits of information, although they do not exist in every format, are nevertheless easily mappable between those formats in which they are defined. An example is the speaker assignment of tiers which is done through a 'participant' attribute in ELAN and a 'speaker' attribute in EXMARaLDA. Mapping between these two is therefore simply a matter of agreeing that their semantics are identical and specifying a unique name for them to be used in a <MetadataElement> in AIF.
- Complex partial correspondences: Other bits of information are also present in several formats, but are encoded in non-isomorphic ways. For example, the parent-child relation between tiers is encoded in both ANVIL and ELAN as an explicit attribute which points from the child tier to the parent tier via a unique ID. In EXMARaLDA, there is no such attribute, but the relation of a tier of type 'Transcription' to all tiers of type 'Annotation' which carry the same speaker assignment is also to be interpreted as a parent-child relation. If the exchange format defines a reliable way of recording information about parent-child relations between tiers, the EXMARaLDA export could transform this information accordingly and thus make it accessible to ANVIL and ELAN for import (and vice versa). The subtle differences between ANVIL-ELAN parent/child relations have been discussed in 3.2.3. A first step towards extended exchange capabilities would be to agree on which of these relationships to include in the tier representation in the <Metadata> tags and to classify them according to properties which transcend the application level (e.g. one-to-many, one-to-one or many-to-one relationships between annotations on parent and child tier).

Going beyond our current approach, we see two ways of further enhancing tool interoperability. The first is to reduce incompatibilities by modifying and assimilating the tools' data formats themselves. However, given that the diversity in tool formats is to a great part motivated by the different specializations of the respective tools, we do not expect (nor do we think it is desirable) to fully standardize the representation of multimodal annotations in that way.

Another strategy has been proposed by a working group at the EMELD/TILR workshop 2007 at which our proposal had been presented: wherever a *format*-based approach to interoperability such as ours meets its limits, it might be worthwhile considering *process*-based methods for data exchange. In such an approach, "interoperability is achieved by having the various annotation tools interact with each other via a well-defined process which mediates the interaction among the tools. Within this process would be the requisite information regarding the data models of each tool that would interact it with as well as methods for detecting (and ideally also for resolving) annotation conflicts." (see [8]). In other words: a higher degree of interoperability could be achieved by letting a third component memorize and restore information which was lost in a conversion between two tools. Such a third component could also act on the basis of the proposed exchange format. We intend to explore this possibility in the future.

Acknowledgments. The initiative described in this paper was sponsored in part by funding from the MITRE Corporation Technology Program. We also gratefully acknowledge the Annotation Graph and Annotation Graph Toolkit projects.

References

[1] Anvil website, http://www.anvil-software.de/
[2] ATLAS Website: http://sourceforge.net/projects/jatlas/
[3] Barras, C., Geoffrois, E., Wu, Z., Liberman, M.: Transcriber: Development and Use of a Tool for Assisting Speech Corpora Production. Speech Communication 33, 5–22 (2000)
[4] Bird, S., Liberman, M.: A formal framework for linguistic annotation. Speech Communication 33, 23–60 (2001)
[5] Boersma, P., Weenik, D.: PRAAT, a system for doing phonetics by computer, version 3.4. Institute of Phonetic Sciences of the University of Amsterdam, Report 132, 182 pages (1996)
[6] Brugman, H., Russel, A.: Annotating Multimedia/Multi-modal resources with ELAN. In: Proceedings of LREC 2004, Fourth International Conference on Language Resources and Evaluation (2004)
[7] C-BAS website, http://www.cmi.arizona.edu/go.spy?xml=cbas.xml
[8] Cochran, M., Good, J., Loehr, D., Miller, S.A., Stephens, S., Williams, B., Udoh, I.: Report from TILR Working Group 1: Tools interoperability and input/output formats (2007),
http://tilr.mseag.org/wiki/index.php?title=Working_Group_1
[9] ELAN website, http://www.lat-mpi.eu/tools/tools/elan
[10] EXMARaLDA website, http://www.exmaralda.org
[11] Kipp, M.: Anvil - A generic annotation tool for multimodal dialogue. In: Proceedings of the 7th European Conference on Speech Communication and Technology (Eurospeech), Aalborg, pp. 1367–1370 (2001)
[12] Kipp, M.: Gesture Generation by Imitation – From human behavior to computer character animation, Boca Raton, Florida: Dissertation.com (2004)
[13] Laprun, C., Fiscus, J., Garofolo, J., Pajot, S.: Recent Improvements to the ATLAS Architecture. In: Proceedings of HLT 2002, Second International Conference on Human Language Technology, San Francisco (2002)
[14] MacVissta website, http://sourceforge.net/projects/macvissta/
[15] Milde, J.-T., Gut, U.: The TASX Environment: An XML-Based Toolset for Time Aligned Speech Corpora. In: Proceedings of the Third International Conference on Language Resources and Evaluation (LREC 2002), Gran Canaria (2002)
[16] Website of the multimodal annotation workshop (2007),
http://www.multimodal-annotation.org
[17] Rohlfing, K., Loehr, D., Duncan, S., Brown, A., Franklin, A., Kimbara, I., Milde, J.-T., Parrill, F., Rose, T., Schmidt, T., Sloetjes, H., Thies, A., Wellinghoff, S.: Comparison of multimodal annotation tools: workshop report. Gesprächsforschung – Online-Zeitschrift zur verbalen Interaktion (7), 99–123 (2006)

[18] MacVissta website, http://sourceforge.net/projects/macvissta/
[19] Maeda, K., Bird, S., Ma, X., Lee, H.: Creating Annotation Tools with the Annotation Graph Toolkit. In: Proceedings of the Third International Conference on Language Resources and Evaluation. European Language Resources Association, Paris (2002)
[20] NITE XML Toolkit Website, http://www.ltg.ed.ac.uk/NITE/
[21] Rose, T.: MacVisSTA: A System for Multimodal Analysis of Human Communication and Interaction. Master's thesis, Virginia Tech. (2007)
[22] Rose, T., Quek, F., Shi, Y.: MacVisSTA: A System for Multimodal Analysis. In: Proceedings of the 6th International Conference on Multimodal Interfaces (2004)
[23] Schmidt, T.: Time-Based data models and the TEI guidelines for transcriptions of speech. Working papers in Multilingualism (56), Hamburg (2005)
[24] Schmidt, T., Wörner, K.: EXMARaLDA – Creating, analysing and sharing spoken language corpora for pragmatic research. In: Pragmatics (to appear, 2009)
[25] Theme website, http://www.noldus.com/site/doc200403003
[26] Transformer website, http://www.oliverehmer.de/transformer/
[27] Wittenburg, P., Brugman, H., Russel, A., Klassmann, A., Sloetjes, H.: ELAN: a Professional Framework for Multimodality Research. In: Proceedings of LREC 2006, Fifth International Conference on Language Resources and Evaluation (2006)

Appendix

Commented Example of an Instance of the Multimodal Annotation Exchange Format

This example was generated by the EXMARaLDA export mechanism. It corresponds to the annotation file illustrated in the screenshot in figure 2.

```
<?xml version="1.0" encoding="UTF-8"?>
<AGSet xmlns="http://www.ldc.upenn.edu/atlas/ag/" xmlns:xlink="http://www.w3.org/1999/xlink"
version="1.0" id="exmaralda">

<Metadata>
   <!-- Each tier is defined in a MetaDataElement with name 'Tier' -->
   <MetadataElement name="Tier">
      <!-- A child MetadataElement with name 'TierIdentifier' spcifies a unique ID for this tier -->
      <!-- This element is obligatory -->
      <MetadataElement name="TierIdentifier">TIE0</MetadataElement>
      <!-- Further child MetadataElements with name 'TierAttribute' -->
      <!-- define further properties of the respective tier -->
      <!-- These elements are optional -->
      <!-- this tier property says that the tier is assigned to the speaker with the (unique) ID 'SPK0' -->
      <MetadataElement name="TierAttribute">
      <!-- This MetadataElement specifies the tool which defined the property -->
         <MetadataElement name="Source">EXMARaLDA</MetadataElement>
         <!-- This MetadataElement specifies the name of the property in the tool's format -->
         <MetadataElement name="Name">speaker</MetadataElement>
         <!-- This MetadataElement specifies the value of the property -->
         <MetadataElement name="Value">SPK0</MetadataElement>
   </MetadataElement>
   <!-- Another tier property defined by EXMARaLDA: -->
   <!-- the tier is of category 'sup' (for 'suprasegmental') -->
```

```
<MetadataElement name="TierAttribute">
    <MetadataElement name="Source">EXMARaLDA</MetadataElement>
    <MetadataElement name="Name">category</MetadataElement>
    <MetadataElement name="Value">sup</MetadataElement>
</MetadataElement>
<!-- Another tier property defined by EXMARaLDA: the tier is of type 'a' (for 'annotation') -->
<MetadataElement name="TierAttribute">
    <MetadataElement name="Source">EXMARaLDA</MetadataElement>
    <MetadataElement name="Name">type</MetadataElement>
    <MetadataElement name="Value">a</MetadataElement>
</MetadataElement>
</MetadataElement>

<!-- another tier definition -->
<MetadataElement name="Tier">
    <MetadataElement name="TierIdentifier">TIE1</MetadataElement>
    <!-- follows another set of EXMARaLDA-specific tier attributes -->
</MetadataElement>

<!-- yet another tier definition -->
<MetadataElement name="Tier">
    <MetadataElement name="TierIdentifier">TIE2</MetadataElement>
    <!-- follows another set of EXMARaLDA-specific tier attributes -->
</MetadataElement>
<!-- follow more tier definitions -->
</Metadata>

<!-- The Timeline to which Anchors refer -->
<Timeline id="exmaralda_Timeline1">
  <!-- The Signal element specifies the media file for this annotation -->
  <Signal id="exmaralda_Timeline1_Signal1" unit="miliseconds" mimeClass=""
        mimeType="video/quicktime" encoding="" xlink:href="pear.mov"/>
</Timeline>

<!-- one AG element holds the actual Annotations and their Anchors -->
<!-- it refers to the Timeline defined above -->
<AG timeline="exmaralda_Timeline1" id="exmaralda_AG1">
  <!-- each Anchor gets a unique ID -->
  <!-- offsets are given in milliseconds -->
  <!-- Anchors should be ordered by offset -->
  <Anchor id="T0" offset="0" unit="milliseconds"/>
  <Anchor id="T1" offset="1900" unit="milliseconds"/>
  <Anchor id="T2" offset="2000" unit="milliseconds"/>
  <Anchor id="T3" offset="3211" unit="milliseconds"/>
  <Anchor id="T4" offset="5000" unit="milliseconds"/>
  <Anchor id="T5" offset="9200" unit="milliseconds"/>
  <Anchor id="T6" offset="10500" unit="milliseconds"/>
  <!-- follow more Anchor definitions -->
  <!-- each Annotation gets a unique ID -->
  <!-- the value of the 'type' attribute refers to the PCDATA value of a -->
  <!-- MetadataElement with name 'TierIdentifier' -->
  <!-- the values of the 'start' and 'end' attribute refer to the 'id' attributes of Anchor elements -->
  <!-- this Annotation element describes an annotation in tier 'TIE0', starting at anchor 'T1', -->
  <!-- ending at anchor 'T3' labelled 'louder' -->
  <Annotation id="TIE0_T1" type="TIE0" start="T1" end="T3">
        <!-- the Feature element(s) contain the actual annotation label(s)-->
        <!-- the value of the 'name' attribute can be freely chosen -->
        <Feature name="description">louder </Feature>
</Annotation>
```

```
<!-- [...] -->

<!-- Three annotation elements from tier 'TIE1', describing verbal behaviour -->
<Annotation id="TIE1_T0" type="TIE1" start="T0" end="T1">
        <Feature name="description">So it starts out with: A </Feature>
</Annotation>
<Annotation id="TIE1_T1" type="TIE1" start="T1" end="T2">
        <Feature name="description">roo</Feature>
</Annotation>
<Annotation id="TIE1_T2" type="TIE1" start="T2" end="T3">
        <Feature name="description">ster crows</Feature>
</Annotation>
<!-- [...] -->

<!-- Three annotation elements from tier 'TIE2', describing non-verbal behaviour -->
<Annotation id="TIE2_T0" type="TIE2" start="T0" end="T1">
        <Feature name="description">rHA on rKN, lHA on lSH</Feature>
</Annotation>
<Annotation id="TIE2_T1" type="TIE2" start="T1" end="T3">
        <Feature name="description">rHA up and to the right </Feature>
</Annotation>
<Annotation id="TIE2_T3" type="TIE2" start="T3" end="T4">
        <Feature name="description">rHA stays up</Feature>
</Annotation>
<!-- more annotations follow -->
</AG>
</AGSet>
```

Author Index